Fro...

P O ...

Berlin

3rd Edition

by Darwin Porter & Danforth Prince

Here's what critics say about Frommer's:

"Amazingly easy to use. Very portable, very complete."

—*Booklist*

"Detailed, accurate, and easy-to-read information for all price ranges."

—*Glamour Magazine*

Wiley Publishing, Inc.

Published by:

WILEY PUBLISHING, INC.

111 River St.
Hoboken, NJ 07030-5744

ISBN 0-7645-4226-4
ISSN 1524-4334

Editor: Caroline Sieg
Production Editor: Blair J. Pottenger
Photo Editor: Richard Fox
Cartographer: Elizabeth Puhl
Production by Wiley Indianapolis Composition Services

For information on our other products and services or to obtain technical
support, please contact our Customer Care Department within the U.S. at
800/762-2974, outside the U.S. at 317/572-3993 or fax 317/572-4002.

Wiley also publishes its books in a variety of electronic formats. Some con-
tent that appears in print may not be available in electronic formats.

Manufactured in the United States of America

5 4 3 2 1

Contents

List of Maps

About the Authors

Veteran travel writers **Darwin Porter** and **Danforth Prince** have written numerous best-selling Frommer's guides, notably to Germany, France, Italy, England, and Spain. Porter, who was bureau chief for the *Miami Herald* when he was 21, wrote the first Frommer's guide to Germany and has traveled extensively in the country. Prince, who began writing with Porter in 1982, worked for the Paris bureau of the *New York Times*.

An Invitation to the Reader

In researching this book, we discovered many wonderful places—hotels, restaurants, shops, and more. We're sure you'll find others. Please tell us about them, so we can share the information with your fellow travelers in upcoming editions. If you were disappointed with a recommendation, we'd love to know that, too. Please write to:

Frommer's Portable Berlin, 3rd Edition

Wiley Publishing, Inc. • 111 River St. • Hoboken, NJ 07030-5744

An Additional Note

Please be advised that travel information is subject to change at any time—and this is especially true of prices. We therefore suggest that you write or call ahead for confirmation when making your travel plans. The authors, editors, and publisher cannot be held responsible for the experiences of readers while traveling. Your safety is important to us, however, so we encourage you to stay alert and be aware of your surroundings. Keep a close eye on cameras, purses, and wallets, all favorite targets of thieves and pickpockets.

FROMMER'S STAR RATINGS, ICONS & ABBREVIATIONS

Every hotel, restaurant, and attraction listing in this guide has been ranked for quality, value, service, amenities, and special features using a **star-rating system.** In country, state, and regional guides, we also rate towns and regions to help you narrow down your choices and budget your time accordingly. Hotels and restaurants are rated on a scale of zero (recommended) to three stars (exceptional). Attractions, shopping, nightlife, towns, and regions are rated according to the following scale: zero stars (recommended), one star (highly recommended), two stars (very highly recommended), and three stars (must-see).

In addition to the star-rating system, we also use **seven feature icons** that point you to the great deals, in-the-know advice, and unique experiences that separate travelers from tourists. Throughout the book, look for:

Finds	Special finds—those places only insiders know about
Fun Fact	Fun facts—details that make travelers more informed and their trips more fun
Kids	Best bets for kids and advice for the whole family
Moments	Special moments—those experiences that memories are made of
Overrated	Places or experiences not worth your time or money
Tips	Insider tips—great ways to save time and money
Value	Great values—where to get the best deals

The following **abbreviations** are used for credit cards:

| AE | American Express | DISC | Discover | V | Visa |
| DC | Diners Club | MC | MasterCard | | |

FROMMERS.COM

Now that you have the guidebook to a great trip, visit our website at **www.frommers.com** for travel information on more than 3,000 destinations. With features updated regularly, we give you instant access to the most current trip-planning information available. At Frommers.com, you'll also find the best prices on airfares, accommodations, and car rentals—and you can even book travel online through our travel booking partners. At Frommers. com, you'll also find the following:

- Online updates to our most popular guidebooks
- Vacation sweepstakes and contest giveaways
- Newsletter highlighting the hottest travel trends
- Online travel message boards with featured travel discussions

The Best of Berlin

As every year of the new millennium goes by, the reunited city of Berlin more firmly establishes itself as the capital of the Germany of the 21st century.

Berlin was almost bombed out of existence during World War II, its streets reduced to piles of rubble, its parks to muddy swampland. But the optimistic spirit and strength of will of the remarkable Berliners enabled them to survive not only the wartime destruction of their city, but also its postwar division, symbolized by the Berlin Wall. Today, structures of steel and glass tower over streets where before only piles of rubble lay, and parks and gardens are again lush.

Before the war, the section of the city that became East Berlin was the cultural and political heart of Germany, where the best museums, the finest churches, and the most important boulevards lay. The walled-in East Berliners turned to restoring their important museums, theaters, and landmarks (especially in the Berlin-Mitte section), while the West Berliners built entirely new museums and cultural centers. This contrast between the two parts of the city is still evident today, though east and west have more or less come together within the immense, fascinating whole that is Berlin.

1 Frommer's Favorite Berlin Experiences

- **Strolling along Unter den Linden and the Kurfürstendamm:** You can't know Berlin until you've strolled the Ku'damm, that glossy, store-lined showcase of Western capitalism, and Unter den Linden, the Prussian centerpiece of the Berlin-Mitte district. See chapters 6 and 7.
- **Kneipen Crawling:** This is the Berlin version of "pub crawling." Whether you want breakfast or a beer at 4am, there's always a Kneipe waiting to claim you, no matter what neighborhood you're in. See "The Bar & Café Scene" in chapter 9.
- **A Touch of Culture:** The baton of the late Herbert von Karajan is no longer raised, but the Berlin Philharmonic is still one of the world's leading orchestras. See p. 144.

- **Wandering the Nikolai Quarter:** A symbol of Berlin's desire to bounce back after war damage, this charming 16th-century neighborhood has been completely rebuilt. Period taverns and churches make it ideal for a leisurely stroll down narrow streets illuminated by gas lanterns. See chapters 6 and 7.

- **Picnicking in the Tiergarten:** What better place for a picnic than the former hunting grounds of the Prussian electors? Wander through this 166 hectare (412-acre) park until you find the ideal spot, but first stop off at KaDeWe's sixth-floor food emporium at Wittgenbergplatz, 20 minutes away, for the makings of a memorable meal. See chapter 6.

2 Best Hotel Bets

- **Best Classic Hotel:** The Waldorf-Astoria of Berlin, **Kempinski Hotel Bristol Berlin,** Kurfürstendamm (© **800/426-3135** or 030/88-43-40), is the classic choice for those seeking time-tested luxury and style. Its rooms are among the city's finest, and the Kempinski Grill offers excellent cuisine. See p. 49.

- **Best Historic Hotel:** Risen from the ashes of 1945, **Hotel Adlon,** Under den Linden 77 (© **800/426-3135** or 030/22-61-0), enjoys one of the most sumptuous addresses in Berlin, right near the Brandenburg Gate. It is a remake of the legendary hotel opened on this spot in 1907 by Lorenz Adlon. See p. 62.

- **Best Boutique Hotel: Dorint am Gendarmenmarkt,** Charlottenstrasse 50–52 (© **030/20375-0**), is one of Berlin's newest and finest boutique hotels, even luring patrons from some old-time deluxe stopovers. It's come a long way since it was a dreary East German youth hostel in 1981. Am Gendarmenmarkt is an ultrahip address in the "new" Berlin. See p. 65.

- **Best Zaniest Hotel: Propeller Island City Lodge,** Albrecht-Achilles-Strasse 58, Charlottenburg (© **030/891-90-16**), is unlike no other in Berlin. Occupying three floors of an old-fashioned apartment building, each room here is different and wacky—perhaps a round bed with a pedal-operated mechanism that can spin on a pivot, or even a Coffin Room where you can sleep like a zombie in a well-ventilated tomb for a Gothic night. See p. 60.

- **Best Pool & Health Club:** Once called in Cold War days a monument to "capitalistic decadence," **The Westin Grand**

Hotel, Friedrichstrasse 158–164 (© **888/625-5144** or 030/2-02-70) has an excellent swimming pool and state-of-the-art fitness club along with a sauna and solarium. Many visitors who like to keep in shape while visiting Berlin check in here. See p. 66.

- **Best Hotel for Avoiding Men:** No men are allowed at the **Artemisia,** Brandenburgischestrasse 13 (© **030/8-73-89-05**), which occupies the fourth and fifth floors of a residential building. The hotel's interior is cozy, warm, and meticulously maintained. See p. 54.

- **Best Location: Sorat Art'otel,** Joachimstalerstrasse 28–29 (© **030/88-44-70**), is chic, discreet, and avant-garde, and the Ku'damm is virtually outside its door. Europe's top designers added their artful touches to the interior. Modernists who want to be central to everything should check in here. See p. 58.

- **Best Moderately Priced Hotel:** For surprisingly reasonable rates, try the **Hotel Sylter Hof Berlin,** Kurfürstenstrasse 114–116 (© **030/2-12-00**), a warmly decorated, traditional place, furnished in Louis XV style. It even has a burlesque-style nightclub. See p. 59.

- **Best Traditional Hotel:** In Grunewald, outside the center of Berlin, stands **Regent Schlosshotel Berlin,** Brahmsstrasse 10 (© **800/545-400** or 030/895-840), an Italian Renaissance–style palace. Kaiser Wilhelm II was once a guest here. Undeniable gloss and sumptuous bedrooms are the highlights. See p. 60.

- **Best Lobby for Pretending You're Rich:** Timeless taste and elegance are found at the **Four Seasons,** Charlottenstrasse 49 (© **800/332-3442** or 030/2-03-38), which attracts some of the world's most sophisticated travelers. Sitting in the lobby enjoying a drink, you're surrounded by Viennese chandeliers, classic antiques, and silk-covered chairs. See p. 62.

- **Best Trendy Hotel: Maritim Pro Arte,** Friedrichstrasse 150–153 (© **030/2-03-35**), a fashionable oasis just a short walk from Unter den Linden, is a place to see and be seen. This "designer hotel" was created by some of Europe's most fabled artists—Philippe Starck was responsible for much of the furnishings. See p. 66.

- **Best-Kept Secret:** Built in 1929, the **Savoy,** Fasanenstrasse 9–10 (© **800/223-5652** or 030/3-11-0-30), used to be better known and now has been overshadowed by more glamorous and famous names. But it's still a winning first-class choice for those who like quiet and luxury without ostentation. See p. 53.

- **Best Bed & Breakfast:** It may call itself a hotel, but **Hotel Luisenhof,** Köpenicker Strasse 92 (© **030/2-41-59-06**), is really more of a glorified B&B. Built in 1822, it has been massively restored and altered over the years and is today one of the city's best small hotels. See p. 68.

- **Best for Value:** It's not state of the art, but **Bogota,** Schlüterstrasse 45 (© **030/8-81-50-01**), has long been a favorite of the budget traveler. High ceilings and an old-fashioned, slightly dated atmosphere are what you get here. No two rooms are alike, but all are comfortable and well maintained. See p. 55.

- **Best Business Center:** An entire floor of the **Berlin Hilton,** Mohrenstrasse 30 (© **800/445-8667** or 030/2-02-30), is devoted to business services. A cavernous, commercial chain palace, the Hilton has the latest equipment and an efficient English-speaking staff adept at receiving messages. See p. 61.

- **Best Service:** What keeps clients returning to the **Grand Hotel Esplanade,** Lützowufer 15 (© **030/25-47-80**), is its unmatched level of service. The Esplanade offers 24-hour room service, an in-house doctor, massages, babysitting, and more. See p. 49.

3 Best Dining Bets

- **Best Neue Deutsche Küche:** Nowhere is modern German cuisine, or *neue Deutsche Küche,* practiced with as much skill as at **Bamberger Reiter,** Regensburgerstrasse 7 (© **030/2-18-42-82**), one of Berlin's leading restaurants. It's known for the quality of its cuisine, for its service, and for the innovation of its chef. See p. 71.

- **Best Newcomer:** **Facil,** in the Madison Hotel, Potsdamer Strasse 3 (© **030/5900-51234**), is found in an 11-story structure near the landmark Potsdamer Platz. For a taste of some of the best continental cuisine in Berlin, head to these refined quarters and sample cutting-edge cuisine that depends on the inspiration of the chef and the best produce in any season. See p. 81.

- **Best Gourmet Restaurant:** **Margaux,** Under den Linden 78 (© **030/22-65-26-11**), is the darling of food critics who hailed

Chef Michael Hoffman's gastronomic delights only a few steps from the Brandenburg Gate. Only the highest quality ingredients go into this perfumed continental cuisine that features—arguably—the best fish dishes in Berlin. See p. 82.

- **Best Avant-Garde Rendezvous: Portalis,** Kronenstrasse 55-58 (✆ **030/20-45-54-96**), attracts the Berlin hipster foodie seeking some of the city's best French and Mediterranean dishes. Textures are light, as most of the clients are proud of their slim waistlines. Expect a delight to your palate consumed in the company of local celebs. See p. 84.

- **Best Rheinish Cuisine: StäV,** 8 Schiffbauerdamm (✆ **030/282-3965**), no longer entertains the politicians of Bonn but has moved to Germany's new capital, a 5-minute walk from the Brandenburg Gate. The diplomats, journalists, and bureaucrats followed, and here they continue to delight their taste buds with Rhineland specialties such as sauerbraten with noodles or braised beef with pumpernickel and raisin sauce. See p. 89.

- **Best Prussian Cuisine:** You're in Prussia, so be sure to sample the finest of that old-fashioned cuisine at **Marjellchen,** Mommsenstrasse 9 (✆ **030/883-26-76**), the only Berlin restaurant that specializes in East Prussian cooking. Amid a Bismarckian decor you'll dine on the likes of pork spareribs stuffed with prunes or potato soup with shrimp and bacon. See p. 75.

- **Best View:** High-altitude views and good German food keep the tables filled at the 213-foot-high **Funkturm Restaurant,** Messedamm 22 (✆ **030/303-829-96**), which offers sweeping panoramas of the new/old German capital. See p. 80.

- **Best Hotel Restaurant: First Floor,** a showcase restaurant within the Palace Berlin Hotel, Budapesterstrasse 42 (✆ **030/25-02-10-20**), stands near the Tiergarten. Its regional German and French cuisine is almost without equal in Berlin. See p. 77.

- **Best International Restaurant: Restaurant Vau,** Jägerstrasse 54 (✆ **030/202-9730**), is Berlin's restaurant of the minute. The short menu features top-notch creations handled with skill and finesse by one of Berlin's best-trained kitchen staffs. Reservations are imperative. See p. 84.

2

Planning Your Trip to Berlin

This chapter covers everything you need to know to make trip-planning a snap, from when to go to how to shop for the best airfare. Browse through it to get started and make sure you've touched all the bases.

1 Visitor Information

INFORMATION

To get visitor information before leaving for Berlin, you might want to contact the headquarters of the **German National Tourist Board** at Beethovenstrasse 69, 60325 Frankfurt am Main (© **069/21-23-8800; www.visits-to-germany.com**). You'll also find a German National Tourist Office in New York at 122 E. 42nd St., 52nd Floor, New York, NY 10168-0072 (© **212/661-7200**); in Toronto at 2 Bloor St. E., Suite 3330, Toronto, ON M4W 3R8 (© **416-967-3381**); in London at P.O. Box 2695, London W1A 3TN (© **020/7317-0908**); and in Australia at P.O. Box A980 Sydney, NSW 12 35 (© **02/9267-8148**). There are also tourist offices in about 20 other international cities, including Hong Kong, Johannesburg, Milan, and Paris.

Berlin Tourism Information Office, Am Karlsbad 11, 10785 Berlin, concentrates specifically on visitor information for Berlin. The organization has no overseas office, but does maintain an excellent website (in English as well as German) at **www.btm.de**.

2 Entry Requirements & Customs

ENTRY REQUIREMENTS

Every U.S., Canadian, British, and Australian traveler entering Germany must hold a **valid passport.** You won't need a visa unless you're staying longer than 3 months. Safeguard your passport in an inconspicuous, inaccessible place like a money belt. If you lose your passport, visit the nearest consulate of your native country as soon as possible for a replacement. It's always a good idea to keep a photocopy of your passport separate from the passport itself; the photocopy helps expedite replacement if your passport gets lost or stolen.

For an up-to-date country-by-country listing of passport require-ments around the world, go the "Foreign Entry Requirement" web page of the U.S. State Department at **http://travel.state.gov/foreign entryreqs.html**.

CUSTOMS
WHAT YOU CAN BRING INTO BERLIN
In general, items required for personal and professional use or con-sumption may be brought into Germany duty-free and without has-sle. No duty is levied for a private car, as long as you report it. You can also bring in gifts duty-free up to a total value of 175€ ($201).

The following items are permitted into Germany duty-free from non-EU counties: 200 cigarettes, or 100 cigarillos, or 50 cigars, or 250 grams of smoking tobacco; 1 liter of liquor above 44 proof, or 2 liters of liquor less than 44 proof, or 2 liters of wine; 50 grams of perfume and 0.25 liters of eau de cologne; 500 grams of coffee; 100 grams of tea. From EU countries the duty-free limits are higher: 300 cigarettes; 1.5 liters of liquor above 44 proof, or 3 liters of liquor less than 44 proof, or 4 liters of wine; 75 grams of perfume and 0.375 liters of eau de cologne; 750 grams of coffee; 150 grams of tea. Duty-free allowances are authorized only when the items are carried in the traveler's personal baggage.

WHAT YOU CAN TAKE HOME FROM BERLIN
Returning **U.S. citizens** who have been away for at least 48 hours are allowed to bring back, once every 30 days, $800 worth of merchan-dise duty-free. You'll be charged a flat rate of 4% duty on the next $1,000 worth of purchases. Be sure to have your receipts handy. On mailed gifts, the duty-free limit is $200. With some exceptions, you cannot bring fresh fruits and vegetables into the United States. For specifics on what you can bring back, download the invaluable free pamphlet *Know Before You Go* online at **www.customs.gov**. (Click on "Travel", and then click on "Know Before You Go!") Or contact the **U.S. Customs Service,** 1300 Pennsylvania Ave., NW, Washing-ton, DC 20229 (© **877/287-8667**) and request the pamphlet.

For a clear summary of **Canadian** rules, write for the booklet *I Declare,* issued by the **Canada Customs and Revenue Agency** (© **800/461-9999** in Canada, or 204/983-3500; www.ccra-adrc. gc.ca). Canada allows its citizens a C$750 exemption, and you're allowed to bring back duty-free one carton of cigarettes, 1 can of tobacco, 40 imperial ounces of liquor, and 50 cigars. In addition, you're allowed to mail gifts to Canada valued at less than C$60 a day, provided they're unsolicited and don't contain alcohol or

Germany

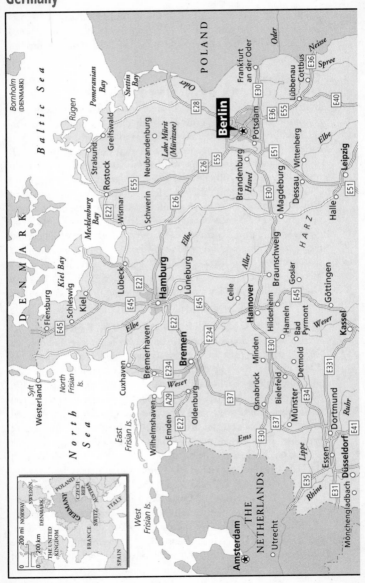

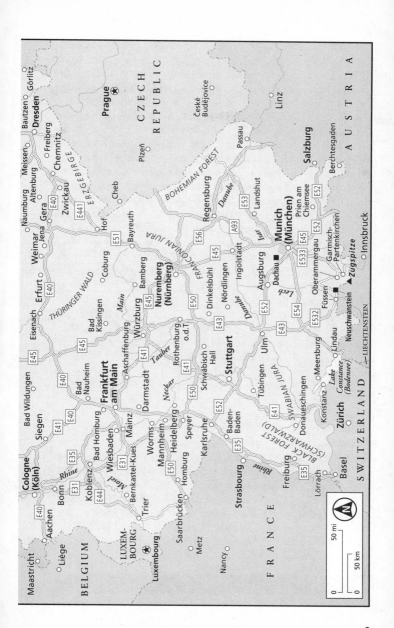

tobacco (write on the package "Unsolicited gift, under $60 value"). All valuables should be declared on the Y-38 form before departure from Canada, including serial numbers of valuables you already own, such as expensive foreign cameras. *Note:* The $750 exemption can only be used once a year and only after an absence of 7 days.

Citizens of the U.K. who are **returning from a European Union (EU) country** will go through a separate Customs Exit (called the "Blue Exit") especially for EU travelers. In essence, there is no limit on what you can bring back from an EU country, as long as the items are for personal use (this includes gifts), and you have already paid the necessary duty and tax. However, customs law sets out guidance levels. If you bring in more than these levels, you may be asked to prove that the goods are for your own use. Guidance levels on goods bought in the EU for your own use are 3,200 cigarettes, 200 cigars, 3 kg of smoking tobacco, 10 liters of spirits, 90 liters of wine, 20 liters of fortified wine (such as port or sherry), and 110 liters of beer.

The duty-free allowance in **Australia** is A$400 or, for those under 18, A$200. Citizens can bring in 250 cigarettes or 250 grams of loose tobacco, and 1,125 milliliters of alcohol. If you're returning with valuables you already own, such as foreign-made cameras, you should file form B263. A helpful brochure available from Australian consulates or Customs offices is *Know Before You Go.* For more information, call the **Australian Customs Service** at ⓒ **1300/363-263,** or log on to www.customs.gov.au.

The duty-free allowance for **New Zealand** is NZ$700. Citizens over 17 can bring in 200 cigarettes, 50 cigars, or 250 grams of tobacco (or a mixture of all 3 if their combined weight doesn't exceed 250g); plus 4.5 liters of wine and beer, or 1.125 ml of liquor. New Zealand currency does not carry import or export restrictions. Fill out a certificate of export, listing the valuables you are taking out of the country; that way, you can bring them back without paying duty. Most questions are answered in a free pamphlet available at New Zealand consulates and Customs offices: *New Zealand Customs Guide for Travellers, Notice no. 4.* For more information, contact **New Zealand Customs,** The Customhouse, 17–21 Whitmore St., Box 2218, Wellington (ⓒ **04/473-6099** or 0800/428-786; www.customs.govt.nz).

3 Money

While this book includes the best hotels, restaurants, and attractions in Berlin, our ultimate aim is to stretch your buying power—to show that you don't need to pay scalpers' prices for charm, top-grade comfort, and quality food.

Although prices are high in Berlin, you generally get good value for your money. The inflation rate, unlike that of most of the world, has remained low. Hotels are usually clean and comfortable, and restaurants generally offer good cuisine and ample portions made with quality ingredients. Public transportation is fast and on time, and most service personnel treat you with respect.

In Germany, many prices for children (generally defined as ages 6–17) are considerably lower than for adults. Children under 6 are often charged no admission or other fee. Always ask about discounts.

CURRENCY

The **euro (€),** the new single European currency, became the official currency of Germany and 11 other participating countries on January 1, 1999. However, the euro didn't go into general circulation until early in 2002. The old currency, the German mark, disappeared into history on March 1, 2002, replaced by the euro, whose official abbreviation is "EUR." Exchange rates of participating countries are locked into a common currency fluctuating against the dollar.

For more details on the euro, check out **www.europa.eu.int/euro**.

All prices are given in euros with conversions into U.S. dollars. As this book went to press, 1€ was worth approximately $1.15 and gaining in strength, so your dollars might not go as far as you'd expect. For up-to-the minute exchange rates between the euro and the dollar, check the currency converter website **www.xe.com/ucc**.

It's a good idea to exchange at least some money—just enough to cover airport incidentals and transportation to your hotel—before you leave home, so you can avoid lines at airport ATMs (automated teller machines). You can exchange money at your local American Express or Thomas Cook office or your bank. If you're far away from a bank with currency-exchange services, American Express offers travelers checks and foreign currency, though with a $15 order fee and additional shipping costs, at www.americanexpress.com or **800/807-6233.**

ATMS

The easiest and best way to get cash away from home is from an ATM (automated teller machine). The **Cirrus** (*C* **800/424-7787;** www.mastercard.com) and **PLUS** (*C* **800/843-7587;** www.visa.com) networks span the globe; look at the back of your bank card to see which network you're on, then call or check online for ATM locations at your destination. Be sure you know your personal identification number (PIN) before you leave home and be sure to find

The Euro, the U.S. Dollar, the British Pound & the Canadian Dollar

In January of 2002, the largest money-changing operation in history led to the deliberate obsolescence of many of Europe's individual national currencies, including the German mark. In its place was substituted the euro, a currency based on the fiscal participation of a dozen nations in Europe.

For American Readers: At this writing, 1 euro equals approximately $1.15, and 1 U.S. dollar equals approximately 0.89 euros. This was the rate of exchange used to calculate the dollar values throughout this book.

For British readers: At this writing, Great Britain still uses the pound sterling, with 1 euro equaling approximately 70 pence, and £1 equaling approximately 1.42€.

For Canadian Readers: At this writing, 1 euro equals approximately $1.53, 1 Canadian dollar equals approximately 0.65€.

€	U.S.$	British£	Canadian$
0.25	0.29	0.18	0.38
0.50	0.58	0.35	0.76
0.75	0.86	0.53	1.15
1.00	1.15	0.70	1.53
2.00	2.30	1.40	3.06
3.00	3.45	2.10	4.59
4.00	4.60	2.80	6.12
5.00	5.75	3.50	7.65
6.00	6.90	4.20	9.18
7.00	8.05	4.90	10.71
8.00	9.20	5.60	12.24
9.00	10.35	6.30	13.77
10.00	11.50	7.00	15.30
15.00	12.65	10.50	22.95
20.00	13.80	14.00	30.60
25.00	28.75	17.50	38.35
30.00	34.50	21.00	45.90
35.00	40.25	24.50	53.55
40.00	46.00	28.00	61.20
45.00	50.60	31.50	67.50
50.00	57.50	35.00	75.00

out your daily withdrawal limit before you depart. Also keep in mind that many banks impose a fee every time a card is used at a different bank's ATM, and that fee can be higher for international transactions (up to $5 or more) than for domestic ones (where they're rarely more than $1.50). On top of this, the bank from which you withdraw cash may charge its own fee. To compare banks' ATM fees within the U.S., use www.bankrate.com. For international withdrawal fees, ask your bank.

You can also get cash advances on your credit card at an ATM. Keep in mind that credit card companies try to protect themselves from theft by limiting the funds someone can withdraw outside their home country, so call your credit card company before you leave home.

TRAVELER'S CHECKS

Traveler's checks are something of an anachronism from the days before the ATM made cash accessible at any time. Traveler's checks used to be the only sound alternative to traveling with dangerously large amounts of cash. They were as reliable as currency, but, unlike cash, could be replaced if lost or stolen.

These days, traveler's checks are less necessary because most cities have 24-hour ATMs that allow you to withdraw small amounts of cash as needed. However, keep in mind that you will likely be charged an ATM withdrawal fee if the bank is not your own, so if you're withdrawing money every day, you might be better off with traveler's checks—provided that you don't mind showing identification every time you want to cash one.

You can get traveler's checks at almost any bank. **American Express** offers denominations of $20, $50, $100, $500, and (for cardholders only) $1,000. You'll pay a service charge ranging from 1% to 4%. You can also get American Express traveler's checks over the phone by calling ⊙ **800/221-7282;** Amex gold and platinum cardholders who use this number are exempt from the 1% fee.

⟮Tips⟯ Small Change

When you change money, ask for some small bills or loose change. Petty cash will come in handy for tipping and public transportation. Consider keeping the change separate from your larger bills, so that it's readily accessible and you'll be less of a target for theft.

What Things Cost in Berlin	U.S.$	British£
Taxi from Tegel Airport to Europa Center	$16–$25	£10.50–£16.50
Underground from Kurfürstendamm to Dahlen	$2.40	£1.58
Local telephone call	45¢	30p
Double room at Brandenburger Hof (expensive)	$276	£180
Double room at Art Nouveau (moderate)	$127	£82.50
Double room at the Bogotà (inexpensive)	$83	£54
Lunch for one at the La Table (moderate)	$27	£18
Dinner for one (without wine) at Ponte Vecchio (expensive)	$41	£27
Dinner for one (without wine) at Alexanderkeller (inexpensive)	$23	£15
Half-liter of beer	$5.20–$6.30	£3.38–£4.13
Coca-cola in a restaurant	$2.05	£1.35
Cup of coffee	$4.05	£2.63
Glass of wine	$3.45–$4.60	£2.25–£3
Roll of ASA 200 color film, 36 exposures	$4.05–$5.75	£2.65–£3.75
Admission to Pergamon Museum (adult)	$4.60	£3
Movie Ticket	$8.05–$9.20	£5.25–£6
Ticket to Berlin Philharmonic Orchestra	$18–$59	£11.50–£38.33

Visa offers traveler's checks at Citibank locations nationwide, as well as at several other banks. The service charge ranges between 1.5% and 2%; checks come in denominations of $20, $50, $100, $500, and $1,000. Call © **800/732-1322** for information. AAA members can obtain Visa checks without a fee at most AAA offices or by calling ✆ **866/339-3378. MasterCard** also offers traveler's checks. Call ✆ **800/223-9920** for a location near you.

Foreign currency traveler's checks are useful if you're traveling to one country, or to the Euro zone; they're accepted at locations such as bed & breakfasts where dollar checks may not be, and they minimize the amount of math you have to do at your destination. **American Express** offers checks in Australian dollars, Canadian dollars, British pounds, Euros and Japanese yen. **Visa** checks come in Australian, Canadian, British and Euro versions; **MasterCard** offers those four plus yen and South African rands.

If you choose to carry traveler's checks, be sure to keep a record of their serial numbers separate from your checks in the event that they are stolen or lost. You'll get a refund faster if you know the numbers.

CREDIT CARDS

Credit cards are safe way to carry money, they provide a convenient record of all your expenses, and they generally offer good exchange rates. You can also withdraw cash advances from your credit cards at banks or ATMs, provided you know your PIN number. If you've forgotten yours, or didn't even know you had one, call the number on the back of your credit card and ask the bank to send it to you. It usually takes 5 to 7 business days, though some banks will provide the number over the phone if you tell them your mother's maiden name or some other personal information. Your credit card company will likely charge a commission (1 or 2%) on every foreign purchase you make, but don't sweat this small stuff; for most purchases, you'll still get the best deal with credit cards when you factor in things like ATM fees and higher traveler's check exchange rates.

In Germany, American Express, Diners Club, MasterCard, and Visa are commonly accepted, with the latter two cards predominating.

For tips and telephone numbers to call if your wallet is stolen or lost, go to "Lost and Found" in the Fast Facts section of this chapter.

4 When to Go

Berlin has a temperate, changeable climate. Winters are generally cool and wet, though temperatures often dip below freezing, and it sometimes snows. Summers are pleasant and rarely blazingly hot; however, for this reason Berlin establishments often lack air-conditioning. Many visitors find fall and late spring to be the best times to come to the city.

Berlin's Average Daytime Temperature & Rainfall (Inches)

	Jan	Feb	Mar	Apr	May	June	July	Aug	Sept	Oct	Nov	Dec
°F	30	32	40	48	53	60	64	62	56	49	40	34
°C	–1	0	4	9	12	16	18	17	13	9	4	1
Rainfall	2.2	1.6	1.2	1.6	2.3	2.9	3.2	2.7	2.2	1.6	2.4	1.9

HOLIDAYS

Public holidays are January 1 (New Year's Day), Easter (Good Friday and Easter Monday), May 1 (Labor Day), Ascension Day (10 days before Pentecost/Whitsunday, the 7th Sunday after Easter), Whitmonday (day after Pentecost), October 3 (Day of German Unity), November 17 (Day of Prayer and Repentance), and December 25 and 26 (Christmas). In addition, the following holidays are observed in some German states: January 6 (Epiphany), Corpus Christi (10 days after Pentecost), August 15 (Assumption), and November 1 (All Saints' Day).

BERLIN CALENDAR OF EVENTS

The German National Tourist Board publishes a free calendar of forthcoming events in Germany three times a year, in April, October, and January; the first two are half-yearly calendars and the latter is a yearly preview. They each give the dates of trade fairs and exhibitions, theatrical and musical performances, local and folk festivals, sporting events, conferences, and congresses throughout Germany. The following are some of the coming highlights in Berlin.

February

International Film Festival. Stars, would-be stars, directors, and almost anyone with a film to peddle show up at this well-attended festival. It lasts for 1 week and is a showcase for the work of international film directors as well as the latest German films. The festival takes place at various theaters around the city; check local newspapers for details. Tickets can be purchased at any box office. Contact the **Full House Service** (© **030/25489-100**) or www.berlinale.de for more information. February 5 to 15.

March

Fasching. Carnival festivals take place throughout Germany, including Berlin, reaching their peak on the Tuesday (Mardi Gras) before Ash Wednesday.

July

The Love Parade. A techno-rave street party in the center of Berlin. This event transforms Berlin into one huge party, starting off with a series of floats carrying Europe's best DJ's. Evening events center around the Tiergarten. Second weekend in July. See p. 146.

September
Berliner Festwochen. One of the high points on the cultural calendar of Germany, the Berlin Festival brings an international array of performing artists to Berlin. It features opera and symphony performances as well as major theatrical presentations. Contact the **Berlin Tourist Information Office** (© **030/25-00-25;** www.berlintourism.de). Early September to mid-October.

October
German Unification Day. Various events throughout the city. Contact the Berlin Tourist Information Office (© **030/25-00-25;** www.berlintourism.de). Oct. 3.

November
Jazz-Fest Berlin. This annual festival staged at the Philharmonie attracts some of the world's finest jazz artists, ranging from traditional to experimental. Contact the **Berlin Tourist Information Office** (© **030/25-00-25;** www.berlintourism.de) for more information. Early November.

December
New Year's Eve party at the Brandenburg Gate. Dec. 31.

5 Travel Insurance

Visiting Berlin is not viewed as a risky destination, but the prudent traveler may want the extra protection of insurance for that unforeseen disaster.

Check your existing insurance policies and credit-card coverage before you buy travel insurance. You may already be covered for lost luggage, cancelled tickets or medical expenses. The cost of travel insurance varies widely, depending on the cost and length of your trip, your age, health, and the type of trip you're taking.

TRIP-CANCELLATION INSURANCE Trip-cancellation insurance helps you get your money back if you have to back out of a trip, if you have to go home early, or if your travel supplier goes bankrupt. Allowed reasons for cancellation can range from sickness to natural disasters to the State Department declaring your destination unsafe for travel. (Insurers usually won't cover vague fears, though, as many travelers discovered who tried to cancel their trips in October 2001 because they were wary of flying.) In this unstable world, trip-cancellation insurance is a good buy if you're getting tickets well in advance—who knows what the state of the world, or of your airline, will be in nine months? Insurance policy details vary, so read the fine print—and especially make sure that your airline or cruise line is on the list of carriers covered in case of bankruptcy.

For information, contact one of the following insurers: **Access America** (✆ 866/807-3982; www.accessamerica.com); **Travel Guard International** (✆ 800/826-4919; www.travelguard.com); **Travel Insured International** (✆ 800/243-3174; www.travelinsured.com); and **Travelex Insurance Services** (✆ 888/457-4602; www.travelex-insurance.com).

MEDICAL INSURANCE   Most health insurance policies cover you if you get sick away from home—but check, particularly if you're insured by an HMO. With the exception of certain HMOs and Medicare/Medicaid, your medical insurance should cover medical treatment—even hospital care—overseas. However, most out-of-country hospitals make you pay your bills up front, and send you a refund after you've returned home and filed the necessary paperwork. And in a worst-case scenario, there's the high cost of emergency evacuation. If you require additional medical insurance, try **MEDEX International** (✆ **800/MEDEX00** or 410/453-6300; www.medex assist.com) or **Travel Assistance International** (✆ **800/821-2828;** www.travelassistance.com; for general information on services, call the company's Worldwide Assistance Services, Inc., at ✆ **800/777-8710**).

LOST-LUGGAGE INSURANCE   On international flights (including US portions of international trips), baggage is limited to approximately $9.07 per pound, up to approximately $635 per checked bag. If you plan to check items more valuable than the standard liability, see if your valuables are covered by your homeowner's policy, get baggage insurance as part of your comprehensive travel-insurance package or buy Travel Guard's "BagTrak" product. Don't buy insurance at the airport, as it's usually overpriced. Be sure to take any valuables or irreplaceable items with you in your carry-on luggage, as many valuables (including books, money and electronics) aren't covered by airline policies.

If your luggage is lost, immediately file a lost-luggage claim at the airport, detailing the luggage contents. For most airlines, you must report delayed, damaged, or lost baggage within 4 hours of arrival. The airlines are required to deliver luggage, once found, directly to your house or destination free.

6 Health & Safety

STAYING HEALTHY

Berlin medical facilities are among the best in the world. If a medical emergency arises, your hotel staff can usually put you in touch with a reliable doctor. If not, contact the American embassy or a consulate; each one maintains a list of English-speaking doctors. Of course, in Frankfurt it is almost impossible to find a doctor who does not speak English. Medical and hospital services aren't free, so be sure that you have appropriate insurance coverage before you travel.

If you suffer from a chronic illness, consult your doctor before your departure. For conditions like epilepsy, diabetes, or heart problems, wear a **Medic Alert Foundation** (© 800/825-3785 or 800/432-5378; www.medicalert.org), which will immediately alert doctors to your condition and give them access to your records through Medic alert's 24-hour hotline. Membership is $35, plus a $20 annual fee.

Pack prescription medication in your carry-on luggage. Carry written prescriptions in generic, not brand-name form, and dispense all prescription medications from their original labeled vials. Also bring along copies of your prescriptions in case you lose your pills or run out.

For more information, contact the **International Association for Medical Assistance to Travelers (IAMAT; © 716/754-4883** in the U.S. or 519/836-0102 in Canada; fax 519/836-3412; www.iamat.org). This organization offers tips on travel and health concerns in foreign countries, and lists many local English-speaking doctors.

STAYING SAFE

Violent crime is rare in Berlin, but can occur, especially around the rail station. Most incidents of street crime consist of theft of unattended items and pickpocketing. There have been a few reports of aggravated assault against U.S. citizens in higher-risk areas. American travelers are advised to take the same precautions against becoming crime victims as they would in any American city.

The loss or theft abroad of a U.S. passport should be reported immediately to the local police and the nearest U.S. Embassy or Consulate. If you are the victim of a crime while overseas, in addition to reporting to local police, please contact the nearest U.S.

Embassy or Consulate for assistance. The Embassy/Consulate staff can, for example, assist you to find appropriate medical care, to contact family members or friends, and explain how funds could be transferred. Although the investigation and prosecution of the crime is solely the responsibility of local authorities, consular officers can help you to understand the local criminal justice process and to find an attorney if needed.

U.S. citizens may refer to the Department of State's pamphlet, *"A Safe Trip Abroad,"* for ways to promote a trouble-free journey. The pamphlet is available by mail from the Superintendent of Documents, U.S. Government Printing Office, Washington, DC 20402, via the Internet at www.access.gpo.gov/su_docs, or via the Bureau of Consular Affairs home page at http://travel.state.gov.

TRAVELERS WITH DISABILITIES

Most disabilities shouldn't stop anyone from traveling. There are more options and resources out there than ever before.

Germany is one of the better countries for travelers with disabilities, and Berlin itself has excellent facilities. The tourist office can issue permits for drivers to allow access to disabled parking areas.

Many travel agencies offer customized tours and itineraries for travelers with disabilities. **Flying Wheels Travel** (© 507/451-5005; www.flyingwheelstravel.com) offers escorted tours and cruises that emphasize sports and private tours in minivans with lifts. **Accessible Journeys** (© 800/846-4537 or 610/521-0339; www.disabilitytravel.com) caters specifically to slow walkers and wheelchair travelers and their families and friends.

Organizations that offer assistance to travelers with disabilities include the **MossRehab Hospital** (www.mossresourcenet.org), which provides a library of accessible-travel resources online; the **Society for Accessible Travel and Hospitality** (© 212/447-7284; www.sath.org; annual membership fees: $45 adults, $30 seniors and students), which offers a wealth of travel resources for all types of disabilities and informed recommendations on destinations, access guides, travel agents, tour operators, vehicle rentals, and companion services; and the **American Foundation for the Blind** (© 800/232-5463; www.afb.org), which provides information on traveling with Seeing Eye dogs.

For more information specifically targeted to travelers with disabilities, the community website **iCan** (www.icanonline.net/channels/travel/index.cfm) has destination guides and several regular columns on accessible travel.

British travelers with disabilities should contact **RADAR** (Royal Association for Disability and Rehabilitation), Unit 12, City Forum, 250 City Rd., London EC1V 8AF (℗ **020/7250-3222;** fax 020/7250-0212; www.radar.org.uk), which publishes vacation "fact packs," selling for £2 to £5 containing information on trip planning, travel insurance, specialized accommodations, and transportation abroad.

GAY & LESBIAN TRAVELERS

Although Germany is one of the "gayest" countries of Europe and Berlin is one of the gayest capitals, there is also prejudice and hostility here. Violence against gays and foreigners (especially nonwhite) is not unknown. On the other hand, homosexuality is widely accepted by a vast number of the country's millions, especially young people. All major cities have a wide and varied gay and lesbian nightlife. Keep in mind western Germany is far more gay-friendly than the more isolated outposts of the former East Germany. The legal minimum age for consensual homosexual sex is 18.

Before you go, consider picking up a copy of *Frommer's Gay & Lesbian Europe,* which contains a chapter on Berlin.

The International Gay & Lesbian Travel Association (IGLTA) (℗ **800/448-8550** or 954/776-2626; www.iglta.org) is the trade association for the gay and lesbian travel industry, and offers an online directory of gay and lesbian-friendly travel businesses; go to their website and click on 'Members.'

Many agencies offer tours and travel itineraries specifically for gay and lesbian travelers. **Above and Beyond Tours** (℗ **800/397-2681;** www.abovebeyondtours.com) is the exclusive gay and lesbian tour operator for United Airlines. **Now, Voyager** (℗ **800/255-6951;** www.nowvoyager.com) is a well-known San Francisco–based gay-owned and operated travel service. **Olivia Cruises & Resorts** (℗ **800-631-6277** or 510/655-0364; www.olivia.com) charters entire resorts and ships for exclusive lesbian vacations and offers smaller group experiences for both gay and lesbian travelers.

The following travel guides are available at most travel bookstores and gay and lesbian bookstores, or you can order them from **Giovanni's Room** bookstore, 1145 Pine St., Philadelphia, PA 19107 (℗ **215/923-2960;** www.giovannisroom.com): *Frommer's Gay & Lesbian Europe,* an excellent travel resource; *Out and About* (℗ **800/929-2268** or 415-644-8044; www.outandabout.com), which offers guidebooks and a newsletter 10 times a year packed with solid information on the global gay and lesbian scene; *Spartacus International Gay Guide* and *Odysseus,* both good, annual English-language guidebooks focused on gay men; the *Damron* guides, with separate, annual books for gay men and lesbians; and *Gay Travel A to Z: The World of Gay & Lesbian Travel Options at Your Fingertips,* by Marianne Ferrari (Ferrari Publications; Box 35575, Phoenix, AZ 85069), a very good gay and lesbian guidebook series.

SENIOR TRAVEL

Mention the fact that you're a senior citizen when you make your travel reservations. Although all of the major U.S. airlines have cancelled their senior discount and coupon book programs, many hotels still offer discounts for seniors. In most cities, people over the age of 60 qualify for reduced admission to theaters, museums, and other attractions, as well as discounted fares on public transportation.

Members of **AARP** (formerly known as the American Association of Retired Persons), 601 E St. NW, Washington, DC 20049 (② **800/424-3410** or 202/434-2277; www.aarp.org), get discounts on hotels, airfares, and car rentals. AARP offers members a wide range of benefits, including *AARP: The Magazine* and a monthly newsletter. Anyone over 50 can join.

Many reliable agencies and organizations target the 50-plus market. **Elderhostel** (② **877/426-8056;** www.elderhostel.org) arranges study programs for those aged 55 and over (and a spouse or companion of any age) in the U.S. and in more than 80 countries around the world. Most courses last 5 to 7 days in the U.S. (2–4 weeks abroad), and many include airfare, accommodations in university dormitories or modest inns, meals, and tuition. **ElderTreks** (② **800/741-7956;** www.eldertreks.com) offers small-group tours to off-the-beaten-path or adventure-travel locations, restricted to travelers 50 and older.

Recommended publications offering travel resources and discounts for seniors include: the quarterly magazine *Travel 50 & Beyond* (www.travel50andbeyond.com); *Travel Unlimited: Uncommon Adventures for the Mature Traveler* (Avalon); *101 Tips for Mature Travelers,* available from Grand Circle Travel (② **800/221-2610** or 617/350-7500; www.gct.com); *The 50+ Traveler's Guidebook* (St. Martin's Press); and *Unbelievably Good Deals and Great Adventures That You Absolutely Can't Get Unless You're Over 50* (McGraw-Hill).

7 Getting There

BY PLANE

The main hub for air traffic in Germany is Frankfurt. Most international visitors, including those from such U.S. cities as New York, use Frankfurt as their gateway city, arriving there and boarding a connecting flight into Berlin. Other cities throughout Europe, such as Amsterdam and London, are also used to route transatlantic passengers to Berlin. Surprisingly, there is only one direct flight from the United States to Berlin. Lufthansa flies daily except Friday from Dulles airport in Washington, D.C., to Berlin.

Flying time to Frankfurt is about 7½ hours from New York, 10 hours from Chicago, and 12 hours from Los Angeles. There are also nonstop flights from the United States to Munich and Düsseldorf.

Lufthansa (© 800/645-3880; www.lufthansa-usa.com) operates the most frequent service and flies to the greatest number of Germany's airports. From North America, Lufthansa serves 16 gateway cities. In any season, there are more than 100 weekly flights from these cities to Germany. The largest of the gateways is the New York City area, where flights depart from both JFK and Newark airports. From JFK there are daily flights to Frankfurt. From Newark, there are daily flights to Frankfurt, Munich, and Düsseldorf. Lufthansa's other gateways include Atlanta, Boston, Chicago, Dallas/Fort Worth, Detroit, Houston, Los Angeles, Miami, Philadelphia, San Francisco, and Washington, D.C. Lufthansa also flies to Germany from Toronto, Vancouver, Calgary, and Mexico City. The airline has a 10% discount for seniors over 60; the reduction applies to a traveling companion as well.

Lufthansa has an alliance with United Airlines and Air Canada to provide seamless air service to Germany and other parts of the globe from North America. Dubbed "Star Alliance," the union allows cross-airline benefits, including travel on one or all of these airlines on one ticket and frequent-flyer credit to the participating airline of your choice. The Star Alliance also includes Scandinavian Airlines System, Thai Airways International, and Varig.

American Airlines (© 800/443-7300; www.aa.com) flies nonstop to Frankfurt daily from both Dallas/Fort Worth and Chicago. Nonstop daily service is also available between Miami and Frankfurt. From Frankfurt, Düsseldorf, and London, among others, American's flights connect easily with ongoing flights to many other German cities on Lufthansa or British Airways.

Continental Airlines (© **800/231-0856;** www.continental.com) offers daily nonstop service between Newark and Frankfurt and Düsseldorf. The airline maintains excellent connections between Newark and its hubs in Cleveland and Houston. Continental also offers discounts and other benefits to seniors 62 and over and to their traveling companions, regardless of age.

From the Delta Flight Center at JFK airport in New York, **Delta Airlines** (© **800/241-4141;** www.delta.com) offers daily service to both Frankfurt and (via Brussels) Hamburg. Delta is especially strong in service to Germany from its home base in Atlanta, with two daily nonstops to Frankfurt and daily nonstops to Munich, as well as Hamburg via Paris, and Stuttgart via Paris. Delta also offers frequent nonstops to Frankfurt from Cincinnati (one of its major Midwestern hubs).

If you fly one of **KLM's** (© **800/374-7747;** www.nwa.com) frequent nonstop flights into Amsterdam from New York's JFK and from Atlanta, you can include a stopover in Holland. From Amsterdam, many flights on both KLM and Lufthansa fly into all the major cities of Germany. Flights to Germany on **Northwest Airlines** (© **800/374-7747;** www.nwa.com), KLM's partner, are available out of Boston and Washington, D.C.

United Airlines (© **800/241-6522;** www.ual.com) offers daily nonstops from Washington, D.C., and Chicago to Frankfurt. Furthermore, because of the Star Alliance, discussed above, all German flights by Lufthansa or Air Canada will also be honored as a part of a United ticket. If you're interested in taking advantage of the Star Alliance, be sure to notify the United ticket agent when you are booking or inquiring about your flight.

From London, **British Airways** (© **0845/773-3377** in London, or 0345/222-111 in the U.K.; www.britishairways.com) and **Lufthansa** (© **0845/773-7747** in the U.K.) are the most convenient carriers to the major German cities, including Düsseldorf, Cologne, Frankfurt, Munich, and Berlin. BA has seven flights a day to Cologne (flying time: 75 min.), five daily flights to Munich (1 hr. 40 min.), and four nonstop and three one-stop to Berlin (1 hr. 40 min.). It also services Bremen, Hannover, and Stuttgart. **British Midland** (© **0870/607-0555**) in London, or 0345/554-554 in the U.K.; www.flybmi.com) has two daily flights to Cologne, four daily to Frankfurt, and one daily to Dresden.

From Ireland, **Aer Lingus** (© **01/886-8888;** www.flyaerlingus. com) flies between Dublin and Frankfurt and Düsseldorf; **Lufthansa** (© **01/844-5544**) flies from Frankfurt to Dublin.

From Australia, **Qantas** (℃ 008-112-121 in Australia; www.qantas. com.au) flies from both Melbourne and Sydney to Frankfurt via Asia. Lufthansa offers cheap fares in conjunction with Qantas.

BY TRAIN

Many passengers travel to Berlin by train from other European cities. In Germany, many cities, including Frankfurt and Hamburg, have good rail connections to Berlin. A trip from Frankfurt to Berlin takes about 7 hours.

British Rail runs four trains a day to Germany from Victoria Station in London, going by way of the Ramsgate-Ostend ferry or jetfoil. Two trains depart from London's Liverpool Street Station, via Harwich Hook of Holland. Most trains change at Cologne for destinations elsewhere in Germany. Tickets can be purchased through British Rail travel centers in London (℃ **0877/677-1066** in the U.K., or 0845/748-4950). See "By the Chunnel," below, for information about the Eurostar service running between London and Brussels via the Channel Tunnel.

Train journeys can be lengthy. If you go by jetfoil, Cologne is 9½ hours away from London; by the Dover-Ostend ferry, it's 12½ hours; and via the Ramsgate-Ostend ferry, it's 13 hours. Berlin can be reached in about 20 hours. Travel from London to Munich, depending on the connection, can take from 18 to 22 hours; it's often cheaper to fly than to take the train.

From Paris several trains depart throughout the day for points east, fanning out across eastern France to virtually every part of Germany. The most glamorous of these is the Orient Express, which departs from the Gare de l'Est around 6pm, arriving in Munich around 3am. For railway information on the French rail lines call ℃ **08-36-35-35-39.** Likewise, trains depart from throughout Austria, Italy, Holland, Denmark, and the Czech Republic for all points in Germany, interconnecting into one of the most efficient, and densely routed, rail networks in the world. For information and timetables before your departure, call **RailEurope** at ℃ **800/848-7245.**

STATIONS IN BERLIN

Most trains from the west arrive at the **Bahnhof Zoologischer Garten,** the main train station, called "Bahnhof Zoo." It lies in the center of the city, close to the Kurfürstendamm, and is well connected with public transportation. Both the U-Bahn and the bus network link this station with the rest of Berlin. Bus no. 109 runs to Berlin-Tegel Airport, if you're making connections.

Facilities at the station include a visitor information counter, which dispenses free maps and brochures. It's open daily from 5am to 10pm. The staff here will also make hotel reservations for a fee of 2€ ($2.30). You can also mail letters, exchange currency, and rent lockers.

Berlin has two other train stations, the **Berlin Ostbahnhof** and **Berlin Lichtenberg.** Many trains from east Europe pull into these two stations, both in the eastern part of Berlin. However, certain trains from the west also stop at one of these, so always make sure you're getting off at the right station. S-Bahn 5 connects both of these stations to Bahnhof Zoo. For information about any railway station in Berlin, call ✆ **01805/99-66-33.**

BY THE CHUNNEL

The $15 billion Channel Tunnel (or "Chunnel"), one of the great engineering feats of all time, is the first link between Britain and the Continent since the Ice Age. The tunnel was built beneath the seabed through a layer of impermeable chalk marl and sealed with a reinforced concrete lining. The 50km (31-mile) journey between Britain and France takes 35 minutes, although actual time in the Chunnel is only 19 minutes. Once on the Continent, you can connect to Germany fairly easily.

Rail Europe sells tickets on the **Eurostar** direct train service between London and Paris or Brussels (✆ **800/4EURAIL**). Round-trip first-class fare between London and Paris costs $369, regular second-class $159. Round-trip first-class fare between London and Brussels costs $279, with regular second class at $159. In the United Kingdom, make reservations for **Eurostar** at ✆ **0870/530-0003;** in Paris at ✆ **08-36-35-35-39;** and in the United States at ✆ **800/ 848-RAIL.** A journey from London to Paris via the Chunnel takes about the same amount of time as flying, if you calculate door-to-door travel time. Trains leave from London's Waterloo Station and arrive in Paris at the Gare du Nord.

The tunnel also accommodates passenger cars, charter buses, taxis, and motorcycles from Folkestone to Calais. It operates 24 hours a day, 365 days a year, running every 15 minutes during peak travel times and at least once an hour at night. Tickets may be purchased at the tollbooth. Contact **Eurotunnel** (✆ **800/4-EURAIL** in the U.S. and Canada; 08705/35-35-35 in the U.K.).

BY CAR & FERRY

If you want to bring your car over from England, you face a choice of ports, from which you'll continue on driving to Germany. **P&O**

Stenna Lines (© 0870/600-0611; www.posl.com in the U.K.) has 30 to 35 ferryboat crossings a day, depending on the season, between Dover and Calais. The crossing can take as little as 1 hour, 15 minutes. Once in Calais, the drive to Cologne takes about 3 hours. Other options involve passage from Harwich to the Hook of Holland, a sea crossing of about 8 hours. You can also take your car via the Chunnel (see above).

BY BUS (COACH)

You can travel by bus to Berlin from London, Paris, and many other cities in Europe. The continent's largest bus operator is **Eurolines,** 52 Grosvenor Gardens, London SW1W 0AU, which operates out of Victoria Coach Station in Central London. In Paris, the Eurolines office is within a 35-minute subway ride from Central Paris, at 28 av. du Général-de-Gaulle, 93541 Bagnolet; Métro stop: Gallieni. For more information about **Eurolines in Britain,** call © 020/773330-8235; www.eurolines.com. For more information about **Eurolines in Germany,** contact **Deutsche Touring,** Am Römerhof 17, 60426 Frankfurt am Main (© 069/7-90-32-40; www.touring-germany.com). Eurolines does not maintain a U.S.-based sales agent, but many travel agents can arrange for a ticket on the bus lines that link Europe's major cities. Buses on long-haul journeys are equipped with toilets and partially reclining seats. They stop for 60-minute breaks every 4 hours for rest and refreshment.

FLYING FOR LESS: TIPS FOR GETTING THE BEST AIRFARE

Passengers sharing the same airplane cabin rarely pay the same fare. Travelers who need to purchase tickets at the last minute, change their itinerary at a moment's notice, or fly one-way often get stuck paying the premium rate. Here are some ways to keep your airfare costs down.

- Passengers who can book their ticket **long in advance,** who can **stay over Saturday night,** or who **fly midweek** or **at less-trafficked hours** will pay a fraction of the full fare. If your schedule is flexible, say so, and ask if you can secure a cheaper fare by changing your flight plans.
- You can also save on airfares by keeping an eye out in local newspapers for **promotional specials** or **fare wars,** when airlines lower prices on their most popular routes. You rarely see fare wars offered for peak travel times, but if you can travel in the off-months, you may snag a bargain.

- Search **the Internet** for cheap fares.
- **Consolidators,** also known as bucket shops, are great sources for international tickets, although they usually can't beat the Internet on fares within North America. Start by looking in Sunday newspaper travel sections; U.S. travelers should focus on the *New York Times, Los Angeles Times,* and *Miami Herald.* For less-developed destinations, small travel agents who cater to immigrant communities in large cities often have the best deals. *Beware:* Bucket shop tickets are usually nonrefundable or rigged with stiff cancellation penalties, often as high as 50% to 75% of the ticket price, and some put you on charter airlines with questionable safety records. Reliable consolidators are worldwide and available on the Net. **STA Travel** is now the world's leader in student travel, thanks to their purchase of Council Travel. It also offers good fares for travelers of all ages. **Flights.com** (© **800/TRAV-800;** www.flights.com) started in Europe and has excellent fares worldwide, but particularly to that continent. It also has "local" websites in 12 countries. **Fly-Cheap** (© **800/FLY-CHEAP;** www.1800flycheap.com) is owned by package-holiday megalith MyTravel and so has especially good access to fares for sunny destinations. **Air Tickets Direct** (© **800/778-3447;** www.airticketsdirect.com) is based in Montreal and leverages the currently weak Canadian dollar for low fares; it'll also book trips to places that U.S. travel agents won't touch, such as Cuba.
- Join **frequent-flier clubs.** Accrue enough miles, and you'll be rewarded with free flights and elite status. It's free, and you'll get the best choice of seats, faster response to phone inquiries, and prompter service if your luggage is stolen, your flight is canceled or delayed, or if you want to change your seat. You don't need to fly to build frequent-flier miles—**frequent-flier credit cards** can provide thousands of miles for doing your everyday shopping.
- For many more tips about air travel, including a rundown of the major frequent-flier credit cards, pick up a copy of *Frommer's Fly Safe, Fly Smart* (Wiley Publishing, Inc.).

3

Getting to Know Berlin

Berlin is a vast and sprawling city, and can be confusing to the visitor. This chapter will give you the basic information you'll need to know once you're in Berlin, including an overview of the city's geography and systems of transportation. In addition, check out the "Fast Facts" section, at the end of the chapter, for details on everything from camera shops to local laundries.

1 Orientation

ARRIVING

BY PLANE   **Tegel** is the city's busiest airport, serving most flights from the west. Historic **Tempelhof** (made famous as the city's lifeline during the Berlin Airlift) has declined in importance, although it's still used for flights from Basel, Brussels, Copenhagen, Prague, and many cities within Germany. **Schönefeld,** the airport in the eastern sector, is used primarily by Russian and eastern European airlines. Private bus shuttles among the three airports operate constantly, so you can make connecting flights at a different airport. For information on any of the three airports call ✆ **0180/500-01-86** or visit www.berlin-airport.de.

   Lufthansa (✆ **800/645-3880;** www.Lufthansa-usa.com) offers direct flights from Washington, D.C. to Berlin. Otherwise transatlantic passengers from other cities are routed to its hubs at Frankfurt and Munich.

   Delta (✆ **800/241-4141;** www.delta.com) has flights to Berlin-Tegel in the evening from New York's JFK airport and from Atlanta. However, daily flights, depending on the season or on business, are not always a sure thing, so you'll need to check with a travel agent or the airline itself.

   The best and most convenient service into Berlin is available aboard **British Airways (BA)** (✆ **800/247-9297;** www.british airways.com), which efficiently funnels dozens of daily flights from North America to Germany, including five a day into Berlin-Tegel, through its vast terminals at London-Heathrow. Connections to

Berlin Today & Tomorrow

Berlin is living up to its reputation as never before as a dynamic, exciting hub of activity. The city's nightlife is among Europe's best and wildest. Since the German government was transferred here from Bonn, Berlin has not only been reborn as the capital of Germany, but wants to become "the capital of Europe."

As befits a new capital, the city continues to receive a major face-lift. More than $120 billion has been invested in new streets, buildings, and railways. The former East Berlin is rapidly being restored and gentrified, particularly in the **Mitte** (central) district. Here new luxury hotels and shopping arcades compete with the litter of the Kurfürstendamm. The opening of the Hotel Adlon, overlooking the Brandenburg Gate, is particularly notable. **Prenzlauer Berg,** a blue-collar eastern neighborhood that escaped the worst of the wartime bombing, is becoming a chic district of cafes and boutiques. The downside of all this for Berliners has been

Berlin are excellent from at least 40 gateways in the U.S. and Canada, more than that offered by any other airline. Frequent transatlantic price wars keep fares to Berlin aboard BA lower than you might have thought, especially in off-season. Stopovers in London can be arranged at minimal cost, and deeply discounted hotel packages are available in either Berlin or London, at rates that are significantly less than what you'd have paid if you'd arranged them yourself. And if you opt for passage in Business Class (BA calls it Club Class), you'll ride on the most comfortable, and one of the largest, airline seats in the industry, in a configuration that can be transformed into something approaching a bed.

Berlin-Tegel Airport (© 01805/000186; www.berlin-airport.de/PubEnglish) is 8km (5 miles) northwest of the city center. Public transportation by bus, taxi, or U-Bahn is convenient to all points in the city. BVG buses X9 and 109 run every 10 to 15 minutes from the airport to Bahnhof Zoo in Berlin's center, departing from outside the arrival hall; a one-way fare is 3€ ($3.45). A taxi to the city center costs 14€ to 22€ ($16–$25) and takes 20 minutes. No porters are available for luggage handling, but pushcarts are free.

the sharp increase in real-estate prices, as well as the inconvenience of living in the world's largest construction site.

Many of Berlin's famous buildings have been restored. The rebuilt **Reichstag** has a glittering glass dome; upon the building stands not the old glowering imperial hunter, but the national symbol, the eagle (locals refer affectionately to the statue as "the fat hen"). The Oranienburger Strasse **synagogue,** wrecked on Kristallnacht and finished off by Allied bombers, has been rebuilt in all its splendor. Likewise, **Berlin Cathedral** and the five state museums on **Museum Island** have been painstakingly returned to their original glory.

Visitors often overlook Berlin's **natural attractions.** Few metropolitan areas are blessed with as many gardens, lakes, woodlands, and parks—these cover an amazing one-third of the city. First-time visitors are often surprised to learn that small farms with fields and meadows still exist within the city limits.

The main terminal has a **visitor information counter** where you can get a free map of the city. The counter is open daily 5am to 10pm. Facilities at the terminal include money-exchange centers, luggage-storage facilities (and locker rentals), a police station, auto-rental kiosks, dining facilities, and a first-aid center. Shops sell gifts, film, and travel paraphernalia.

Berlin-Schönefeld Airport (© **01805/000186;** www.berlin-airport.de/PubEnglish), once the main airport for East Berlin, now receives many flights from Asia, as well as Russia and other European countries. It lies in Brandenburg, 19km (12 miles) southeast of the city center. The city center is a 55-minute ride on the S-Bahn. You can also take bus 171 from the airport to Rudow, where you transfer to the U-Bahn. Either means of transport costs 3€ ($3.45).

Berlin-Tempelhof Airport (© **01805/000186;** www.berlin-airport.de/PubEnglish) is the city's oldest airport, 6km (4 miles) southeast of the city center. Tempelhof now receives several flights a day from German and European cities. Take the U-Bahn or bus 119. All bus trips from Tempelhof into the center cost 3€ ($3.45).

BY TRAIN As Berlin strengthens its role as capital, increasing numbers of trains are speeding their way into town. All points of the country, especially Frankfurt, Munich, and Bonn, maintain excellent rail connections, with high-tech, high-speed improvements being made to the country's railway system virtually all the time. One recent major improvement is that Berlin and the great port of Hamburg are now 15 minutes closer thanks to high-speed (250kmph/155 mph) InterCity Express service (the trip is now 2 hr. and 8 min.). Since reunification, Berlin has improved the facilities of railway stations in both the western zone (Bahnhof Zoologischer Garten) and eastern zone (Berlin Ostbahnhof), installing improved S-Bahn links to interconnect them. The station you'll use depends on the destination or origin of your train, or the location of your hotel within the city. Some, but not all, trains make arrivals and departures from both stations. A third station, Berlin Lichtenberg, within the city's eastern half, is used for trains pulling in from small towns. For information about any railway station, call © **00810/599-66-33.**

BY BUS (COACH) Regularly scheduled buses operate from 250 German and continental cities, including Frankfurt, Hamburg, and Munich. Long-distance bus companies servicing Berlin include **Autokraft GmbH, Haru-Reisen,** and **Bayern Express & P. Köhn** (© **030/8-60-96-0** or 030/8-60-21-1).

Arrivals and departures are at the **ZOB Omnibusbahnhof am Funkturm,** Masurenalle, Charlottenburg. Taxis and bus connections are available at the station, U-Bahn at nearby Kaiserdamm station.

BY CAR From Frankfurt, take the E451 north until it connects with the E40 going northeast. Follow this Autobahn past Jena and then head north on the E51 into Berlin. From Nürnberg, also take the E51 into Berlin. From Dresden, take the E55 north to Berlin. Expect heavy traffic on the autobahns on weekends and sunny days when everybody is out touring.

VISITOR INFORMATION

For visitor information and hotel bookings, head for the **Berlin Tourist Information Center,** Europa Center (near Memorial Church); the entrance is on the Budapesterstrasse side. It's open Monday to Saturday 8am to 8pm and Sunday 10am to 6:30pm. There's also a branch at the south wing of the Brandenburg Gate, open daily 9:30am to 6pm. Neither branch accepts telephone calls from the general public. Instead, dial © **030/25-00-25** for hotel reservations within Germany. If you're calling from outside of

Germany, you'll have to access a different number: ℂ **01805/75-40-40.** The cheapest and most up-to-date way to access tourist information about Berlin is on the Internet at **www.berlin-tourism.de**.

CITY LAYOUT

Berlin is one of the largest and most complex cities in Europe. Since it's so spread out, you'll need to depend on public transportation. No visitor should try to explore more than two neighborhoods a day, even superficially.

The center of activity in the western part of Berlin is the 4km (2½-mile) long **Kurfürstendamm,** called the Ku'damm by Berliners, who seem to have a habit of irreverently renaming every street and building in the city. Along this wide boulevard you'll find the best hotels, restaurants, theaters, cafes, nightclubs, shops, and department stores. It's the most elegant and fashionable spot in Berlin, but, like much of the city, it combines chic with sleaze in places. Walkers can stop off at one of the popular cafes lining the boulevard.

From the Ku'damm you can take Hardenbergstrasse, which crosses Bismarckstrasse and becomes Otto-Suhr-Allee, which will lead to the **Schloss Charlottenburg** area and its museums, a major sightseeing area. The **Dahlem Museums** are in the southwest of the city, often reached by going along Hohenzollerndamm.

The huge **Tiergarten** is the city's largest park. Running through it is **Strasse des 17 Juni,** which leads to the famed **Brandenburg Gate** (just south of the Reichstag). On the southwestern fringe of the Tiergarten is the **Berlin Zoo.**

⌒Tips Finding an Address

As for the numbering of streets, keep in mind the city sometimes assists you by posting the range of numbers that appears within any particular block, at least within major arteries such as the Kurfürstendamm. These numbers appear on the street signs themselves, which is a great help in finding a particular number on long boulevards. You won't find these numbers on street signs of smaller streets, however. Although some streets are numbered with the odds on one side and the evens on the other, many (including the Ku'damm) are numbered consecutively up one side of the street and back down the other. *Warning:* The names of some eastern Berlin streets and squares with links to the old East German regime have been changed.

The Brandenburg Gate is the start of eastern Berlin's most celebrated street, **Unter den Linden,** the cultural heart of Berlin before World War II. It runs from west to east, leading to **Museumsinsel (Museum Island),** where the most outstanding museums of eastern Berlin, including the Pergamon Museum, are situated. Unter den Linden crosses another major artery, **Friedrichstrasse.** If you continue south along Friedrichstrasse, you'll reach the former location of **Checkpoint Charlie,** a famous border site of the Cold War days. No longer a checkpoint, it now has a little museum devoted to memories of the Berlin Wall. Unter den Linden continues east until it reaches **Alexanderplatz,** the center of eastern Berlin, with its soaring television tower (Fernsehturm). A short walk away is the newly restored **Nikolai Quarter (Nikolaiviertel),** a neighborhood of bars, restaurants, and shops that evoke life in the prewar days.

MAPS   Good maps of Berlin can be purchased at bookstores or news kiosks, such as the Europa Press Center (a magazine and newspaper store in the Europa Center). One of the best maps is the **Falk** map, which offers full-color detail and comprehensive indexes (consequently, it's sometimes awkward to unfold and refold). Be sure to obtain an up-to-date map showing the most recent changes.

NEIGHBORHOODS IN BRIEF

Visitors who knew Berlin during the Cold War are amazed at the way traffic now zips between sectors that once were rigidly segregated by border guards. Today, your taxi will blithely drive beneath the Brandenburg Gate or along the Friedrichstrasse, without regard to barriers that once used to be virtually impenetrable. Names you're likely to hear as you navigate your way through the reunited city include the following:

In the Western Zone

Charlottenburg   Despite being renamed by Berlin wits as Klamottenburg (Ragsville) after the bombings of World War II, this is still the wealthiest and most densely commercialized district of western Berlin. Its centerpiece is Charlottenburg Palace. One of the most interesting subdivisions of Charlottenburg is the neighborhood around **Savignyplatz,** a tree-lined square a short walk north of the western zone's most visible boulevard, Kurfürstendamm. Lining its edges and the streets nearby are a profusion of bars, shops, and restaurants, an engaging aura of permissiveness, and an awareness that this is the bastion of the city's prosperous bourgeoisie.

Dahlem   Now the university district, Dahlem was originally established as an independent village to the southwest of Berlin's center.

Ku'damm In the 1950s and '60s, during the early stages of the Cold War, the Ku'damm emerged as a rough-and-tumble boom-town, bristling with boxy-looking new constructions, and per-meated with a maverick sense of parvenu novelty. Since reunification, when vast neighborhoods within Mitte opened for real-estate speculation and instant gentrification, the Ku'damm has reinvented itself as a bastion of capitalistic and corporate con-servatism, with a distinct sense of old and established money that's waiting for public perceptions to grow bored with the nov-elties that have been associated with the opening of the former East Berlin. The poignancies of the Weimar Republic and the Cold War are not lost, however, even upon the corporate spon-sors of the big-money real-estate ventures that line the Ku'damm. If you look at the Hochhaus entrance of the Europa Center, on the Tauentzienstrasse side, whose glossy chrome-trimmed interior decor might remind you of an airport waiting lounge, you'll find a plaque honoring the long-ago site of the private home of Weimar statesman Gustav Stresemann, which used to stand at 12A Tauentzienstrasse. Immediately adjacent to that plaque is an artfully graffitied chunk of the former Berlin Wall, encased in Plexiglas like an irreplaceable work of ancient archaeology. It is dedicated to the people who lost their lives trying to escape over the Wall during the peak of the Cold War.

Grunewald Many newcomers are surprised by the sheer sprawl of Grunewald's 49sq. km (19 sq. miles) of verdant forest. The area serves as a green lung for the urbanites of Berlin. It lies west/southwest of the city center.

Hansaviertel This neighborhood, northwest of Tiergarten park, contains a series of residential buildings designed by different archi-tects (including Le Corbusier, Walter Gropius, and Alvar Aalto).

Kreuzberg Originally built during the 19th century to house the workers of a rapidly industrializing Prussia, this has tradi-tionally been the poorest and most overcrowded of Berlin's dis-tricts. Today, at least 35 percent of its population is composed of guest workers from Turkey, the former Yugoslavia, and Greece. Before the city's reunification, the district evolved into the head-quarters for the city's artistic counterculture. Since reunification, however, the fast-changing neighborhoods within Mitte, espe-cially Hackescher Höfe (see below) have offered stiff competition.

Schöneberg Like Kreuzberg, it was originally an independent suburb of workers' housing, but after the war it was rebuilt as a solidly middle-class neighborhood that also happens to include

Berlin at a Glance

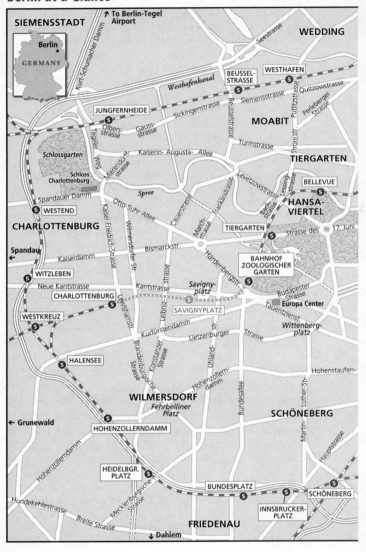

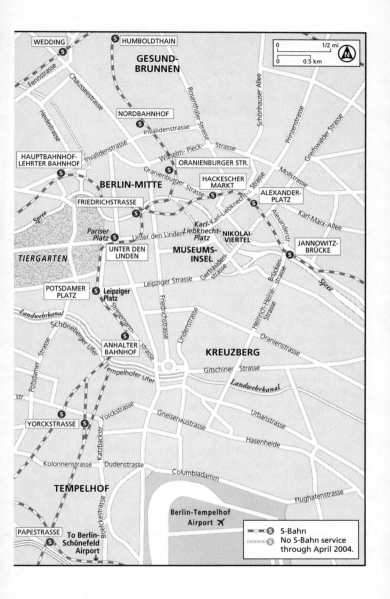

WEDDING

HUMBOLDTHAIN

GESUND-
BRUNNEN

Fennstrasse

Chausseestrasse

Heidestrasse

NORDBAHNHOF

Invalidenstrasse

Rosenthaler Strasse

Schönhauser Allee

Prinzenstrasse

Greifswalder Strasse

HAUPTBAHNHOF-
LEHRTER BAHNHOF

Invalidenstrasse

Wilhelm- Pieck- Strasse

ORANIENBURGER STR.

Oranienburger Strasse

BERLIN-MITTE

HACKESCHER
MARKT

Mollstrasse

ALEXANDER-
PLATZ

Karl-Marx-Allee

FRIEDRICHSTRASSE

Karl-Karl-Liebknecht-

Karl-
Liebknecht-
Platz

NIKOLAI-
VIERTEL

Alexanderstr.

Spree

Pariser
Platz

Unter den Linden

UNTER DEN
LINDEN

MUSEUMS-
INSEL

Gertraudenstrasse

JANNOWITZ-
BRÜCKE

TIERGARTEN

Leipziger Strasse

Heinrich-Heine- Brücken- strasse

Spree

POTSDAMER
PLATZ

Leipziger
Platz

Stresemann

Friedrichstrasse

Lindenstrasse

Landwehrkanal

Schöneberger Ufer

strasse

ANHALTER
BAHNHOF

Tempelhofer Ufer

KREUZBERG

Oranienstrasse

Potsdamer Strasse

Gitschiner Strasse

Landwehrkanal

YORCKSTRASSE

Yorckstrasse

Katzbackstr.

Gneisenaustrasse

Urbanstrasse

Hasenheide

str.

Kolonnenstrasse

Dudenstrasse

Columbiadamm

Flughafenstrasse

TEMPELHOF

Boelckestrasse

Berlin-Tempelhof
Airport ✈

PAPESTRASSE

To Berlin-
Schönefeld
Airport
↓

S-Bahn

No S-Bahn service
through April 2004.

37

the densest concentration of gay bars and clubs (between Nollen-dorfplatz and Victoria-Luise-Platz).

Spandau Set near the junction of the Spree and Havel rivers, about 10km (6 miles) northwest of the city center, Spandau boasts a history of medieval grandeur. Though it merged with Berlin in 1920, its Altstadt (old city) is still intact. The legendary Spandau prison was demolished in the early 1990s.

Tiergarten The name Tiergarten (which means "Animal Garden") refers both to a massive urban park and, to the park's north, a residential district of the same name. The park was originally intended as a backdrop to the grand avenues laid out by the German kaisers. The neighborhood contains the Brandenburg Gate, the German Reichstag (Parliament), the Berlin Zoo, and some of the city's grandest museums.

In The Eastern Zone

Alexanderplatz The former East German regime threw up lots of rather ugly modern buildings and defined Alexanderplatz as the centerpiece of its government. Today the large and sterile-looking square is dominated by the tallest structure in Berlin, the Sputnik-inspired TV tower.

Hackesche Höfe A warren of brick-sided factories during the 19th century, this neighborhood is evolving into one of the city's most visible counterculture strongholds. Part of this derives from the fact that it wasn't too badly mangled by the former East German regime. Another factor in its renaissance involves a thirst by cutting-edge, often youthful Berliners to recolonize what used to be the heart of the DDR. You'll get a sense of rising real-estate values and an aura that combines aspects of Paris's Latin Quarter and New York's Greenwich Village.

Mitte (Center) Closed to capitalist investment for nearly 50 years, this monumental district in the heart of Berlin is the one that's on every speculator's mind these days. It was originally conceived as the architectural centerpiece of the Prussian kaisers. Its fortunes declined dramatically as the Communist regime infused it with starkly angular monuments and architecturally banal buildings. Although some of Mitte's grand structures were destroyed by wartime bombings, unification has exposed its remaining artistic and architectural treasures. The district's most famous boulevard is Unter den Linden. Famous squares within the district include Pariser Platz (the monumental square adjacent to the Brandenburg Gate), Potsdamer Platz (see below), and Alexanderplatz (see above).

Museumsinsel (Museum Island)   This island in the Spree River hosts a complex of museums housed in neoclassical buildings that always seem to be under renovation. Its most famous museum, the Pergamon, contains magnificent reconstructions of ancient temples.

Nikolaiviertel   Near the Alexanderplatz, the Nikolaiviertel is the most perfectly restored medieval neighborhood in Berlin, and a triumph of the restoration skills of the former East German regime.

Potsdamer Platz   Before World War II, this was the thriving heart of Berlin. Blasted into rubble by wartime bombings, it was bulldozed into a "no man's land" when the Wall went up on its western edge in 1961. After reunification, it was transformed into the biggest building site in Europe, out of which emerged a glittering, hypermodern square dominated by such corporate giants as Daimler-Chrysler. It's often cited as a symbol of the corporate culture of a reunited Germany.

2 Getting Around

BY PUBLIC TRANSPORTATION

The Berlin transport system consists of buses, trams, and U-Bahn (underground) and S-Bahn (elevated) trains. The network is run by the **BVG** or Public Transport Company Berlin-Brandenburg. Public transportation throughout the city operates from about 4:30am to 12:30am daily (except for 62 night buses and trams, and U-Bahn lines U-9 and U-12). For information about public transport, call © **030/1-94-49** or visit www.bvg.de. For a plan of Berlin's **U-Bahn and S-Bahn system,** see the inside back cover of this guide.

The **BVG standard ticket** *(Einzelfahrschein)* costs 2.40€ ($2.75) and is valid for 2 hours of transportation in all directions, transfers included. A 24-hour ticket for the whole city costs from 6.30€ ($7.25). Only standard tickets are sold on buses. Tram tickets must be purchased in advance. All tickets should be kept until the end of the journey; otherwise you'll be liable for a fine of 31€ ($35). Unless you buy a day pass, don't forget to time-punch your ticket into one of the small red boxes prominently posted at the entrance to city buses and underground stations.

If you're going to be in Berlin for 3 days, you can purchase for 19€ ($22) a **Berlin-Potsdam WelcomeCard,** which entitles holders to 72 free hours on public transportation in Berlin and Brandenburg. You'll also get free admission or a price reduction of up to 50% on

Berlin U-Bahn & S-Bahn

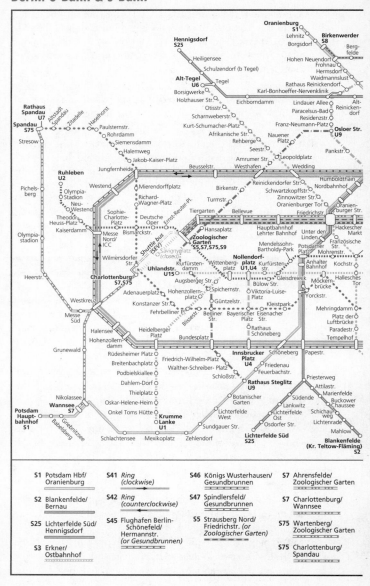

S1 Potsdam Hbf/ Oranienburg	**S41** *Ring (clockwise)*	**S46** Königs Wusterhausen/ Gesundbrunnen	**S7** Ahrensfelde/ Zoologischer Garten
S2 Blankenfelde/ Bernau	**S42** *Ring (counterclockwise)*	**S47** Spindlersfeld/ Gesundbrunnen	**S7** Charlottenburg/ Wannsee
S25 Lichterfelde Süd/ Hennigsdorf	**S45** Flughafen Berlin-Schönefeld/ Hermannstr. *(or Gesundbrunnen)*	**S5** Strausberg Nord/ Friedrichstr. *(or Zoologischer Garten)*	**S75** Wartenberg/ Zoologischer Garten
S3 Erkner/ Ostbahnhof			**S75** Charlottenburg/ Spandau

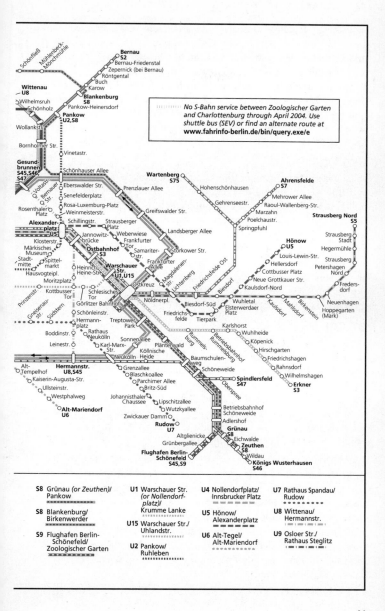

No S-Bahn service between Zoologischer Garten and Charlottenburg through April 2004. Use shuttle bus (SEV) or find an alternate route at **www.fahrinfo-berlin.de/bin/query.exe/e**

S8 Grünau (or Zeuthen)/ Pankow	**U1** Warschauer Str. (or Nollendorf- platz)/ Krumme Lanke	**U4** Nollendorfplatz/ Innsbrucker Platz	**U7** Rathaus Spandau/ Rudow
S8 Blankenburg/ Birkenwerder	**U15** Warschauer Str./ Uhlandstr.	**U5** Hönow/ Alexanderplatz	**U8** Wittenau/ Hermannstr.
S9 Flughafen Berlin- Schönefeld/ Zoologischer Garten	**U2** Pankow/ Ruhleben	**U6** Alt-Tegel/ Alt-Mariendorf	**U9** Osloer Str./ Rathaus Steglitz

sightseeing tours, museums, and other attractions, and a 25% reduction at 10 theaters as well. The card is sold at many hotels, visitor information centers, and public-transportation sales points. It's valid for one adult and three children under the age of 13.

Two **excursion bus lines** make some beautiful scenic spots accessible. Bus 218 operates from the Theodor-Heuss-Platz U-Bahn station (near the radio tower) via Schildhorn, Grunewald Tower, and Wannsee Beach to the Wannsee S-Bahn station, and bus 216 runs from the Wannsee S-Bahn station to Pfaueninsel via Moorlake.

BY TAXI

Taxis cruise restlessly along the major boulevards, indicating their availability by an illuminated roof light. The meter begins ticking at 3.05€ ($3.50). A 1.55€ ($1.80) supplement is added if you call a cab to a specific address by phone. Within the city center, each kilometer costs around 1.60€ ($1.85), depending on the time of day. Prolonged taxi rides that you arrange to distant suburbs are factored at a per-kilometer rate of 1.02€ ($1.20). Staff members at hotels and restaurants can easily summon a cab for you, in some cases simply by throwing a switch on their phone. Otherwise, dial ⓒ21-02-02, 69-41-099, or 24-63-25-63.

BY CAR

U.S. rental companies have outlets in Berlin. If possible, you should make reservations in advance. You'll find **Hertz** at Berlin-Tegel Airport (ⓒ 030/41-70-46-74) and at Budapesterstrasse 39 (ⓒ 030/2-61-10-53). **Avis** is also at Berlin-Tegel (ⓒ 030/4-10-13-148) and at Budapesterstrasse 43 (ⓒ 030/23-09-370).

But in general, touring Berlin by car is not recommended. Traffic is heavy, and parking is very difficult to come by. Use the excellent public transportation network instead.

PARKING   If you're driving into Berlin, chances are that you'll want to safely store your car once you arrive. Many hotels offer parking facilities; otherwise, you'll find parking garages that remain open throughout the day and night. Those located near the Ku'-damm and the Europa Center include the **Parkhaus Metropol,** Joachimstaler Strasse 14–19; **Parkhaus Los-Angeles-Platz,** Augsburger Strasse 30; **Parkhaus Europa Center,** Nürnberger Strasse 5–7; and the **Parkhaus am Zoo,** Budapesterstrasse 38. Charges start at 2€ ($2.30) per hour.

CITY DRIVING   One problem that often infuriates drivers in Berlin is that it's almost impossible to turn left on major avenues (except at major intersections in the east), because of the position-ing of metal barriers and tram lines. Oversize signs tell you to drive straight on. Drivers have to make a right-hand turn, swing around the block, and then proceed straight across the tram lines wherever a traffic light will allow.

BY BICYCLE

Bicycling in Berlin's crushing traffic is not a very appealing prospect, but you might want to rent a bike to explore the city's outlying parks and forests. Both the U-Bahn and S-Bahn provide specific com-partments for bicycles for an extra 2.55€ ($2.95). Transport of bicy-cles, however, is not permitted during rush hour: Monday to Friday before 9am and again in the afternoon between 2 and 5:30pm. In the city and suburbs, try to confine your bicycling to cycle zones, delineated with solid red lines running between the pedestrian side-walks and the traffic lanes.

A good place for bike rentals is **Fahrradstation,** Readrathstrasse 40–41 (✆ **030/28-38-4848;** S-Bahn: Hackescher Markt), open Monday to Friday 10am to 7pm, Saturday and Sunday 10am to 4pm. A 24-hour rental costs from 13€ to 25€ ($15–$29) on up.

FAST FACTS: Berlin

American Express Reiseland American Express offices at Alte Potsdamer Strasse 7 (✆ **030/25-29-74-74;** U-Bahn: Hüttenweg), Am Borsigturm 2 (✆ **030/21-47-62-92;** U-Bahn: Borischverger), Bayreuthstrasse 37–38 (✆ **030/30-17-400;** U-Bahn: Wittenberg-platz), and Friedrichstrasse 172 (✆ **030/20-17-40-12;** U-bahn: Friedrichstrasse), are all open Monday to Friday 9am to 7pm.

Business Hours Most **banks** are open Monday to Friday 9am to either 1 or 3pm. Most other **businesses** and **stores** are open Monday to Friday 9 or 10am to either 6 or 6:30pm and Satur-day 9am to 2pm. On *langer Samstag,* the first Saturday of the month, shops stay open until 4 or 6pm. Some stores close late on Thursday (usually 8:30pm).

Currency Exchange You can exchange money at all airports, at major department stores, at any bank, and at American Express offices (see above) and other currency exchange out-lets. There is also a currency exchange office at the Bahnhof Zoo; it's open Monday to Saturday from 8am to 9pm and on

Sunday from 10am to 6pm. ATM machines proliferate in Berlin at virtually every branch of the Dresdner or Deutsche Bank, post offices, and railway stations. Two particularly convenient branches with 24-hour ATM service are **Deutsche Bank** at Wittenbergplatz (U-Bahn: Wittenbergplatz) and **Dresdner Bank** at Kurfürstendamm 237 (U-Bahn: Kurfürstendamm).

Dentists/Doctors The Berlin tourist office in the Europa-Center (see "Visitor Information," above) keeps a list of English-speaking dentists and doctors in Berlin. In case of a medical emergency, call © **030/31-00-31.**

Drugstores If you need a pharmacy *(Apotheke)* at night, go to one on any corner. There you'll find a sign in the window giving the address of the nearest drugstore open at night; such posting is required by law. A central pharmacy is **Europa-Apotheke,** Tauentzienstrasse 9–12 (© **030/2-61-41-42;** U-Bahn: Kurfürstendamm), by the Europa-Center. It's open Monday to Friday 9am to 8pm and Saturday to 6pm.

Embassies & Consulates The following embassies and consulates are all located in Berlin. The embassy of the **United States** is in Dahlem at Clayallee 170 (© **030/832-92-33;** U-Bahn: Dahlem-Dorf), open Monday to Friday 8:30am to noon. The **U.K. Embassy** is at Unter den Linden 32-34 (© **030/20-18-40;** U-Bahn: Unter den Linden), open Monday to Friday 9am to 4pm. The **Australian Embassy** is at Friedrichstrasse 200 (© **030/880-08-80;** U-Bahn Uhlandstrasse), open Monday to Friday 9am to noon. The **Canadian Embassy** is at Friedrichstrasse 95 (© **030/20-31-20;** U-Bahn: Friedrichstrasse), open Monday to Friday 9am to noon. The **Irish Embassy** is at Friedrichstrasse 200 (© **030/22-07-20;** U-Bahn: Uhlandstrasse), open Monday to Friday 9:30am to noon and 2:30 to 3:45pm. The **New Zealand Embassy** is at Friedrichstrasse 60 (© **030/206-210;** U-Bahn: Friedrichstrasse), open Monday to Friday 9am to 1pm and 2 to 5:30pm. The **South African Embassy** is at Friedrichstrasse 60 (© **030/22-07-30;** U-Bahn: Friedrichstrasse), open Monday to Friday 9am to noon.

Emergencies To call the police, dial © **110.** To report a fire or to summon an ambulance, dial © **112.**

Hospitals Hotel employees are usually familiar with the locations of the nearest hospital emergency room. In an emergency, call © **112** for an ambulance.

Hot Lines If you're the victim of rape or sexual assault, call **LARA,** Tempelhoferufer 14 (© **030/216-88-88**). For problems relating to drug use or drug addiction, call the drug help line at ℂ **030/1-92-37.** Gays seeking legal or health-related advice should call **Schwüles Uberfall** (ℂ 030/216-33-36). Gays can also call the **Café Positif** (ℂ 030/216-8654) for advice about AIDS and its treatment and prevention; and **Man-o-Meter** (ℂ 030/216-8008) for information about anything to do with gay life or gay events in Berlin or the rest of Germany. All of the above are staffed with some English speakers.

Internet Access You can get internet access all over town—ask at your hotel for the one closest to you. For a good place in the center of town, visit **Karstadt Sports,** Joachimstaler 5–6 (ℂ 030/8802-41-89; U-Bahn: Bahnhof Zoologisher Garten). Open Monday to Saturday 10am to 8pm.

Laundry/Dry Cleaning Deluxe and first-class hotels offer laundry service, but prices tend to be high. You'll find laundromats *(Wascherei)* and dry-cleaning outlets *(Reiningung)* all over town. One that's relatively convenient is **Wascherei Lindenberg,** Curtius Strasse 13–14 (ℂ 030/833-1056; S-Bahn Lichterfelder West). Otherwise, ask at your hotel for additional options.

Lost Property For items lost on the bus or U-Bahn, go to **BVG Fündbüro,** Frauenhoferstrasse 33–36 (ℂ 030/25-62-30-40; U-Bahn: Ernst-Reuter-Platz); open Monday to Thursday 9am to 6pm and Friday 9am to 2pm. For items lost on the S-Bahn, go to **Deutsches Bahn AG/8-Bahn Berlin GmbH,** Mittelstrasse 20 (ℂ 030/2-97-296-12; U-Bahn: Friedrichstrasse), Monday, Wednesday, or Thursday 10am to 4pm, Tuesday 10am to 6pm, or Friday 8am to noon. The general lost-property office, **Zentrales Fündbüro,** is at Platz der Luftbrücke 6 (ℂ 030/69-95; U-Bahn: Platz der Luftbrücke). Hours are Monday and Tuesday 7:30am to 2pm, Wednesday noon to 6:30pm, and Friday 7:30am to noon.

Passports **For residents of the United States:** Whether you're applying in person or by mail, you can download passport applications from the U.S. State Department website at **http://travel.state.gov**. For general information, call the **National Passport Agency** (ℂ 202/647-0518). To find your regional passport office, either check the U.S. State Department website or call the **National Passport Information Center** (ℂ 900/225-5674); the fee is 55¢ per minute for automated information and $1.50 per minute for operator-assisted calls.

For Residents of Canada: Passport applications are available at travel agencies throughout Canada or from the central **Passport Office,** Department of Foreign Affairs and International Trade, Ottawa, ON K1A 0G3 (© **800/567-6868;** www.dfait-maeci.gc.ca/passport).

For Residents of the United Kingdom: To pick up an application for a standard 10-year passport (5-yr. passport for children under 16), visit your nearest passport office, major post office, or travel agency or contact the **United Kingdom Passport Service** at © 0870/521-0410 or search its website at www.ukpa.gov.uk. **For Residents of Ireland:** You can apply for a 10-year passport at the **Passport Office,** Setanta Centre, Molesworth Street, Dublin 2 (© 01/671-1633; www.irlgov.ie/iveagh). Those under age 18 and over 65 must apply for a 3-year passport. You can also apply at 1A South Mall, Cork (© **021/272-525**) or at most main post offices.

For Residents of Australia: You can pick up an application from your local post office or any branch of Passports Australia, but you must schedule an interview at the passport office to present your application materials. Call the **Australian Passport Information Service** at © **131-232,** or visit the government website at www.passports.gov.au. **For Residents of New Zealand:** You can pick up a passport application at any New Zealand Passports Office or download it from their website. Contact the **Passports Office** at © 0800/225-050 in New Zealand or 04/474-8100, or log on to www.passports.govt.nz.

Post Office The post office at the Bahnhof Zoo is open Monday to Saturday 6am to midnight and Sunday 8am to midnight. If you have mail sent here, have it marked Hauptpostlagernd, Postamt 120, Bahnhof Zoo, D-10612, Berlin. There's also a post office at Hauptbahnhof, open Monday to Friday 7am to 8pm and Saturday 8am to 1pm. For postal information, call © **030/31-00-80.** You can make long-distance calls at post offices at far cheaper rates than at hotels.

Radio Radio programs in English can be heard on 87.9 FM (or 94 on cable) and 1197 AM for the American Forces Network, and on 30 FM (87.6 on cable) for the BBC.

Restrooms A restroom is called a *Toilette* and is often labeled wc, with either F (for *Frauen,* "women") or H (for *Herren,* "men"). Public facilities are found throughout Berlin and at all terminals, including the Europa Center on Tauentzien-strasse. It's customary to tip attendants at least .25€ (20¢).

Safety One unfortunate side effect of reunification has been an increase in muggings, bank robberies, hate crimes, and car break-ins. Residents of Berlin sometimes feel unsafe at night, especially in the dimly lit streets of Kreuzberg. Nonetheless, Berlin is still much safer than most large American cities. In case of a robbery or an attack, report the problem immediately to the police. You'll need a police report for any insurance claims.

Taxis See "Getting Around," earlier in this chapter.

Telegrams/Fax These can be sent from the post office (see "Post Office," above).

Water The tap water in Berlin, as in all German cities, is safe to drink. However, most Berliners prefer to ask for bottled water, either carbonated or noncarbonated.

4

Where to Stay

Berlin is the scene of frequent international trade fairs, conferences, and festivals, and during these times, vacancies in the city will be hard to find. The greatest concentration of hotels, from the cheapest digs to the most expensive, lies in the center near the **Kurfürstendamm** (Ku'damm), the main boulevard of western Berlin. Most good-value pensions and small hotels are in the western part of the city; note that many such accommodations are in older buildings where plumbing is rarely state of the art.

The business convention crowd still anchors primarily in the west, as do the hordes of summer visitors on whirlwind tours of Europe. **Eastern Berlin** often attracts Germans from other parts of the country who want a glimpse of the Berlin that was shut away behind the Wall for so long. The eastern sector still doesn't have the visitor structure and facilities of the west, although several first-class and deluxe hotels have opened there, notably the Grand, Adlon, and Hilton.

Travelers can also head for hotels in **Grunewald,** close to nature in the Grunewald Forest, or **Charlottenburg,** near Olympic Park. If you like biking, jogging, and breathing fresh air and don't mind the commute into central Berlin for shopping and attractions, you'll enjoy both these areas.

Tegel Airport is only 20 minutes from Berlin by taxi, but if you have a very early departure or late arrival, and want the added security of an airport hotel, you can check into **Novotel Berlin Airport,** Kurt-Schumacher-Damm 202, 13405 Orsteil-Reinickendorf (© **030/41060;** fax 030/4106700; www.novotel.com). Doubles are medium-size and furnished in standard motel-chain format. The

---

Tips **Dialing Germany**

Remember that the phone numbers in this book contain an initial 0 in the German city code. That 0 is only used within Germany. Omit it when calling from abroad.

rate for a double is 153€ ($176), dropping to 78€ ($90) on Friday and Saturday. There's also a restaurant on-site, plus a free shuttle service that runs back and forth between the hotel and airport. American Express, Diners Club, MasterCard, and Visa are accepted.

1 On or Near the Kurfürstendamm

VERY EXPENSIVE

Grand Hotel Esplanade ★★★   Strikingly contemporary, this luxe hotel lies in a quiet and verdant neighborhood near several foreign embassies, some concert halls, and the massively expanding Potsdamer Platz. Thanks to river views and a swath of park, you might get the feeling that you're far from the city. It competes effectively with other Berlin hotels in its class, with a well-conceived collection of modern art. It is, in fact, the hypercontemporary alternative to the more traditional Kempinski. The starkly contemporary, bright, sun-flooded, and cheerful rooms pay strict attention to sound insulation. Bathrooms are generously sized with shower-tub combinations. Corner rooms are among the most spacious and have some of the best views of the surrounding area.

Lützowufer 15, 10785 Berlin. © **030/25-47-80.** Fax 030/265-11-71. www. esplanade.de. 400 units. 110€–305€ ($127–$351) double; from 420€ ($483) suite. AE, DC, MC, V. Parking 16€ ($18). U-Bahn: Kurfürstenstrasse, Nollendorfplatz, or Wittenbergplatz. **Amenities:** Harlekin restaurant (see p. 74), 2 bars; indoor pool; whirlpool; solarium; sauna; room service; babysitting; laundry/dry cleaning; nonsmoking rooms. *In room:* A/C, TV/VCR, minibar, hair dryer, bathrobes.

Kempinski Hotel Bristol Berlin ★★★   This hotel reigns as one of Berlin's most prestigious and visible hotels, enjoying a reputation equivalent to some of the best hotels in the world. But the emergence of such luxe Berlin Mitte properties as Adlon and Four Seasons has shaken the Kempinski crown. It occupies a bulky, boxy-looking building that was originally erected during the peak of the Cold War, but whose interior has benefited from ongoing improvements and renovations. The staff is superbly trained and the shamelessly rich-looking decor is more opulent and better designed than that of many comparably priced competitors. Rooms contain high-quality reproductions of English and Continental antiques, enough insulation to retain an almost reverential hush, and spacious bathrooms with shower-tub combinations. Overall, this is the most opulent hotel in what used to be defined as Berlin's Western Zone.

Kurfürstendamm 27, 10719 Berlin. © **800/426-3135** in the U.S., or 030/88-43-40. Fax 030/88-360-75. www.kempinski.com. 301 units. 135€–312€ ($155–$359) double; from 180€ ($207) suite. AE, DC, MC, V. Parking 21€ ($24). U-Bahn: Kurfürstendamm.

Where to Stay in Western Berlin

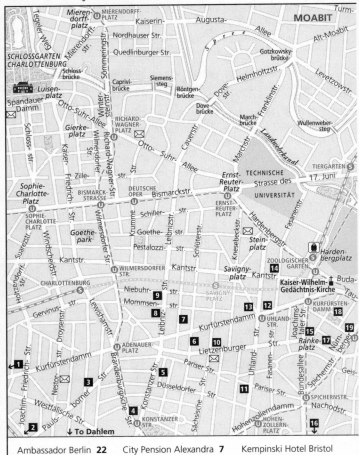

Propeller Island City Lodge **3**
Regent Schlosshotel Berlin **2**
Savoy **14**
Sorat Art'otel **15**
Steigenberger Berlin **18**

⊠	Post Office
----⑤	S-Bahn
---⑪	U-Bahn
⑤	No S-Bahn service through April 2004.
🚉	Train station

> ### (Kids) Family-Friendly Hotels
>
> **Ambassador Berlin** (p. 58)   Rooms, for the most part, are spacious and exceedingly comfortable for families.
>
> **Palace Berlin** (p. 57)   For the family traveling upmarket, this hotel near the zoo is a good choice, with both indoor and outdoor pools, and a helpful family-friendly staff.
>
> **Artemisia** (p. 54)   Although in theory this well-run and affordable hotel is for women only, children, including boys up to age 14, can stay here with their mothers.

Amenities: 3 restaurants; indoor pool; fitness center; sauna; solarium; room service; massage; babysitting; laundry/dry cleaning. *In room:* A/C, TV, minibar, hair dryer.

Steigenberger Berlin 🌟🌟   One of Berlin's most visible luxury hotels lies on a formal, gracefully proportioned plaza a few steps from the Kaiser Wilhelm Memorial Church. Originally built behind a nondescript facade in 1981, it caters to a demanding clientele of relatively conservative clients. This place represents western Berlin's sense of the status quo more visibly than virtually any other hotel in town. Public areas are large, well-designed, open spaces with high ceilings. Overall, expect a sense of bustling conservatism, plush and contemporary comfort, and corporate Europe at its most deeply entrenched. Rooms, for the most part, are medium in size, each maintained in good condition with a tasteful modern decor and generous-size beds. Bathrooms have combination tubs and showers, makeup mirrors, and robes.

Los-Angeles-Platz 1, 10789 Berlin. ℂ 800/223-5652 in the U.S. and Canada, or 030/21-27-0. Fax 030/2-12-71-17. www.berlin.steigenberger.de. 397 units. 245€– 350€ ($282–$403) double; from 435€ ($500) suite. AE, DC, MC, V. Parking 18€ ($21). U-Bahn: Kurfürstendamm. **Amenities:** 2 restaurants; 2 bars; pool; sauna; solarium; room service; massage; babysitting; laundry/dry cleaning. *In room:* A/C, TV, dataport, minibar, hair dryer, safe.

EXPENSIVE
Brandenburger Hof/Relais & Châteaux 🌟🌟🌟   This hotel lies on a dignified street in the commercial heart of the city and dates from 1991 when it was built in the classic Bauhaus style beloved by so many Germans. As a Relais & Châteaux property, it offers better food and service than most hotels of its price. Rooms range from medium-size to spacious and are among the most stylish in the city.

The decor, with torchier lamps, black leather upholstery, and platform beds, may appear a touch minimalist, but everybody will appreciate the original artworks that adorn the walls. Another bonus is the state-of-the-art security system and the French doors that open up onto balconies on all but the top floor. The spacious bathrooms have large shower/tub combinations, plenty of shelf space, and scales. Housekeeping here is among the finest in Berlin. A popular gathering place for guests is the "Wintergarten," an unusual combination of an Italian monastery garden and a Japanese garden.

Eislebener Strasse 14, 10789 Berlin. © **030/21-40-50.** Fax 030/21-40-51-00. www.brandenburger-hof.com. 82 units. 240€–280€ ($276–$322) double; from 450€ ($518) suite. Rates include breakfast buffet. AE, DC, MC, V. Parking 18€ ($21). U-Bahn: Kurfürstendamm or Augsburger Strasse. S-Bahn: Zoologischer Garten. **Amenities:** 2 restaurants, piano bar; room service; babysitting; laundry/valet. *In room:* TV, minibar, hair dryer.

Savoy 🐾   If you don't demand grand, full-service facilities, this might be the hotel for you. Built in 1929, the quiet, unassuming Savoy is a reliable and durable favorite. It's better than many in its category, and although it has lost some of its old-Berlin flavor, it remains the choice for the die-hard traditionalist. Its beautifully furnished rooms and luxurious suites come complete with generous desk space, upholstered armchairs, and cocktail tables.

Fasanenstrasse 9–10, 10623 Berlin. © **800/223-5652** in the U.S. and Canada, or 030/3-11-0-30. Fax 030/3-11-03-333. www.savoy-hotels.com. 125 units. 182€– 242€ ($209–$278) double; 212€–459€ ($244–$298) suite. Children under 12 stay free in parents' room. AE, DC, MC, V. Parking 10€ ($12). U-Bahn: Kurfürstendamm. **Amenities:** Restaurant, bar; fitness club; sauna; room service; babysitting; laundry. *In room:* TV, minibar, hair dryer, safe, trouser press.

MODERATE

Art Nouveau   On the fourth floor of an Art Nouveau apartment house, this little known hotel is an atmospheric choice. Even the elevator is a historic gem of the upmarket and desirable neighborhood. Established in the late 1970s, Art Nouveau was fully renovated in 1998. The well-furnished and comfortable rooms are pleasantly decorated and high-ceilinged, all with excellent beds. Rooms in the rear are more tranquil except when the schoolyard is full of children at play. There's an honor bar in the lobby where guests keep track of their own drinks. A generous breakfast is the only meal served.

Leibnizstrasse 59, 10629 Berlin. © **030/3-27-74-40.** Fax 030/327-744-40. www. hotelartnouveau.de. 16 units. 110€–165€ ($127–$190) double; 175€–230€ ($201–$265) suite. Parking 4€ ($4.60). Rates include breakfast. U-Bahn: Adenauerplatz. **Amenities:** Breakfast room; bar; lounge. *In room:* TV, hair dryer.

Artemisia *(Finds* This hotel *for women only* occupies the fourth and fifth floors of a residential building with an elevator. In cold weather, there's often a cozy fire in one of the sitting rooms. Women's conferences and consciousness-raising sessions sometimes take place here. Rooms are medium in size and meticulously maintained, each with a quality mattress and fine linen. Two rooms share a bathroom, but the rest have a good-size bathroom with shower or tub. Children, including boys up to age 14, can stay here with their mothers.

Brandenburgischestrasse 18 (near the Ku'damm), 10707 Berlin. ✆ 030/8-73-89-05. Fax 030/8-61-86-53. www.frauenhotel-berlin.de. 12 units, 10 with shower or bath. 92€ ($106) double without shower or bath; 106€ ($122) double with shower or bath. Children under 8 stay free in mother's room. Rates include continental breakfast. AE, DC, MC, V. Free parking. U-Bahn: Konstanzerstrasse. **Amenities:** Breakfast room; bar; lounge. *In room:* TV, hair dryer.

Bleibtreu Hotel *(R* The facade of this trend-conscious hotel isn't easily recognizable from the street, as the tiny lobby is accessible via an alleyway that leads past an avant-garde garden and a big-windowed set of dining and drinking facilities. The setting is the labyrinthine premises of what was built long ago as a Jugendstil-era apartment house. Rooms are small, minimalist, and furnished in carefully chosen natural materials. Extras include dataports and cordless phones. Bathrooms are cramped but well designed, and equipped with showers. Tables spill from the cafe into the tiny garden, where shrubs and flowers are surrounded with smooth-polished pieces of colored glass—a definite conversation piece.

Bleibtreustrasse 31, 10707 Berlin (1 block south of the Kurfürstendamm). ✆ 030/88474-0 or 800/223-5652 for reservations in the U.S. and Canada. Fax 030/88474-444. www.bleibtreu.com. 60 units. 192€–242€ ($221–$279) double, 302€–352€ ($347–$405) suite. AE, MC, V. U-Bahn: Kurfürstendamm. **Amenities:** Restaurant (vegetarian and organic); bar; room service; laundry. *In room:* TV, minibar, hair dryer, safe.

Hotel Domus *(Value* Clean, streamlined, and unpretentious, this government-rated three-star hotel dates from 1975. It was created from an older core whose elaborate detailing couldn't be salvaged. The result is an enduringly stylish, uncluttered piece of architecture that rises from a prestigious neighborhood a few blocks from the Ku'damm. It's a favorite of business travelers, who appreciate its good value and respectability. As such, it has a high proportion of single rooms, which cost 79€ to 91€ ($91–$105). Rooms are well designed, well scrubbed, and although not particularly large, very comfortable, each with a neat, shower-only bathroom. There are virtually no extras on-site, and other than breakfast and a drink that the receptionist might sell you within the lobby, no meals are served. But overall, it's a worthy, albeit simple choice, with good value and a helpful staff.

Uhlandstrasse 49, 10719 Berlin. (© **030/880-3440.** Fax 030/880344-44. www. hotel-domus-berlin.de. 70 units. 120€–145€ **($138–$147)** double; 140€–150€ **($161–$173)** suite. Discounts sometimes available Fri–Sun, depending on bookings. AE, DC, MC, V. Parking 7€ ($8.05). U-Bahn: Hohenzollernplatz or Spichernstrasse. **Amenities:** Breakfast room; bar. *In room:* TV, hair dryer.

Kronprinz Berlin This hotel is located away from Berlin's center at the far western edge of the Ku'damm. In spite of its many discreet charms and features, it remains relatively little known or publicized. All rooms have balconies and fine appointments (often tasteful reproductions of antiques). If you want a little extra comfort, ask for one of the Bel-Etage rooms. All units are equipped with compact bathrooms, many with tub and shower combination. Many guests congregate in the garden under the chestnut trees in summer.

Kronprinzendamm 1, 10711 Berlin. (© **030/89-60-30.** Fax 030/8-93-12-15. www. kronprinz-hotel.de. 80 units. 145€ **($167)** double; 220€ **($253)** suite. Children 12 and under stay free in parents' room. Rates include buffet breakfast. AE, DC, MC, V. Free parking. U-Bahn: Adenauerplatz. Bus: 104, 110, 119, 129, or 219. **Amenities:** Breakfast room; bar; babysitting; laundry/dry cleaning. *In room:* TV, dataport, mini-bar, hair dryer, safe.

INEXPENSIVE

Bogota Since 1964, this hotel has been a local favorite for the frugal traveler when a quartet of four separate hotels on four floors were combined into a cohesive whole. Typical for older Berlin apartment houses, bedrooms come in various shapes and sizes, but all of them have been recently restored.

The building more or less withstood WWII bombardments. Constructed in 1911, it had been a famous address known for its frequent parties, at which a young Benny Goodman appeared on occasion. The famous entrepreneur, Oskar Skaller, lived here and was known for his collection of Impressionists, including paintings by van Gogh.

What is now the lounge and TV room was once the office of the infamous director, Hans Hinkel, of the Reich Chamber of Culture. Charlie Chaplin named the title character in his film, *The Great Dictator,* after Hinkel. Bedrooms are well cared for and comfortable, the best opening onto an inner courtyard. Bathrooms with shower units are small but efficiently organized.

Schlüstrasse 45, 10707 Berlin. ✆ **030/8-81-50-01.** Fax 030/8-83-58-87. www.hotelbogota.de. 125 units, 60 with bathroom (12 with shower but no toilet). 72€ ($83) double without bath; 80€ ($92) double with shower but no toilet; 96€–100€ ($110–$115) double with bathroom. Rates include continental breakfast. AE, DC, MC, V. Parking 10€ ($12). U-Bahn: Adenauerplatz or Uhlandstr. S-Bahn: Savignyplatz. **Amenities:** Breakfast room; lounge. *In room:* TV, hair dryer.

City Pension Alexandra

This three-floor hotel is comfortable, centrally located, and quiet. The building dates from 1900 and was converted into a hotel in the 1920s. Certain rooms are lined with photographs of old Berlin—perfect for acquainting yourself with what to look for as you tour the streets of the city. Most rooms have modern furniture; some are more classic.

Wielandstrasse 32, 10629 Berlin. ✆ **030/8-81-21-07.** Fax 030/88-57-78-18. www.alexandra-berlin.de. 9 units, 4 with shower only. 75€ ($86) double with shower only; 99€ ($114) double with bathroom. Rates include buffet breakfast. AE, MC, V. S-Bahn: Savignyplatz or Oliveplatz. **Amenities:** Breakfast room; lounge; babysitting. *In room:* TV, hair dryer.

Hotel-Pension Bregenz

This dignified pension occupies the fourth and sunniest floor of a four-story, century-old apartment building, accessible by elevator. The owner, Mr. Zimmermann, works hard to maintain the cleanliness and charm of his comfortably furnished, relatively large rooms. Double doors help to minimize noise from the public corridors. The staff gladly assists guests in reserving tickets for shows and tours.

Bregenzer Strasse 5, 10707 Berlin. ✆ **030/8-81-43-07.** Fax 030/8-82-40-09. 14 units, 11 with bathroom (shower only). 60€ ($69) double without bathroom, 88€ ($101) double with bathroom. Rates include breakfast. MC, V. Parking 3€ ($3.45). S-Bahn: Savignyplatz. U-Bahn: Adenauerplatz. *In room:* TV, minibar, hair dryer, safe.

Pension München

This pension occupies only part of the third floor of a massive four-story elevator building erected as an apartment house in 1908. It offers a simple but tasteful decor of modern furnishings accented with fresh flowers. Rooms are clean, with contemporary furniture and prints and engravings by local artists. Each comes with a compact, shower-only bathroom. Look for sculptures by the owner in some of the public areas as well. *Note:* If there are no rooms available here, you're likely to be recommended to a similar pension, **Pension Güntzel** (✆ **030/8-57-90-20**), on the building's street level and cellar.

Guntzelstrasse 62 (close to Bayerischer Platz), 10717 Berlin. ✆ **030/8-57-91-20.** Fax 030/85-79-12-22. 8 units. 78€ ($90) double. AE, DC, MC, V. Parking is available on the street. U-Bahn: Guntzelstrasse. *In room:* TV.

Pension Niebuhr   Clean, safe, and sophisticated, this gay-friendly hotel occupies 1½ floors of a century-old apartment building. Willi Heidasch is your amiable host, maintaining simple but clean rooms, seven with phone and TV. Beds are a bit worn but still have comfort in them, and shower bathrooms are small. Paintings by aspiring Berlin artists (many for sale) decorate the public areas. About half the clientele is gay, a percentage that's growing, according to the owner.

Niebuhrstrasse 74, 10629 Berlin. (C) 030/3-24-95-95. Fax 030/3-24-80-21. www. pension-niebuhr.de. 12 units, 7 with bathroom. 65€ ($75) double without bathroom; 90€ ($104) double with bathroom. Rates include breakfast. AE, MC, V. Parking 2.50€ ($2.90). S-Bahn: Savignyplatz. **Amenities:** Room service. *In room:* TV.

Pension Nürnberger Eck   This reliable pension is refreshingly old-fashioned. It occupies the second floor of a four-story building on a relatively quiet side street. Rooms are large, with high ceilings, massive doors, and in many cases, reproductions of Biedermeier-style furniture, including comfortable beds with soft mattresses, plus small shower bathrooms. This is the kind of place where Sally Bowles from *Cabaret* might have stayed.

Nürnberger Strasse 24a (near the Europa Center), 10789 Berlin. (C) 030/2-35-17-80. Fax 030/235-178-99. 8 units, 5 with bathroom. 72€ ($83) double without bathroom; 95€ ($109) double with bathroom. MC, V. Rates include breakfast. Parking 6€ ($6.90). U-Bahn: Augsburgerstrasse. **Amenities:** Breakfast room. *In room:* TV.

2 Near the Memorial Church & Zoo

VERY EXPENSIVE

Palace Berlin *Kids*   Although it isn't at the level of the Kempinski or the Grand Hotel Esplanade, this well-managed hotel outranks such landmarks as the Berlin Hilton and the Steigenberger Berlin. Don't be surprised by its boxy exterior (ca. 1968) that rises immediately adjacent to the equally boxy-looking Europa Center. Inside, thanks to dozens of improvements made throughout the 1990s, the setting is very comfortable, and at times even opulent. Rooms range in size from medium to spacious. All have fine beds, superb lighting, quality carpeting, and conservatively traditional styling. The best of the lot are those that benefited from a radical upgrade in the late 1990s. Known as "new deluxe rooms," they're for the most part on the third, fourth, and fifth floors. About 90 of the rooms are set aside for nonsmokers. Most bathrooms feature tub-shower combinations. The glamorous in-house restaurant, First Floor, is the only gourmet deluxe restaurant in Berlin that's open every day for lunch and dinner. Families will appreciate this hotel's proximity to the zoo as well as the fact that many of the rooms are spacious enough to accommodate extra beds and because children under 12, who share a room with their parents, can stay at no extra charge.

In the Europa-Center, Budapesterstrasse 45, 10787 Berlin. ℂ 800/457-4000 in the U.S., or 030/2-50-20. Fax 030/2502-1161. www.palace.de. 282 units. 225€–300€ ($259–$345) double; from 455€ ($523) suite. AE, DC, MC, V. Parking 21€ ($24). U-Bahn: Zoologischer Garten. **Amenities:** 3 restaurants (see First Floor, p. 77), 2 bars; large health club; nonsmoking rooms. *In room:* A/C, TV, minibar, hair dryer, safe, trouser press.

EXPENSIVE

Ambassador Berlin 🐾 *Kids*   This hotel is an attractive choice if you'd like to lodge near the Ku'damm. The heated tropical pool on the eighth floor, with its retractable dome and a waterfall, is an unusual feature, attracting the family trade. Rooms are, for the most part, spacious and exceedingly comfortable and include traditional furnishings. Bathrooms are rather small, and only a fifth have showers; the rest have tubs. Soundproof windows are always a relief in noisy central Berlin, and nonsmokers get a floor to themselves. The hotel is sometimes overrun with large groups.

Bayreutherstrasse 42–43, 10787 Berlin. ℂ 030/21-90-20. Fax 030/21-90-23-80. www.sorat-hotels.com. 198 units. 99€–185€ ($114–$213) double; 200€ ($230) suite. Rates include buffet breakfast. AE, DC, MC, V. Parking 13€ ($15). U-Bahn: Wittenbergplatz. **Amenities:** Bar; massage; babysitting; laundry. *In room:* A/C, TV, minibar, hair dryer.

Hecker's Hotel   For years this establishment enjoyed a reputation as a small, private hotel, but now it's expanded. Although not in the same league as the Sorat (see below), this is still a winning choice. It's conveniently located near the Ku'damm and the many bars, cafes, and restaurants around Savignyplatz. The original 42 rooms are smaller than the newer units, which are medium-size. The rather severe and somewhat somber modern style may not suit everyone—certainly not those seeking romantic ambience. Each unit comes with a compact, shower-only bathroom. There is a sterility here but also up-to-date comfort and top-notch maintenance.

Grolmanstrasse 35, 10623 Berlin. ℂ 030/8-89-00. Fax 030/8-89-02-60. www.heckers-hotel.de. 69 units. 150€–200€ ($173–$230) double; 300€–330€ ($345–$383) suite. AE, DC, MC, V. Parking 11€ ($13). U-Bahn: Uhlandstrasse. Bus: 109 from Tegel Airport to Uhlandstrasse or 119 from Tempelhof Airport. **Amenities:** Small restaurant; bar (roof dining in summer); room service; dry cleaning/laundry; nonsmoking rooms. *In room:* TV, minibar, hair dryer, safe.

Sorat Art'otel 🐾   Chic, discreet, and avant-garde, the Sorat is unlike any other Berlin hotel. The location is ideal, in the heart of cosmopolitan Berlin, with the Ku'damm action virtually outside the

front door. The decor, strictly minimalist, includes touches from top designers. You'll find Philippe Starck bar stools, Arne Jacobsen chairs, and artwork by Berliner Wolf Vostell. Modernists will be at home here, amid chrome-legged furnishings and pedestal tables that look like cable spools. Traditionalists might not be so pleased. Rooms are all comfortable, with soundproofing, deluxe mattresses on large beds, and tasteful lighting. Bathrooms are generous in size with shower-tub combinations. The service here is among Berlin's finest.

Joachimstalerstrasse 29, 10719 Berlin. (℃ **030/88-44-70.** Fax 030/88-44-77-00. www.sorat-hotels.com. 133 units. 147€–267€ ($169–$307) double. Rates include buffet breakfast with champagne. Parking 11€ ($13). AE, DC, MC, V. U-Bahn: Kurfürstendamm. **Amenities:** Restaurant (Greek/international); room service; laundry. *In room:* A/C, TV, minibar, hair dryer.

MODERATE

Hotel Sylter Hof Berlin This hotel, built in 1966, offers rich trappings at good prices. The main lounges are warmly decorated in Louis XV style, with chandeliers, provincial chairs, and antiques. Well-maintained rooms—mostly singles—may be too small for most tastes but are good for business travelers. All the compact, tiled bathrooms are equipped with shower-tub combinations. The staff pays special attention to your comfort.

Kurfürstenstrasse 116, 10787 Berlin. (℃ **030/2-12-00.** Fax 030/214-28-26. www. sylterhof-berlin.de. 161 units. 125€–140€ ($144–$161) double; from 180€ ($207) suite. Rates include buffet breakfast. AE, DC, MC, V. Parking 11€ ($12). U-Bahn: Wittenbergplatz. Bus: 119, 129, 146, or 185. **Amenities:** Restaurant; bar, coffee bar; nightclub next door. *In room:* TV, minibar, hair dryer.

INEXPENSIVE

Arco Hotel Although some of its competitors are more visible and more heavily promoted, this is one of the most consistently reliable and fairly priced gay hotels in Berlin. It occupies part of a former old-Berlin apartment building that was completely renovated in 1999. Rooms are mostly white, well scrubbed, and well organized, with tasteful albeit simple artwork and furnishings. Each comes with a small shower bathroom. There's a garden in back, site of breakfasts during clement weather. A polite and hardworking staff is alert to the location of emerging neighborhood bars and restaurants, many of whose owners recommend this place. Much of its business derives from repeat guests from as far away as Los Angeles.

Geisbergstrasse 30, 10777 Berlin. (℃ **030/23-51-480.** Fax 030/21-47-51-78. www. arco-hotel.de. 22 units. 85€–94€ ($98–$108) double. Rates include breakfast. AE, DC, MC, V. U-Bahn: Wittenberg-Platz, Viktoria-Luise-Platz or Nollendorferplatz. **Amenities:** Breakfast room; lounge. *In room:* TV, hair dryer, safe.

3 In Grunewald

VERY EXPENSIVE

Regent Schlosshotel Berlin ✿✿✿   With only 54 gem-like rooms, this is one of the most historic and plushest hotels in Berlin. It was built in the 19th century by a friend and advisor of Kaiser Wilhelm II, who entertained him from time to time on the premises. For anyone who can afford it and prefers a stay in the city's verdant suburbs, the experience can be elegant, historic, and charming. Service is superb and invariably cheerful. Although changes have been made to the decor, its original inspiration was by German-born fashion superstar Karl Lagerfeld. The structure's monumental staircase, minstrel's gallery, and other Belle Epoque trappings remain, but Mr. Lagerfeld's contributions have added an undeniable gloss to the hotel's interior. Beds are sumptuous, with great pillows, fine linen, and elegant fabrics. Bathrooms have shower-and-tub combos, plush towels, radiantly heated floors, slippers, scales, and robes.

Brahmsstrasse 10, 14193 Berlin-Grunewald. ℭ **800/545-4000** in U.S. and Canada, or 030/895-840. Fax 030/895-84800. www.schlosshotelberlin.com. 54 units. 225€–430€ ($259–$495) double; from 520€ ($598) suite. AE, DC, MC, V. S-Bahn: Grunewald. **Amenities:** 2 restaurants; bar; health club; spa; sauna; salon; room service; massage; babysitting; laundry/dry cleaning. *In room:* A/C, TV/VCR, dataport, stereo and CD player, minibar, hair dryer, safe.

4 In Charlottenburg

MODERATE

Propeller Island City Lodge ✿ *Finds*   The zaniest hotel we recommend in this guide will appeal to clients who understand in advance exactly what's available. We heartily advise readers—more forcefully than at any other hotel—to phone and check out the establishment's website before moving in.

Associated with a record producer and songwriting studio *(Propeller Island GmbH),* this hotel occupies three high-ceilinged floors of an old-fashioned apartment house originally built in the 1880s. Each of the bedrooms is both radical and radically different in its décor, its theme, and its presuppositions, and each might delight or appall you—depending on your values, expectations, and personality—with its quirks. *Therapie* is an all-white, minimalist room whose mood changes with the color of the lighting, which you can adjust at will. *Flying Bed* places a mattress as an iconic temple at the top of an inclined ramp, giving your bed a cultish importance you're not likely to feel in a roadside Howard Johnson's on the U.S. mainland. *Galerie* features a round bed, a pedal-operated mechanism that can spin it on a pivot, and lots of empty picture frames wherein you can superimpose your fantasies on an otherwise blank space. Weirdest of all (and not recommended) is the *Coffin Room,* where cult freaks can sleep in either of two (well-ventilated) closed coffins for a night of gothic pensiveness, or whatever.

There's a staff in attendance only during the mornings. If your arrival is scheduled for any other time, phone in advance to arrange a rendezvous time with a local student, who will give you the key. None of the rooms has a phone or a minibar, and amenities vary widely, according to the *zeitgeist* of the individual accommodation (some have TVs, two have basic kitchens). Owner and creative developer Berlin-born Lars Stroschen has composed music intended for specific rooms of this hotel.

Albrecht-Achilles-Strasse 58, Charlottenburg, 10709 Berlin. Tel. 030/891-9016 (daily from 8am to noon) and 0163/256-5909 (a mobile phone for all other hours of the day). Fax 030/891-9016. www.propeller-island.de. 30 units. 85€–125€ ($98–$144) double; 195€ ($224) suite. DC, MC, V. U-Bahn: Adenauerplatz.

5 In Berlin-Mitte

VERY EXPENSIVE

Berlin Hilton 𝒜   The Four Seasons and Westin Grand are finer hotels, attracting some of the Hilton's former clients, but this durable landmark is still going strong. Set within one of the city's most expensive and desirable neighborhoods (Gendarmenmarkt), this deluxe hotel was the first to open in what was East Berlin following the collapse of the Berlin Wall. Today it's the third largest hotel in the city and one of the most popular. The seven-floor hotel contains enough accessories and facilities to keep you jumping for a week. Thanks to all the visual distraction in the lobby, there's even a vague sense that you might be in a resort hotel that's eager to cater to the needs of both large groups and business travelers alike. Rooms are conservatively modern and very comfortable, with double-glazed windows, comfortable beds, bedside controls, and well-equipped bathrooms with tub/shower combos. At least half overlook the twin churches of the dramatic Gendarmenmarkt.

Mohrenstrasse 30, 10117 Berlin. © 800/445-8667 in the U.S. and Canada, or 030/2-02-30. Fax 030/20-23-42-69. www.hilton.com. 589 units. 199€–450€ ($229–$518) double; 330€–500€ ($380–$570) suite. Special weekend packages available. AE, DC, MC, V. U-Bahn: Stadtmitte. **Amenities:** 4 restaurants; bar; pool; health spa; Jacuzzi; sauna; room service; babysitting; laundry. *In room:* A/C, TV, minibar, hair dryer, safe.

Four Seasons ✦✦✦   This hotel lacks the historical pedigree of its major competitor, the newly rebuilt Adlon, but the Four Seasons is Berlin's most sumptuous address. One of Berlin's most opulent hotels, it was built in 1996 on the site of a bombed-out parking lot about a block from the Gendarmenmarkt. From the look of things, you'd never realize the venue is relatively new, as everything about it evokes Versailles and an undeniable sense of well-established and very plush prosperity. Decor, illuminated with light from two separate courtyards, includes Viennese crystal chandeliers and antiques from throughout Europe, giving you the sense that you've entered a private and very upscale home. Rooms are furnished with timeless taste and elegance, with very large bathrooms, each with walk-in showers, deep tubs, and a relentlessly upscale selection of toiletries.

Charlottenstrasse 49, 10117 Berlin. ℂ **800/332-3442** in the U.S., or 030/2-03-38. Fax 030/203-36-009. www.fourseasons.com. 204 units. 300€–360€ ($345–$414) double; from 395€ ($454) suite. AE, MC, V. Parking 21€ ($24). U-Bahn: Französis-chestrasse. **Amenities:** Restaurant; bar; health club; 24-hr. room service; massage; babysitting; dry cleaning/laundry. *In room:* A/C, TV, minibar, hair dryer, safe.

Grand Hyatt Berlin ✦✦✦   This is the most exciting, best-designed, and most iconoclastic hotel in Berlin, a government-rated five-star mecca. Don't expect rococo frills: Interior designer Hannes Wettstein permeated this hotel with a minimalist simplicity that might remind you of a Zen temple. Ceilings soar toward surreal-looking inverted pyramids, upstairs hallways run off into futuristic-looking infinities, and light derives from rambling expanses of glass or translucent slabs of alabaster. The large and sun-flooded rooms are among the hotel's best features. Suites are often commandeered by fashion photographers as backgrounds for cutting-edge fashion layouts. *Hint:* For a surcharge of 45€ ($52), you can upgrade your accommodation to the Regency Club. There, the value of free breakfasts, afternoon tea, evening cocktail hour, daytime snacks, and enhanced services will more than compensate you for the supplement you'll pay.

Marlene-Dietrich-Platz 2, 10785 Berlin. ℂ **030/25-53-12-34.** Fax 030/25-53-12-35. www.hyatt.com. 340 units. 210€–305€ ($242–$351) double; 45€ ($52) supplement, per room, for upgrade to Regency Club; from 365€ ($420) suite. AE, DC, MC, V. Parking 16€ ($18). U-Bahn: Potsdamer Platz. **Amenities:** 2 restaurants; bar; cafe; pool; tennis court; health club; sauna; room service; laundry/dry cleaning; computer rental. *In room:* A/C, TV, dataport, Sony Playstation, minibar, hair dryer, safe.

Hotel Adlon ✦✦✦   Berlin's most historic hotel is a phoenix freshly risen from the ashes of 1945. Only the Four Seasons (see above) is a more sumptuous address in Berlin. No other hotel sits as close to the

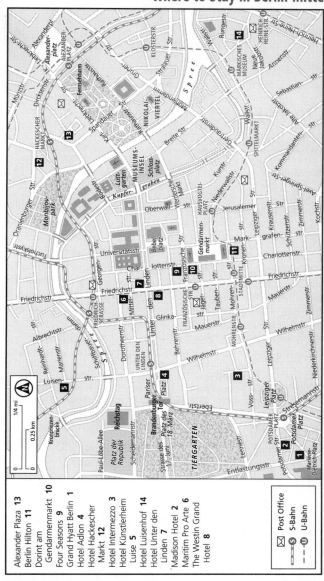

Alexander Plaza **13**
Berlin Hilton **11**
Dorint am
Gendarmenmarkt **10**
Four Seasons **9**
Grand Hyatt Berlin **1**
Hotel Adlon **4**
Hotel Hackescher
Markt **12**
Hotel Intermezzo **3**
Hotel Künstlerheim
Luise **5**
Hotel Luisenhof **14**
Hotel Unter den
Linden **7**
Madison Hotel **2**
Maritim Pro Arte **6**
The Westin Grand
Hotel **8**

⊠ Post Office
Ⓢ S-Bahn
Ⓤ U-Bahn

Fun Fact **The Grand Hotel**

Time was, Greta Garbo and Marlene Dietrich could be seen checking into the **Hotel Adlon** (which Vicki Baum's novel *The Grand Hotel* was based on), as well as Charlie Chaplin luring a young Polish girl (later screen vamp and Gloria Swanson's chief rival Pola Negri) to his bedchamber. The Adlon lasted until Berlin fell in 1945. Maestro Herbert von Karajan was eating caviar in the Adlon's dining room when Hitler shot himself in his bunker.

Brandenburg Gate, at the top of an avenue that's reasserting its claim on the city's sense of chic. Grand and historic, and permeated with the legends of the glamour and tragedies that befell it during various eras of its life, it was originally built by legendary hotelier Lorenz Adlon in 1907, then reopened with a well-publicized flourish in 1997 after a massive expenditure of funds. Public areas, some of them illuminated with lavishly detailed stained-glass domes, contain coffered ceilings, mosaics, inlaid paneling, and lots of Carrara marble. Rooms are mostly large and have lots of state-of-the-art electronic extras, such as CD players. Those on the top floor offer the best views but are a bit more cramped and lack some extras. All come equipped with spacious bathrooms containing shower-tub combinations.

Unter den Linden 77, 10117 Berlin. (C) 800/426-3135 in the U.S., or 030/22-61-0. Fax 030/22-61-11-16. www.hotel-adlon.de. 337 units. 280€–620€ ($322–$713) double; 375€–415€ ($431–$477) junior suite. AE, DC, MC, V. Parking 23€ ($26). S-Bahn: Unter den Linden. **Amenities:** 3 restaurants; bar; health club; spa; room service; babysitting; laundry/dry cleaning. *In room:* A/C, TV, CD player, minibar, hair dryer, safe.

EXPENSIVE

Alexander Plaza *$* This hotel is set a short walk from both Alexanderplatz and the historic district of Hackescher Höfe. It originated around 1900 as an office building. In 1997, in combination with another building next door, it was converted into one of the neighborhood's most charming and best-managed hotels. A labyrinth of hallways open into rooms with unique floor plans. Each has parquet floors, high ceilings, and neo-Biedermeier blond-wood furniture. The "executive rooms" are very large. Low-end rooms are smaller and less dramatic, but still very comfortable. Each midsize unit comes with a private bathroom equipped with tub and shower. The staff here is among the most attentive in Berlin.

Rosenstrasse 1, 10178 Berlin. © 800/223-5652 for reservations in North America, or 030/240-010. Fax 030/240-01-777. www.hotel-alexander-plaza.de. 92 units. 155€–205€ ($178–$236) double; 215€–285€ ($247–$328) suite. S-Bahn: Hackescher Markt. **Amenities:** Restaurant; bar; health club; sauna; solarium; steamroom; room service. *In room:* TV, minibar, hair dryer.

Dorint am Gendarmenmarkt ✦✦

This is one of the latest boutique hotels to open, and it's so good it lures visitors from such old favorites as the Berlin Hilton. The shell that contains this hotel was designed by the then–East German government in 1981 as a youth hostel, and set behind a faux-Jugendstil facade that has since then been declared a historic monument. After reunification, the Dorint chain carefully converted the structure into an upscale hotel of artfully simple, Zen-like minimalism. The result is a soothing blend of high-tech accessories and a restful kind of neutrality administered in an upbeat way that usually appeals to anyone working in the field of media, the arts, or high-tech science. Small and choice, and presenting an ultra-hip version of "new Berlin" to the antique setting of the Gendarmenmarkt, it's one of the genuinely unusual upscale hotels in Berlin. The best rooms overlook the Gendarmenmarkt from behind tiny balconies. Most units have showers.

Charlottenstrasse 50–52, 10117 Berlin. © 030/20375-0. Fax 030/20375-100. www.dorint.com. 92 units. 215€–305€ ($247–$351) double; 305€–400€ ($351–$460) suite. AE, DC, MC, V. U-Bahn: Stadtmitte. **Amenities:** Restaurant; cafe; health club; sauna; steamroom; meditation room; room service; laundry. *In room:* A/C, TV, dataport, minibar, hair dryer, safe.

Madison Hotel ✦

One of the most posh and elegant hotels in the pivotal Potsdamer Platz neighborhood was built in 1999 in an 11-story format that's sheathed in steel and warmly textured Italian brick. Each of the units inside is configured as a suite, not as a conventional room, and each is upholstered in discreetly plush fabrics, decorated with top-of-the-line stone, tile, or marble, and ringed with big windows that flood the postmodern interiors with sunlight. One of this hotel's most charming features is on its fifth floor, where a bamboo and tree-studded garden, replete with waterfalls, provides a verdant and very calm oasis in the middle of one of Berlin's newest showcase neighborhoods.

Staff here tends to be extremely alert, capable, and well-mannered, and since the suites are all supremely comfortable and stylish, we highly recommend this hotel as a genuine winner. All baths come with a shower-tub combination and, in the case of the larger suites, separate shower and separate bathtubs. ***Hint:*** Don't be surprised by the small scale of this hotel's street-level reception facility.

The upper levels, including the lounge (Qiu) one floor above lobby level, are spacious and opulent, in vivid contrast to the discreet and non-flamboyant scale of the reception area.

Potsdamer Strasse 3, 10785 Berlin. © 030/590-05-0000. Fax 030/590-05-0500. www.madison-berlin.de. 167 units (all suites). 190€–490€ ($219–$564) double. U-bahn: Potsdamer Platz. **Amenities:** Facil restaurant (see p. 81), Qiu Lounge for upscale snacks and drinks; 11th-floor exercise room and health club, two saunas, laundry/dry cleaning, babysitting, room service (6:30am–midnight); concierge. *In-room:* A/C, minibar, TV.

Maritim Pro Arte ⟨ℱ⟩   This is a more luxe version of Sorat Art'o-tel (see above). Set about a block from Unter den Linden, this hotel was built as an avant-garde architectural showcase in the mid-1970s by the then–East German government. Today, despite frequent ren-ovations, it still evokes a jazzy, "moderno," and vaguely dated kind of architecture that features lots of chrome and stainless steel. There's a bustle here, however, thanks in part to a hardworking and polite staff, and a regular clientele of business clients and conven-tioneers. Avant-garde artwork is exhibited throughout, and some of the furniture was created by Phillipe Starck. Rooms are individually designed, soothing, uncluttered, and comfortable. Most provide a fax outlet and all have reclining chairs. Each unit comes with a good-size private bathroom with tub and shower.

Friedrichstrasse 151–153 (across from Friedrichstrasse station), 10117 Berlin. © 030/ 2-03-35. Fax 030/20-33-42-09. www.maritim.de. 403 units. 172€–242€ ($198–$278) double; from 300€ ($345) suite. AE, DC, MC, V. Parking 15€ ($17). S-Bahn: Friedrichstrasse. **Amenities:** 3 restaurants; bar; pool; fitness studio; sauna; solarium; room service; babysitting; laundry. *In room:* A/C, TV, minibar, hair dryer, safe.

The Westin Grand Hotel ⟨ℱℱℱ⟩   This is a monument to "capi-talistic decadence," as they used to say during the Cold War era, but amazingly, it was first constructed on socialist soil by the then-com-munist East German government. Now under management by the Westin group, and devoid of its original sense of stiffness, it's one of Berlin's finest hotels, though it pales in comparison to its major rival, the Four Seasons. Belle Epoque features blend with contem-porary styling. Rooms, radically renovated and upgraded in 1998, come in a wide range of styles, from beautifully appointed standard doubles all the way up to the lush-looking Schinkel Suite. Beds con-tain wonderfully soft linens, down pillows and comforters, and firm mattresses. Other features include terrycloth robes, combination tub and shower, and fresh flowers.

Friedrichstrasse 158–164, 10117 Berlin. © 888-625-5144 in the U.S., or 030/ 2-02-70. Fax 030/20-27-33-62. www.westin.com/berlin. 364 units. 286€–305€

($329–$351) double; 458€ ($527) suite; from 920€ ($1058) apt. suite. AE, DC, MC, V. Parking 20€ ($23). U-Bahn: Französische Strasse. S-Bahn: Friedrichstrasse. **Amenities:** Restaurant; bar; pool; fitness club; sauna; solarium; salon; 24-hr. room service; massage; babysitting; laundry/dry cleaning. *In room:* A/C, TV, minibar, hair dryer.

MODERATE

Hotel Hackescher Markt *☆* You'd never know this nugget of charm was newly built in 1998, as everything about it evokes a late 19th-century landmark. Inside, there's a quiet, flagstone-and-ivy-covered courtyard that clients use for reading, and a polite and helpful staff that knows virtually everything about what's happening in the hotel's cutting-edge neighborhood. There's a bar on street level where hipsters might feel supremely comfortable, and where live music is presented Wednesday and Saturday nights. Rooms are soothing, partially oak-paneled, and outfitted with comfortable and practical furniture. Standard singles tend to be just a bit small—a better bet might be one of the more upscale doubles. Bathrooms have heated floors, and combination tub and shower. Some guests appreciate the romantic overtones of rooms on the uppermost floor, whose walls are angled thanks to the building's mansard roof.

Grosse Präsidentenstrasse 8, 10178 Berlin. © **030/28-00-30.** Fax 030/28-00-31-11. www.hackescher-markt.com. 31 units. 135€–170€ ($155–$196) double; 175€–202€ ($201–$232) suite. AE, MC, V. U-Bahn: Hackescher Markt. **Amenities:** Bar; room service; laundry. *In room:* TV, minibar, hair dryer, safe.

Hotel Intermezzo *(Finds)* In the center of a quiet street, this hotel *for women only* lies only a 5-minute walk from the Brandenburg Gate, the Reichstag, and Unter den Linden. The back of the hotel looks onto the landmark Potsdamer Platz and the new Sony Centre. In other words, you couldn't be more central in Berlin. The interior design looks like a showroom at IKEA. Bedrooms are attractively and comfortably furnished, each with a tidy shower. Female guests meet like-minded souls in the breakfast room, which looks like it was transplanted from a Swedish B&B to Berlin. A freshly made and excellent buffet is prepared every morning. The hotel is a clean, well maintained, and an inviting haven for women, especially those traveling alone. Most guests are solo travelers.

An der Kolonnade 14, 10117 Berlin. © **030/224-890.** Fax 030/224-890-97. www.hotelintermezzo.de. 16 units. 42€ single; 70€ ($48–$81) double; 88€ ($101) triple; 118€ ($136) quad. Children up to 12 years old, 25€ ($29). Boys allowed up to 12 years old. AE, MC, V. S-Bahn: Potsdamer Platz. **Amenities:** Breakfast room. *In room:* TV, hair dryer.

Hotel Künstlerheim Luise *☆ (Finds)* Its German name translates into English as "home for artists." No, it's not a communal crash-pad for the bohemian fringe, but a choice and select boutique hotel where every accommodation was designed and individually furnished by a different German artist. There's nothing quite like this. Under historical preservation, the hotel is installed in a restored 1825 city palace. Clients from the arts, media, and even the political or business world are drawn to this unusual hostelry. Each room comes as a total surprise, and you know, of course, that you're going to be treated to some of the artist's work, which runs the gamut from Andy Warhol-like pop to even classicism. Some units evoke modern minimalism, whereas others are much more quirky.

Luisenstrasse 19, 10117 Berlin. ℭ 030/284-480. Fax 030/2844-8448. www. kuenstlerheim-luise.de. 43 units. 121€ ($139) without bathroom, 135€ ($155) double with bathroom. 124–130€ ($143–$150) suite. AE, DC, MC, V. U-Bahn: Friedrichstrasse. **Amenities:** Restaurant bar next door. *In room:* A/C in some units, TV, minibar in suites, safe in suites.

Hotel Luisenhof ⍟   This is one of the most desirable small hotels in eastern Berlin. It lies within a severely dignified house, built in 1822. Its five floors of high-ceilinged rooms have been outfitted in a conservative and traditional style, a welcome escape from modern Berlin. The upgraded units range in size from small to spacious, but all are equipped with fine beds and individual fax machines. Bathrooms, though small, are beautifully appointed, most with a tub and shower. The neighborhood around this hotel, like many other parts of the once-dour eastern zone, is undergoing a rapid renovation.

Köpenicker Strasse 92, 10179 Berlin. ℭ 030/2-41-59-06. Fax 030/2-79-29-83. www. luisenhof.de. 27 units. 136€ ($156) double; from 195€ ($224) suite. Rates include breakfast. AE, DC, MC, V. U-Bahn: Märkisches Museum. **Amenities:** Restaurant; room service (6am–midnight); laundry/dry cleaning. *In room:* TV, minibar, hair dryer.

Hotel Unter den Linden   An architectural fright erected by Cold War commies, this hotel is softening under capitalist control. The location, at the corner of Unter den Linden and Friedrichstrasse, is almost unbeatable for Berlin-Mitte convenience. You can walk out the door and stroll over to the Reichstag or the Brandenburger Tor. It's banal but affordable. Its guest rooms are comfortable and a bit small, each with newly installed plumbing including tiled shower-only bathrooms.

Unter den Linden 14, 10117 Berlin. ℭ 030/238-110. Fax 030/238-11-100. www. hotel-unter-den-linden.de. 331 units. 98€–143€ ($116–$164) double. Rates include breakfast. AE, DC, MC, V. U-Bahn: Friedrichstrasse. **Amenities:** Breakfast salon; bistro bar with summer terrace; room service; laundry. *In room:* TV.

5

Where to Dine

If it's true that optimism and appetite go hand in hand, Berliners must be among the most optimistic people in Europe. But just because Berliners like to eat doesn't mean that they like to spend a lot on food. Locals know that you can often have a memorable dinner here in an unheralded wine restaurant or sidewalk cafe. Rising food costs in the east, however, mean that in the new Berlin, the eastern section can no longer be viewed as a bargain basement in the food department.

If a restaurant bill says *Bedienung,* that means a service charge has already been added, so just round up to the nearest euro.

Examples of typical dishes are the Berliner *Schlachteplatte* (cold plate); pigs' trotters cooked with sauerkraut and pea purée; and *Eisbein* (pickled knuckle of pork with sauerkraut). Venison, wildfowl, and wild boar also appear frequently, as do carp and trout, along with an infinite variety of sausages.

But Berlin does not limit itself to traditional cuisine. A new wave of restaurants has swept across the city, from east to west. More and more are going ethnic, serving everything from Indonesian or French to Thai or Japanese. Eastern European wines are now almost as popular as those from Germany itself.

1 Restaurants by Cuisine

AMERICAN
Hard Rock Cafe (Near the Kurfürstendamm, $, p. 77)

ARABIC
Oren (Berlin-Mitte, $, p. 89)

AUSTRIAN
Keller-Restaurant im Brecht-Haus-Berlin (Berlin-Mitte, $, p. 88)

CONTINENTAL
Aigner (Berlin-Mitte, $$, p. 85)

Key to Abbreviations: $$$$ = Very Expensive $$$ = Expensive $$ = Moderate
$ = Inexpensive

Alt-Luxemburg ★★★
(Greater Charlottenburg,
$$$$, p. 79)

Bamberger Reiter ★★★
(Near the Kurfürsten-
damm, $$$$, p. 71)

Dressler (Berlin-Mitte, $,
p. 88)

Facil ★★★ (Grünewald,
$$$$, p. 81)

Kaefer's Restaurant
Dachgarten (Near the
Kurfürstendamm, $$,
p. 75)

Lubitsch (On or Near the
Kurfürstendamm, $,
p. 77)

Margaux ★★★ (Berlin-
Mitte, $$$, p. 82)

Schwarzengraben ★ (Berlin-
Mitte, $$$, p. 87)

EAST PRUSSIAN

Marjellchen ★ (Near the
Kurfürstendamm, $$,
p. 75)

FRENCH

First Floor ★★★ (Near the
Memorial Church &
Zoo, $$$$, p. 77)

Harlekin ★★ (Near the
Kurfürstendamm, $$$$,
p. 74)

Paris Bar ★ (Near the
Kurfürstendamm, $$$,
p. 74)

Portalis ★★ (Berlin-Mitte,
$$$, p. 84)

GERMAN

Alexanderkeller (Berlin-
Mitte, $, p. 87)

Bierhaus Luisen-Bräu
(Greater Charlottenburg,
$, p. 80)

First Floor ★★★ (Near the
Memorial Church & Zoo,
$$$$, p. 77)

Französischer Hof (Berlin-
Mitte, $$$, p. 82)

Ganymed (Berlin-Mitte, $$,
p. 86)

Keller-Restaurant im Brecht-
Haus-Berlin (Berlin-
Mitte, $, p. 88)

Mutter Hoppe (Berlin-
Mitte, $, p. 89)

Seidler Restaurant (Near the
Kurfürstendamm, $$,
p. 76)

Zur Letzten Instanz (Berlin-
Mitte, $$, p. 90)

INTERNATIONAL

Funkturm Restaurant
(Greater Charlottenburg,
$$, p. 80)

Ganymed (Berlin-Mitte, $$,
p. 86)

Guy ★ (Berlin-Mitte, $$$$,
p. 81)

Harlekin ★★ (Near the
Kurfürstendamm, $$$$,
p. 74)

Langhans ★★ (Berlin-Mitte,
$$, p. 86)

Paris-Moskau ★ (Near the
Tiergarten, $$$, p. 78)

Restaurant Vau ★★ (Berlin-
Mitte, $$$, p. 84)

The Seasons Restaurant ★
(Berlin-Mitte, $$$,
p. 85)

Vivaldi ★ (Grunewald,
$$$$, p. 80)

Vox ☞ (Berlin-Mitte, $$$, p. 85)

YVA Suite ☞ (Near the Kurfürstendamm, $, p. 76)

ISRAELI

Oren (Berlin-Mitte, $, p. 89)

ITALIAN

Ana e Bruno ☞ (Greater Charlottenburg, $$$, p. 79)

La Gaiola (Berlin-Mitte, $, p. 88)

Ponte Vecchio ☞☞ (Greater Charlottenburg, $$$, p. 79)

Restaurant Mario (Near the Kurfürstendamm, $$, p. 76)

JAPANESE

Daitokai ☞ (Near the Memorial Church and Zoo, $$$, p. 78)

MEDITERRANEAN

Portalis ☞☞ (Berlin-Mitte, $$$, p. 84)

RHENISH

StäV ☞ (Berlin-Mitte, $, p. 89)

2 Near the Kurfürstendamm

VERY EXPENSIVE

Bamberger Reiter ☞☞☞ CONTINENTAL Bamberger Reiter, serving French, German, and Austrian dishes in the style of *neue Deutsche Küche,* is still the choice of savvy local foodies. Don't judge it by its location in an undistinguished 19th-century apartment house. The decor evokes old Germany, with lots of mirrors and fresh flowers. The quality is beyond question here—only Rockendorf's or Alt-Luxemburg can even pretend to have better food. The menu changes daily according to the availability of fresh ingredients and the inspiration of the chef, but might include a roulade of quail, bass with Riesling sauce, cream of fresh asparagus soup, lamb with beans and potato croutons, and date strudel with almond ice cream. German seafood aficionados go here for the fresh fish, which is caught with hook and line—not netted. Chef Cristoph Fischer believes that fish caught in a net die of shock, whereas the hooked fish fights until the bitter end and the meat is stronger. "It tastes like fish," he says. The wine list is enormous, with a dozen varieties of champagne alone.

Regensburgerstrasse 7. ✆ **030/2-18-42-82.** Reservations required. Main courses 20€–33€ ($23–$38); 4- or 5-course fixed-price menu 48€–52€ ($55–$60). AE, DC, MC, V. Tues–Sat 5:30pm–1am (last order 10:30pm). U-Bahn: Spichernstrasse.

Where to Dine in Western Berlin

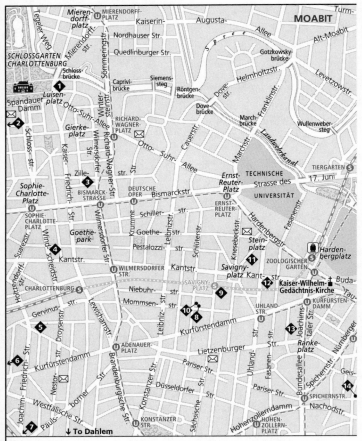

Alt-Luxemburg **4**

Ana e Bruno **2**

Bamberger Reiter **14**

Bierhaus Luisen-Bräu **1**

Daitokai **15**

First Floor **16**

Funkturm Restaurant **6**

Hard Rock Café **13**

Harlekin **19**

Kaefer's Restaurant Dachgarten **18**

Lubitsch **9**

Marjellchen **8**

Paris Bar **12**

Paris-Moskau **17**

Ponte Vecchio **3**

Restaurant Mario **11**

Seidler Restaurant **5**

Vivaldi **7**

YVA Suite **10**

Kids **Family-Friendly Restaurants**

Funkturm Restaurant (p. 80)   Kids delight in ascending this radio tower on Messedam, open daily 10:30am to 11:30pm. The food at the restaurant is good, and later you can go to the observation platform for a truly grand view. The elevator costs 3.05€ ($3.50) for adults, 1.55€ ($1.80) for children.

Hard Rock Cafe (p. 77)   After enough sauerkraut and wurst, kids may want a familiar American hamburger, and this place dispenses them by the truckload.

Harlekin *ŘŘ* FRENCH/INTERNATIONAL   This is among the top three restaurants of Berlin, ranking up there with First Floor and Bamberger Reiter. This restaurant's rise to prominence chagrined jealous chefs at old favorites like the Kempinski. The menu is perfectly balanced between tradition and innovation. For example, appetizers are likely to include such dishes as calves' consommé with crayfish or osso bucco consommé with lobster Spätzle. For your main course, you might be won over by the saddle of lamb baked in a spring roll or turbot roasted with mixed root vegetables. All dishes are made with fresh local produce and are perfectly prepared. Set menus are always delightful and often pleasantly surprising.

In the Grand Hotel Esplanade, Lützowufer. ⓒ **030/254-78-858.** Reservations recommended. Main courses 25€–32€ ($29–$37); 4- to 6-course fixed-price menu 68€–86€ ($78–$99). AE, DC, MC, V. Tues–Sat 6:30–11pm. Closed 3½ weeks in July (dates vary). U-Bahn: Nollendorfplatz or Wittenbergplatz.

EXPENSIVE

Paris Bar *Ř* FRENCH (TRADITIONAL)   This French bistro has been a local favorite since it cheered up the postwar years in dismal bombed-out Berlin. It's crowded with elbow-to-elbow tables like a Montmartre tourist trap but is a genuinely pleasing little place on the see-and-be-seen circuit, close to the Theater des Westens. The food is invariably fresh and well prepared, but not particularly innovative.

Kantstrasse 152. ⓒ **030/313-80-52.** Reservations recommended. Main courses 13€–35€ ($15–$40). AE. Daily noon–3am. U-Bahn: Uhlandstrasse.

MODERATE

Kaefer's Restaurant Dachgarten CONTINENTAL   When a team of cutting-edge architects redesigned the most famous building in Berlin, the Reichstag (Parliament House), they added a restaurant on the uppermost floor, just behind the soaring metallic dome that inspires so many photographs. Lines leading to this edgy setting merge sightseers and diners into the same queues, so here's how to shorten the potential wait: Phone for a table and note the reservation number. Head for the Reichstag's handicapped entrance on the building's west side (facing the Platz der Republik), give the attendant your number, and ride an elevator directly to the restaurant. Your meal will include a close-up view of the dome and the building's interior, plus a sweeping view over former East Berlin. Frankly, a visit here might be best at breakfast, when there's a business-like aura consistent with the Reichtag's august role as a Teutonic icon. The "Berliner" lunch menu includes house-style meatballs with potato salad, grilled steaks, and wursts, while the Continental/Asian dinner menus are more exotic, focusing on dishes like fried filet of duck with Austrian-style scalloped potatoes, Asian asparagus, and water chestnuts; and filet of turbot with a purée of truffles and herb-flavored risotto.

In the Reichstag, Platz der Republik. (✆ **030/2262-9933.** Reservations necessary. Breakfast 5.30€–19€ ($6.10–$22) per person. Lunch main courses 12€–19€ ($14–$22); dinner main courses 18€–24€ ($21–$27). Fixed-price lunch 29€ ($33); fixed-price dinner 39€–63€ ($45–$72). AE, DC, MC, V. Daily 9–11am; 11:30am–2:30pm and 6:30–10:30pm (last food order). S-Bahn: Unter den Linden.

Marjellchen ⋪ EAST PRUSSIAN   This is the only restaurant in Berlin specializing in the cuisine of Germany's long-lost province of East Prussia, along with the cuisines of Pomerania and Silesia. The restaurant's unusual name comes from an East Prussian word meaning "young girl." Ramona Azzaro, whose East Prussian mother taught her many of the region's famous recipes, is the creative force here. Amid a Bismarckian ambience of vested waiters and oil lamps, you can enjoy a savory version of red-beet soup with strips of beef, East Prussian potato soup with shrimp and bacon, *Falscher Gänsebraten* (pork spare ribs stuffed with prunes and bread crumbs "as if the cook had prepared a goose"), marinated elk, and *Mecklenburger Kümmelfleisch* (lamb with chives and onions). This is the type of food Goethe or Schiller liked; perhaps you'll be a convert, too. Of course, Marjellchen isn't the place to go if you want to keep tabs on the cholesterol intake.

Mommsenstrasse 9. ℂ **030/883-26-76.** Reservations required. Main courses 12€–22€ ($14–$25). AE, DC, MC, V. Mon–Sat 5pm–midnight. Closed Dec 23, 24, and 31. U-Bahn: Adenauerplatz or Uhlandstrasse. Bus: 109, 119, or 129.

Restaurant Mario NORTHERN ITALIAN Here you'll find Berlin's most imaginative northern Italian food. The innovative chefs shop for the best and most market-fresh ingredients. Begin with a platter of the most delectable antipasti in town. At least two different kinds of pastas are offered nightly, including a favorite made with a green-pepper pesto. Also on hand are more traditional dishes such as chicken breast stuffed with mozzarella and herbs, tantalizing herb-seasoned lamb cutlets, and fresh fish simply grilled and perfectly seasoned.

Carmerstrasse 2. ℂ **030/312-31-15.** Reservations recommended. Main courses 10€–18€ ($12–$21); fixed-price menus 14€–35€ ($16–$40). AE, DC, MC, V. Mon–Fri noon–midnight; Sat 4pm–1am. S-Bahn: Savignyplatz.

Seidler Restaurant GERMAN   This restaurant enjoys a reputation as a select dining spot and social center. Your host, Mr. Seidler, has a devoted local following among theater and media personalities. The chef believes in strong flavors and good hearty cookery. Savor the *Kohlroulade,* a stuffed cabbage roll—few chefs would want to compete with it. The *Tafelspitz,* boiled beef with vegetables, would have pleased Emperor Josef of Austria (it was his favorite dish). Another highlight is the rack of lamb with honey onions and rosemary potatoes. Look also for market-fresh daily specials. The ambience is that of a Berlin bistro, charmingly cluttered with kitsch from all over the world.

Damaschkestrasse 26. ℂ **030/3-23-14-04.** Reservations required. Main courses 9€–22€ ($10–$25). MC. Mon–Sat 5pm–midnight. U-Bahn: Adenauerplatz.

YVA Suite ⓡ *Finds* INTERNATIONAL   There's an excellent restaurant associated with this club, a meeting place for friendly and ultra-hip denizens of Berlin's inner sanctum of writers, artists, and cultural icons. The setting is on the ground floor of the building near the Savignyplatz, within a stylish and almost surgically minimalist, high-ceilinged decor. Expect walls that are almost entirely sheathed in slabs of volcanic lava rock, elegant table settings, well-prepared food for both hearty and delicate appetites, and a formidable tradition of welcoming stars and starlets from Germany's world of high fashion, sports, and the arts. Many *Mitteleuropa* household names have shown up here, including tennis star Boris Becker, models Heidi Klum and Nadia Auermann, and Berlin TV personality Verona Feldbusch. Menu items vary with the season and the chef's inspiration, but are likely to include lemon-coconut soup with chicken satay; goose liver terrine; curried breast of duck with chorizo sausages; and Thai-style bouillabaisse. Incidentally, the name of this place is derived from the building's former resident, photographer Elsa ("YVA") Simon, a well-known teacher and inspiration for such latter-day artists as Helmut Newton.

Schlüterstrasse 52. © 030/88-72-55-73. Reservations recommended. Main courses 7€–21€ ($8–$24). AE, MC, V. Bar and full menu daily 6pm–midnight; bar and limited menu daily midnight–3 or 4am. U-Bahn: Savignyplatz.

INEXPENSIVE

Hard Rock Cafe *Kids* AMERICAN   This is the local branch of the familiar worldwide chain that mingles rock-'n'-roll nostalgia with American food. Menu choices range from a veggie burger to a "pig" sandwich (hickory smoked pork barbecue) like you might find in rural Georgia. The food is unexceptional, but service is friendly.

Meinekestrasse 21. © 030/88-46-20. www.hardrockcafe.com. Reservations accepted for groups of 10 or more. Main courses 9€–20€ ($10–$23). AE, MC, V. Sun–Thurs noon–midnight; Fri–Sat noon–1am. U-Bahn: Kurfürstendamm.

Lubitsch CONTINENTAL   Lubitsch is deeply entrenched in the consciousness of many local residents, and it's considered in some quarters to have a degree of conservative chic. That reputation was enhanced in 1999 when Chancellor Schröder dropped in for lunch and a photo-op, causing ripples of energy to reverberate through the neighborhood. Menu items include lots of cafe drinks, with glasses of wine priced at 4.50€ to 7€ ($5.20–$8), and steaming pots of afternoon tea, but if you drop in for a meal, expect platters of chicken curry salad with roasted potatoes; Berlin-style potato soup; braised chicken with salad and fresh vegetables; a roulade of suckling pig; and Nürnberger-style *wursts*. Count on a not so friendly staff, a black-and-white decor with Thonet-style chairs, and a somewhat arrogant environment that despite its drawbacks, is very, very *Berliner*.

Bleibtreustrasse 47. © 030/882-37-56. Reservations not necessary. Main courses 6€–21€ ($6.90–$24). AE, DC, MC, V. Mon–Sat 9:30am–midnight. U-Bahn: Kurfürstendamm.

3 Near the Memorial Church & Zoo

VERY EXPENSIVE

First Floor *Finds* REGIONAL GERMAN/FRENCH   This is the showcase restaurant of the Palace Berlin Hotel. Located near the Tiergarten and set one floor above street level, it features a perfectly orchestrated service and setting that revolves around the cuisine of a master chef. Carefully rehearsed staff members smooth over the logistics and details of an upscale meal. Winning our praise are such dishes as a terrine of veal with arugula-flavored butter; sophisticated variations of Bresse chicken; guinea fowl stuffed with foie gras and served with a truffled vinaigrette sauce; a cassoulet of lobster and broad beans in a style vaguely influenced by the culinary precepts of southwestern France; filet of sole with champagne sauce; and a mascarpone mousse with lavender-scented honey.

In the Palace Berlin, Budapesterstrasse 42. © 030/25-02-10-20. Reservations recommended. Main courses 28€–39€ ($32–$45). Set menus 42€ ($48) at lunch only; and 68€–105€ ($78–$121) at lunch and dinner. AE, DC, MC, V. Daily noon–2pm and 8–11pm. U-Bahn: Zoologischer Garten.

EXPENSIVE

Daitokai ☆ JAPANESE   Think of it as a less-institutionalized Benihana's. Vermilion carp lanterns illuminate the labyrinth of reflecting pools. Chefs prepare the meals before your eyes at several long tables. This teppanyaki restaurant offers some of the city's finest grilled steak—tender, juicy, and never overcooked. The seafood and vegetables are served with an artistic flair, and the fish is always fresh and beautifully presented. Quality is never skimped. The flawless service features kindly, almost overly polite waitresses in kimonos. To dine here inexpensively and still eat well, take advantage of the set luncheons.

Europa Center. © 030/2-61-80-99. Reservations recommended. Main courses 10.50€–30€ ($12–$35); fixed-price meals 46€–75€ ($53–$86). AE, DC, MC, V. Tues–Sun noon–3pm and 6–midnight. U-Bahn: Bahnhofzoo.

4 Near the Tiergarten

EXPENSIVE

Paris-Moskau ☆ INTERNATIONAL   The grand days of the 19th century are alive and well at this restaurant in the beautiful Tiergarten area, where good dining spots are scarce. The menu features both classic and more cutting-edge dishes. The fresh tomato soup is excellent. Some of the dishes are mundane—the grilled filet of beef in mushroom sauce comes to mind—but other lighter dishes with delicate seasonings are delightful. We recommend the grilled North Sea salmon with herbs accompanied by basil-flavored noodles. The chef should market his recipe for saffron sauce, which accompanies several dishes. You'll receive attentive service from the formally dressed staff.

Alt-Moabit 141. ℂ **030/3-94-20-81.** Reservations recommended. Main courses 16€–26€ ($18–$30); fixed-price menus 56€–80€ ($64–$92). No credit cards. Daily 6–11:30pm. S-Bahn: Bellevue.

5 In Greater Charlottenburg

VERY EXPENSIVE

Alt-Luxemburg ✶✶✶ CONTINENTAL   Bamberger Reiter is still the leader among Berlin restaurants, but Alt-Luxemburg is nipping at its heels. Karl Wannemacher is one of the outstanding chefs of Germany. Try the honey-glazed duck breast or the saddle of venison with juniper sauce. His Bavarian cream of eel and sturgeon terrine is also excellent. For dessert, don't miss the memorable semolina dumplings with orange ragout or the orange sorbet. The service is both unpretentious and gracious. The dark paneling, evenly spaced mirrors, antique chandeliers, and old-fashioned ambience create a Belle Époque aura.

Windscheidstrasse 31. ℂ **030/3-23-87-30.** Reservations required. Fixed-price 4-course menu 68€ ($78); 5-course menu 76€ ($87). AE, DC, MC, V. Mon–Sat 5–11pm. U-Bahn: Sophie-Charlotte-Platz.

EXPENSIVE

Ana e Bruno ✶ ITALIAN   This is one of Berlin's most charming Italian restaurants. Ana and Bruno turn out a delectable cuisine that takes full advantage of the freshest ingredients and produce in any season. *Nuova cucina* is emphasized here more strongly than traditional Italian classics, and the chefs like to experiment. The combinations of food offer delicious flavors and the creations a harmonious medley. Expect dishes such as a radicchio-studded pasta with perfectly cooked shrimp or an Italian filet of veal with a tuna sauce. Regular customers and gourmets keen on experimenting always seem satisfied with the results. A large, reasonably priced wine selection complements the well-chosen menus.

Sophie-Charlotten-Strasse 101. ℂ **030/325-71-10.** Reservations recommended. Main courses 29€–35€ ($33–$40); fixed-price menus 65€–99€ ($75–$114). AE, V. Tues–Fri 6–10:30pm. U-Bahn: Bismarckstrasse.

Ponte Vecchio ✶✶ ITALIAN   We've dined here many times before and were moderately pleased, but the kitchen is so improved that we now view it as the finest Italian restaurant in Berlin. Market-fresh ingredients produce a winning cuisine with a Tuscan focus. If you don't opt for the excellent fresh fish of the day, you'll find any number of other tempting dishes, such as several variations of veal. Shellfish is deftly handled according to Tuscan style, with fresh basil and olive oil. For a succulent, savory, and spicy pasta, we'd recommend the *penne all'arrabiata,* that old Roman favorite.

Spielhagenstrasse 3. ℂ 030/3-42-19-99. Reservations required. Main courses 18€–36€ ($21–$41). DC. Wed–Mon 6:30–11pm. Closed 4 weeks in summer. U-Bahn: Bismarckstrasse.

MODERATE

Funkturm Restaurant *(Kids* INTERNATIONAL   This restaurant at the radio tower's 65m (213-ft.) midway point provides both good food and sweeping, high-altitude views. You'll first have to pay 1.50€ ($1.75) for the elevator ride up. Inside the restaurant's metallic, glossy interior, every table sits near a window, which is entertaining for kids. Menu items include saddle of lamb with vegetables, pepper steak, and seafood. If you just want to enjoy the view without the food, consider paying 3€ ($3.45) for a ride up to the observation platform near the top of the 136m- (446-ft.-) high tower. The higher platform is open daily 10am to 11:30pm. For information about the tower and its upper-tier observation platform, call ℂ **030/30-38-0996.**

Messedamm 22. ℂ 030/303-829-96. Reservations not necessary. Fixed-price lunch 20€ ($23); buffet dinner 29€ ($33). Main course 9€–18€ ($10–$21). AE, DC, MC, V. Tues–Sun 11am–11pm. U-Bahn: Kaiserdamm.

INEXPENSIVE

Bierhaus Luisen-Bräu GERMAN   One of the city's largest breweries, Luisen-Bräu dates from 1987. The decor includes enormous stainless-steel vats of the fermenting brew, from which the waiters refill your mug. There is no subtlety of cuisine here; it's robust and hearty fare. You serve yourself from a long buffet table. The seating is indoor or outdoor, depending on the season, at long picnic tables that encourage a sense of beer-hall *Bruderschaft* (camaraderie).

Luisenplatz 1, Charlottenburg (close to Charlottenburg Palace). ℂ 030/3-41-93-88. Reservations recommended on weekends. Salads, snacks, and platters 6.80€–15€ ($7.80–$17). MC, V. Sun–Thurs 9am–1am; Fri–Sat 9am–2am. U-Bahn: Richard-Wagner-Platz.

6 In Grunewald

VERY EXPENSIVE

Vivaldi 𝒢 INTERNATIONAL   This is the culinary showcase of one of the most unusual small hotels in Berlin, a neo-Renaissance palace built in 1912 by an advisor to Kaiser Wilhelm II. Vivaldi serves, with panache, some of the most elegant hotel food in Berlin, within a paneled and antique-strewn setting that's as grand as anything you're likely to find in Europe. Most diners opt for one of two fixed-price menus, although there's also a limited a la carte list. A clear soup of lentils with smoked duck breast might be followed by gratinated oysters and scallops resting on a bed of spinach salad, Turbot braised with green asparagus. Venison with black Perigord truffles are triumphs of subtle flavors. Service is impeccable. For dessert, consider a honey and clementine orange parfait.

In the Regent Schlosshotel Berlin, Brahmsstrasse 10. © **030/89-58-40.** Reservations recommended. Main courses 33€–51€ ($38–$59). Fixed-price 4-course dinner 80€ ($92); fixed-price 6-course dinner 115€ ($132). AE, DC, MC, V. Tues–Fri 6–10:30pm. S-Bahn: Grunewald.

7 In Berlin-Mitte

VERY EXPENSIVE

Facil ✸✸✸ CONTINENTAL   The Madison Hotel received one of the most exciting—and expensive—new restaurants in Berlin. A crane lifted a vast tonnage of glass, steel, and garden supplies to the fifth floor terrace of a modern, 11-story hotel near the Potsdamer Platz. Don't expect a view of the skyline of Berlin, as you'll probably get something even better: a verdant oasis of Zen-like calm smack in the middle of one of Berlin's most frenetic neighborhoods, replete with stone floors, mahogany trim, copses of bamboo, trees, seasonal flowers, and waterfalls. A glass roof, tightly closed for midwinter views of the falling rain and snow, opens dramatically during clement weather for a view of the moon and stars, to a mere 14 tables. A formal, alert, and attentive staff serves a medley of sophisticated menu items that change with the seasons and the chef's inspiration. Starters may include marinated tuna with lime oil, pine nuts, and olives; foie gras terrine with stewed South African gooseberries; sliced octopus with wild fennel and olive oil; and bread salad with slices of fried quail. Main courses offer braised shoulder of beef with cêpes and polenta; lamb with artichokes and potatoes; and sea bass with tomatoes and romaine lettuce leaves. The fabulous desserts include curd dumplings with chocolate sauce and apricots.

In the Madison Hotel, Potsdamer Strasse 3. Tel. 030/5900-51234. Reservations recommended. Main courses 32€–40€ ($37–$46); set menus 75€–120€ ($86–$138). AE, DC, MC, V. Mon–Fri noon–3pm and 7–11pm. U-Bahn: Potsdamer Platz.

Guy ✸ INTERNATIONAL   This is gastronomy as theater. You'll understand this as you proceed to any of three separate balconies, each supporting at least one row of artfully decorated tables. The overall effect can be compared to the balconies of an old-fashioned opera house, where sightlines tend to focus on whatever's happening on the stage, or on the occupants of other balconies. Don't expect beer and schnitzels, as the cuisine is very haute, even to the point of seeming experimental. The menu changes frequently but might include a medley of marinated quail and goose liver; mussels served on a purée of arugula; lobster and sweetbreads cooked in puff pastry with tarragon-flavored cream sauce; and braised breast of goose with a roulade of potatoes and herbs. If you're in the mood for strong doses of *Gemütlichkeit,* ask for one of the limited number of tables within its cozy wine cellar. During clement weather, there's additional seating on the terrace in front.

Jägerstrasse 59–60. ℭ **030/20-94-26-00.** Reservations recommended. Main courses 26€–30€ ($30–$35). Fixed-price lunch 15€–20€ ($17–$23); fixed-price dinner 51€–74€ ($59–$85). AE, DC, MC, V. Mon–Fri noon–3pm and 6pm–1am; Sat 6pm–1am. U-Bahn: Stadtmitte or Französischer Strasse.

EXPENSIVE

Französischer Hof GERMAN   If you want a reasonable meal in a relaxed atmosphere, this is the place. Französischer Hof fills two floors connected by a Belle Epoque staircase, evoking a century-old Parisian bistro. The kitchen may not be the finest, but ingredients are fresh and deftly handled. One recent memorable dinner included roast duck breast with calvados along with zucchini and potato pancakes. You can begin with the delectable selection of fish canapés. Saddle of lamb is always admirably done, although you may prefer the rather theatrical flambéed filet Stroganoff with almond-studded dumplings.

Jagerstrasse 56. ℭ **030/2-04-35-70.** Reservations recommended. Main courses 20€–38€ ($23–$44). AE, DC, MC, V. Daily noon–midnight. Closed Dec 24. U-Bahn: Hausvogteiplatz.

Margaux 🏵🏵🏵 CONTINENTAL   Chef Michael Hoffman will dazzle your palate with his seductive, inventive dishes and his brilliant wine cellar. Only a few steps from the Brandenburg Gate, Margaux has won raves from several gourmet magazines, many of which have called it "best gourmet restaurant in Berlin" in the 21st century. Noted architect Johanne Nalbach designed the stunning modern interior, and the paintings of Ingeborg zu Schleswig—Andy Warhol's assistant in 1980s New York—grace the walls. The exceptional food is based on only the highest quality of ingredients. Our party of four recently launched our repast with such perfectly prepared starters as marinated duck liver and Breton lobster appearing with curry and surprisingly with watermelon. Hoffman's star shines brightest with his fish, such as John Dory with a Mediterranean "aroma" that turned out

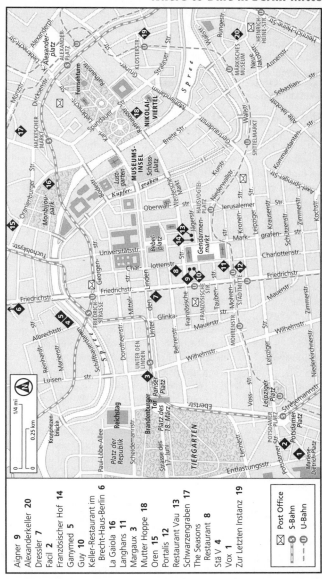

Post Office
S-Bahn
U-Bahn

to be anchovies, olives, tomatoes, and pepper. Frog legs are perfectly—even delectably—perfumed with parsley and garlic, and a roasted saddle of venison won our hearts with a red wine sauce flavored with basil, pepper, and peach.

Unter den Linden 78. © 030/22-65-26-11. Reservations required. Main courses 28€–38€ ($32–$44). Set lunch menus 48€–120€ ($55–$138). Fixed price dinner 75€ ($86). Mon–Sat noon–2pm and 7–11pm. S-Bahn: Unter den Linden.

Portalis (finds) (finds) FRENCH/MEDITERRANEAN This is one of the best examples in Berlin of the sophisticated, worldly, and hip restaurants that import ideas from sunnier, usually Mediterranean, climes. Don't be fooled by its resemblance to a bistro: the cuisine is far more ambitious than that. The color scheme meshes earth tones with dark grays, cherrywood floors, black leather, and stainless steel, providing an artful showcase for the avant-garde cuisine. Textures here are light, without extravagant uses of cream or butter, well suited to palates and waistlines jaded with frequent exposure to *mitteleuropäische* (Central European) food. High-energy chef Volker Drkosch's cuisine varies with the seasons, but may include lobster and lemongrass tempuras; scallops with fresh peas and kohlrabi; a perfectly braised filet of sole with spinach; polenta-stuffed ravioli and morels; sorbets flavored with the juice of prickly pear or obscure French cheeses. When available, freshwater crayfish might be simply but flavorfully seared and seasoned with salt, pepper, and butter. Expect a scattering of well-heeled *Berliner* insiders here, including politicians and personalities from the stage and screen.

Kronenstrasse 55–58. © 030/20-45-54-96. Reservations recommended. Main courses 20€–24€ ($23–$27); fixed-price lunch menu 28€ ($32); fixed-price dinner menu 94€–106€ ($108–$122). AE, MC, V. Tues–Fri noon–2pm and 6:30–11pm. U-Bahn: Stadtmitte.

Restaurant Vau (finds)(finds) INTERNATIONAL This restaurant is the culinary showcase of up-and-coming chef Kolja Kleeburg. You can select from well-chosen international wine list and a menu based on fresh and seasonal ingredients. Choices include terrine of salmon and morels with rocket salad; smoked sturgeon with white beans and caviar; aspic of suckling pig with sauerkraut; salad with marinated red mullet, mint, and almonds; crisp-fried duck with marjoram; ribs of suckling lamb with thyme-flavored polenta; and desserts such as woodruff soup with champagne-flavored ice cream.

Jägerstrasse 54. © 030/202-9730. Reservations recommended. Main courses 26€–36€ ($30–$41) each. Set price lunch 48€–52€ ($55–$60). Fixed-price 4-course dinner 75€–100€ ($86–$115). AE, DC, MC, V. Mon–Sat noon–2:30pm and 7–10:30pm. U-Bahn: Hausvoigteiplatz.

The Seasons Restaurant 🍴 INTERNATIONAL   One of the most appealing hotel dining rooms in Berlin, The Seasons Restaurant exudes a sense of prosperity, thanks to a decor that might have been inspired by Versailles, a sheathing of carefully oiled and partially gilded oak, an open fireplace, and a color scheme of champagne and brown. Despite the upscale decor, the restaurant maintains a deliberately reasonable price-to-value ratio. An impeccably trained staff offers elaborate versions of tuna carpaccio with sesame; smoked breast of pheasant with wild mushrooms, black nuts, and farmer's salad; filet and liver of veal with truffled mashed potatoes and glazed apples; and quail stuffed with goose liver baked in a clay pot. Consider prefacing a meal here with a drink in the hotel's supremely elegant bar.

In the Four Seasons Hotel, Charlottenstrasse 49. ⓒ **030/2-03-38.** Reservations recommended. Lunch main courses 15€–29€ ($17–$33); dinner main courses 26€–39€ ($30–$45); fixed-price menu 49€–94€ ($56–$108). AE, DC, MC, V. Daily noon–2pm and 6:30–11pm. U-Bahn: Französische Strasse.

Vox 🍴 INTERNATIONAL   This is one of the most exciting and creative restaurants in Berlin, far outshining any competition within the vast architectural complex at Potsdamer Platz. One of Switzerland's best design teams created the minimalist decor, with lots of visual emphasis on a stainless steel dominated, open- view kitchen. A team of uniformed chefs concoct artfully present Mediterranean and Asian cuisines in ways you might not expect, such as platters of braised goose liver with apple-flavored vinaigrette; filet of lamb cooked in a wood-burning oven with goat cheese, pepper oil, and Mediterranean vegetables; rotisserie-cooked breast of Barbary duck with mango chutney; and roasted sturgeon on a frothy sauce of white rosemary. One corner of the restaurant features the best sushi bar in Berlin. The venue is enhanced by an attentive and very hip staff, some of whom shuttle between the restaurant and a stylish cocktail lounge that features jazz and blues every night beginning at 10pm. During clement weather, tables spill out onto the terrace, beneath verdant rows of linden trees.

In the Grand Hyatt Berlin, Marlene-Dietrich-Platz 2. ⓒ **030/25-53-12-34.** Reservations recommended. Lunch main courses 14€–20€ ($16–$23); dinner main courses 29€–36€ ($33–$41); platters of sushi 12€–31€ ($14–$36). AE, DC, MC, V. Daily noon–2:30pm and 6:30pm–11:30pm. U-Bahn: Potsdamer Platz.

MODERATE

Aigner CONTINENTAL   Habsburg Austria lives on here. In the late 1990s, the Dorint chain bought the furnishings from one of Vienna's oldest cafes, the Aigner, and moved them into the ground floor of one of Berlin's newest hotels. The result is a black-and-white Jugendstil setting replete with Thonet chairs. There's a lot of ambience here, thanks partly to a location that overlooks the Gendarmenmarkt, and a staff that provides old-fashioned service with a modern flair. The restaurant's signature dish is *Tafelspitz,* the boiled-beef-with-horseradish dish. Here, it's served in a big brass kettle with both haunch and shoulder of beef, with lots of soup, vegetables, savoy cabbage, crème fraîche, and apple-flavored horseradish. Other choices include baked and crusty pike-perch; octopus carpaccio; Wiener schnitzel; and codfish filet with white beans and chorizo.

In the Das Hotel am Gendarmenmarkt, Charlottenstrasse 50–52. © 030/20375-0. Reservations recommended. Main courses 12€–23€ ($14–$26). AE, DC, MC, V. Daily noon–2am. U-Bahn: Stadtmitte.

Ganymed GERMAN/INTERNATIONAL There's nothing trendy or immediately fashionable about this restaurant, which occupied these premises beginning in 1929 and stalwartly continued doing business within East Berlin throughout the Cold War. The setting includes two formal dining rooms, one with an ornate plaster ceiling of great beauty; the other a more modern, big-windowed affair that overlooks the Spree. Food arrives in worthy portions, with plenty of flavor, albeit without too much concern for modern culinary fancies or trends. Examples include the house assortment of appetizers *(Vorspeisen),* laden high with smoked fish, smoked ham, stuffed dumplings, and fish mousse; goose liver terrine; *Eisbein*—the pork shank specialty of 19th-century Berlin; schnitzels made from organically raised veal; mussels in Choron sauce; and breast of pheasant wrapped in Black Forest cured ham.

Schiffbauerdamm 5. © 030/28-59-90-46. Reservations recommended. Main courses 12€–20€ ($14–$23). Fixed-price menus 25€–50€ ($29–$58). AE, MC. Daily noon–2am. U-Bahn: Friedrichstrasse.

Langhans 𝕣𝕣 INTERNATIONAL (MODERN) Few other restaurants combine the culinary traditions of Italy and Japan with such skill and style. Named after the 18th-century designer of the Brandenburg Gate, and created by Detlef Bernhardt, a German-born long-time resident of Japan, it occupies two floors of a grandly proportioned building that flanks the Gendarmenmarkt. Downstairs is a convivial and hip bar loaded with well-dressed patrons, some of whom munch on Spanish-inspired tapas. The most visible culinary zest, however, is upstairs, within a long, minimalist dining room whose views sweep simultaneously out over the twin domes of the square's two churches and a panorama of the brightly lit kitchen.

Here, an international team produces dishes whose flavors are as intriguing as they are delicious. They include lemongrass-and-coconut soup with shrimp; veal carpaccio with sesame and arugula; spaghettini with salmon caviar, Japanese wakame, and lemongrass; braised dorado with green curry and mango; and a superb version of free-range hen with ginger-flavored risotto and sukiyaki sauce. Desserts, as well as virtually everything else on the menu, change frequently, but if it's available you'd probably be richly satisfied with a pear charlotte with tonka bean ice cream.

Charlottenstrasse 59. ℂ **030/20-94-50-70.** Reservations recommended. Main courses 7.50€–19€ ($8.65–$21); set-price menus 26€–29€ ($30–$33). AE, MC, V. Daily 10am–2am. U-Bahn: Gendarmenmarkt.

Schwarzengraben ℛ CONTINENTAL   This is the watering hole of the Berlin *schickeria* or chic crowd. One Berlin paper defined these trendies as "media honchos and their overblond dates." The see-and-be-seen scene might be more important than the cuisine, but two Italian brothers, Ivo and Rudolf Girolo, succeed admirably with superfresh ingredients that are well prepared. Sea bass baked between slices of eggplant is a most credible dish, as is the Italian gnocchi with sausage and green olives. "Black Crows" (its English name) evokes a Soho-style restaurant in New York. Remarkably, the kitchen is prepared to make 300 pasta dishes on short notice, and the chefs know 150 fish recipes by heart. There are even 20 different types of salami that may rest on your plate. Our dining companion for the evening hailed the gnocchi with rabbit ragout and truffles dish as "orgasmic." We're fond of the duck and rabbit pastele. The main dining is upstairs; downstairs for whisky and cigars.

Neue Schonhauswer Schonhauser Strasse 13. ℂ **030/2839-1698.** Reservations recommended. Main courses 14€–23€ ($16–$26). AE, MC, V. Daily 10am–3:30pm and 6–midnight. U-Bahn: Weinmeister.

INEXPENSIVE

Alexanderkeller GERMAN   This reasonably priced, unpretentious restaurant is a lunchtime favorite of neighborhood residents and office workers. The generous meals might include filet of roast beef served with potatoes and artichoke hearts; filet of zander with parsley and new potatoes; or roast pork with red-wine sauce. Food is rich and the meat dishes heavy, but the people in this area love this type of food.

In the cellar of the Hotel Luisenhof, Köpenicker Strasse 92. ℂ **030/2-75-01-42.** Main courses 10€–15€ ($12–$17). MC, V. Daily 11am–midnight. U-Bahn: Märkisches Museum.

Dressler CONTINENTAL   No other bistro along Unter den Linden as successfully re-creates Berlin's prewar decor and style. Designed to resemble an arts-conscious bistro of the sort that might have amused and entertained tuxedo-clad clients in the 1920s, it's set behind a wine-colored façade, and outfitted with leather banquettes, black-and-white tile floors, mirrors, and film memorabilia from the great days of early German cinema. Waiters with vests and aprons scurry around carrying trays of everything from caviar to strudel, as well as three kinds of oysters and hefty portions of lobster salad. You can always drop in to ogle the racks of elegant pastries, consuming them with steaming pots of tea or coffee. Otherwise, more substantial menu items include turbot with champagne vinaigrette; pheasant breast with Riesling sauce; local salmon trout with white wine sauce and braised endive; stuffed breast of veal; and calf's liver with apples.

Unter den Linden 39. ⓒ **030/204-44-22**. Reservations recommended. Main courses 19€–23€ ($21–$26). AE, DC, MC, V. Daily 8am–midnight. S-Bahn: Unter den Linden.

Keller-Restaurant im Brecht-Haus-Berlin SOUTH GERMAN/ AUSTRIAN   This is a dining oddity. From 1953 until his death in 1956, Bertolt Brecht lived here with his wife, Helene Weigel. Today the building houses the Brecht-Weigel-Museum (see "Exploring Berlin-Mitte" in chapter 6). The restaurant, with white plaster and exposed stone, is decorated with photographs of the playwright's family, friends, and theatrical productions. No one will mind if you just stop in for a glass of wine—the place specializes in eastern German wines, French and New World wines. Traditional south German and Austrian food is served, such as an Austrian recipe for *Fleisch Laberln,* meatballs made from minced pork, beef, green beans, and bacon and served with dumplings. In good weather, the seating area includes an enclosed courtyard upstairs.

Chausseestrasse 125. ⓒ **030/2-82-38-43**. Reservations recommended. Main courses 9€–17€ ($10–$20). AE, DC, MC, V. Daily 6pm–midnight, and from May–Oct 11am–3pm and 6pm–midnight. U-Bahn: Zinnowitzer Strasse.

La Gaiola ITALIAN   The owner of this restaurant, an Italian immigrant, wanted to bring the rich flavor of his country's cuisine to Berlin and has done so admirably. Food is served in generous portions. We're especially fond of the fresh seafood or the pasta with sautéed calamari. Two of our favorite dishes include the halibut sautéed or grilled and the lobster ravioli, which is only featured on weekends.

Monbijouplatz 11–12. ℭ **030/28-53-98-90.** Reservations recommended. Main courses 10€–18€ ($12–$21). AE, MC, V. Mon–Sat 6pm–midnight. U-Bahn: Hackescher Markt.

Mutter Hoppe *(Value* GERMAN   This cozy, wood-paneled restaurant still serves the solid Teutonic cuisine favored by a quasi-legendary matriarch (Mother Hoppe) who used to churn out vast amounts of food to members of her extended family and entourage. Within a quartet of old-fashioned dining rooms, you'll enjoy heaping portions of such rib-sticking fare as sauerbraten with roasted potatoes; creamy goulash with wild mushrooms; filet of zander with dill-flavored cream sauce; and braised filet of pork in mushroom-flavored cream sauce. Wine is available, but most guests opt for a foaming mug of beer.

Rathausstrasse 21, Nikolaiviertel. ℭ **030/241-56-25.** Reservations recommended. Main courses 9€–20€ ($10–$23). MC, V. Daily 11:30am–midnight. U-Bahn/S-Bahn: Alexanderplatz.

Oren ISRAELI/ARABIC   You'll notice a similarity in architecture between this restaurant and the massive reconstruction of the Oranienburger synagogue, next door. The cream-colored, high-ceilinged premises are owned by, and rented from, Berlin's Jewish community. Savory aromas of old-fashioned Jewish cooking permeate the restaurant. As such, the site tends to exert a powerful and immediate emotional appeal on customers, most of whom are visitors making a pilgrimage to the nearby synagogue. Prices are reasonable, and the vegetarian and fish platters are both wholesome and plentiful. The menu includes cream of garlic soup; vegetarian platters with hollandaise or choron sauce; filet of zander with fresh cucumber salad; falafel with hummus, tahini, olives, and pita; cold gefilte fish with red-beet salad; and a ragout of zucchini and mushroom with herbed rice. Red or white meat rarely appears on the menu.

Oranienburger Strasse 28. ℭ **030/282-8228.** Reservations recommended. Main courses 6€–16€ ($6.90–$18). AE, MC, V. Mon–Sat noon–1am; Sun 10am–3am. S-Bahn: Oranienburger Tor or Hackescher Markt.

StäV 🏵 *(Finds* RHENISH   For years, this upscale tavern entertained politicians and reporters in Germany's former capital of Bonn. Its owners opposed the re-inauguration of Berlin as the German capital, but they valiantly pulled out of the Rhineland after the switch and followed their clientele to new digs within a 5-minute walk of the Brandenburg Gate. In addition to a taste of Rhenish kitsch, you'll find some of the most politically savvy and astute elected officials, journalists, and bureaucrats in Berlin lining the walls of this high-energy place which only serves one beer, Kölsch,

a brew closely associated with the Rhineland. Expect Rhenish food items like *Himmel and Ärd* (heaven and hell), a mass of apples, onions, and blood sausage; braised beef with pumpernickel and raisin sauce; and sauerbraten with noodles; as well as *Berliner* braised liver with bacon and onions, a crisp Alsatian pizza known as *Flammenküche*, and potato cakes topped with apples and shredded beets or smoked salmon and sour cream.

8 Schiffbauerdamm. ℰ **030/282-3965.** Reservations recommended. Main courses 9€–14€ ($10–$16); fixed-price menu 16€–22€ ($18–$25). AE, DC, MC, V. Daily 11am–1am. U-Bahn: Friedrichstrasse.

Zur Letzten Instanz GERMAN   Reputedly this is Berlin's oldest restaurant, dating from 1525. Zur Letzten Instanz has been frequented by everybody from Napoléon to Beethoven. Prisoners used to stop off here for one last beer before going to jail. The place is located on two floors of a baroque building just outside the crumbling brick wall that once ringed medieval Berlin. Double doors open on a series of small woodsy rooms, one with a bar and ceramic *Kachelofen* (stove). At the back, a circular staircase leads to another series of rooms, where every evening at 6pm, food and wine (no beer) are served. The menu is old-fashioned, mainly limited to Berlin staples.

Waisenstrasse 14–16 (near the Alexanderplatz). ℰ **030/2-42-55-28.** Soup 4€–7€ ($4.60–$8.05); main courses 8€–13€ ($9.20–$15); fixed-price dinner from 20€–29€ ($23–$33). AE, DC, MC, V. Mon–Sat noon–1am; Sun noon–11pm. U-Bahn: Klosterstrasse.

6

Exploring Berlin

Berlin offers a wealth of sightseeing attractions, relating both to the city's venerable past and to its exciting, turbulent present. As befits a new capital, Berlin is undergoing a major face-lift. More than $150 billion has been invested in new streets, railways, and buildings. Half the fun of sightseeing in Berlin today comes from simply wandering the streets to see what the city's thousands of architects are currently up to. The former East Berlin, in particular, is rapidly being restored and gentrified, most notably in the **Berlin-Mitte** district.

Many of the city's most famous older buildings have been restored as well. The rebuilt **Reichstag** has a glittering glass dome; upon the building now stands not the old glowering imperial hunter, but the national symbol, the eagle (locals refer to the statue affectionately as "the fat hen"). Likewise, **Berlin Cathedral** and the five state museums on **Museum Island** have been painstakingly returned to their original glory.

Berlin's magnificent museums may be the city's most famous attractions, but there are some less well-known treasures here as well. For example, few metropolitan areas are blessed with as many gardens, lakes, woodlands, and parks—these cover an amazing one-third of the city. First-time visitors are often surprised to learn that small farms with fields and meadows still exist within the city limits. A picnic in the Tiergarten can be as memorable as an afternoon in the Pergamon Museum.

SUGGESTED ITINERARIES

If You Have 1 Day Get up early and visit the **Brandenburg Gate,** symbol of Berlin, then walk down **Unter den Linden** and have coffee and pastry at the Operncafé. Visit the **Gemäldegalerie** to see some of the world's greatest masterpieces. Afterward, go to **Charlottenburg Palace** and its museums to view the celebrated bust of Queen Nefertiti in the **Ägyptisches Museum.** In the evening, walk along the Kurfürstendamm, visit the **Kaiser Wilhelm Memorial Church,** and dine in a local restaurant.

If You Have 2 Days On Day 2, visit the **Pergamon Museum** on Museum Island; be sure to see the Pergamon Altar. Explore the **National Gallery** and the **Bode Museum,** then head for Alexanderplatz. Take the elevator up for a view from its TV tower, before exploring the **Nikolai Quarter** on foot.

If You Have 3 Days On Day 3, go to **Potsdam** (see chapter 10, "Side Trips from Berlin").

If You Have 4 or 5 Days On Day 4, take a walk through the restored Nikolai Quarter. In the afternoon return to Charlottenburg Palace and explore the **Historical Apartments,** and in the evening visit the **Europa Center** for drinks and dinner. On Day 5, see some of the sights you might have missed. Take some walks through Berlin and stop at the Cold War's **Checkpoint Charlie,** with its museum. If time remains, visit the **Berlin Zoo,** stroll through the **Tiergarten,** and attend a cabaret in the evening.

1 The Top Museums

The great art collections of old Berlin suffered during and after World War II. Although many paintings were saved by being stored in salt mines, many larger works were destroyed by fire. Part of the surviving art stayed in the east, including a wealth of ancient treasures that remind us of the leading role played by German archaeologists during the 19th and early 20th centuries. The paintings that turned up in the West and were passed from nation to nation in the late 1940s have nearly all been returned to Berlin.

CHARLOTTENBURG PALACE & MUSEUMS

Charlottenburg lies just west of the Tiergarten. Plan on spending the day here, since the area contains several museums as well as the royal apartments. After seeing the main attractions you can enjoy a ramble through **Schlossgarten Charlottenburg.** These formal gardens look much as they did in the 18th century. A grove of cypresses leads to a lake with swans and other waterfowl.

North of the palace stands the **Mausoleum,** which holds the tombs of King Friedrich Wilhelm II and Queen Luise, sculptured by Rauch, as well as several other interesting funerary monuments of the Prussian royal family.

Ägyptisches Museum *ℛ* The western Berlin branch of the Egyptian Museum is housed in the palace's east guardhouse. It's worth the trip just to see the famous colored bust of Queen Nefertiti, which dates from about 1360 B.C. and was discovered in 1912.

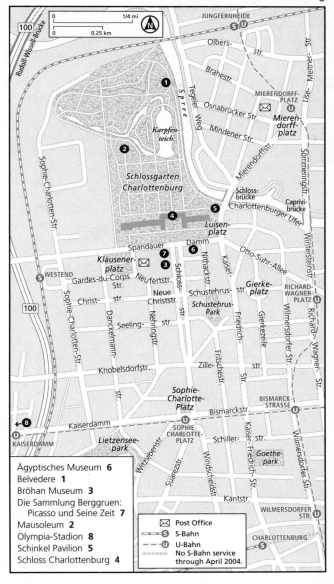

Ägyptisches Museum **6**
Belvedere **1**
Bröhan Museum **3**
Die Sammlung Berggruen:
Picasso und Seine Zeit **7**
Mausoleum **2**
Olympia-Stadion **8**
Schinkel Pavilion **5**
Schloss Charlottenburg **4**

⊠	Post Office
···Ⓢ···	S-Bahn
···Ⓤ···	U-Bahn
▨▨▨	No S-Bahn service through April 2004.

The bust, stunning in every way, is all by itself in a dark first-floor room, illuminated by a spotlight. It's believed that the bust never left the studio in which it was created but served always as a model for other portraits of the queen. In addition, look for the head of Queen Tiy, the world-famous head of a priest in green stone, and the monumental Kalabasha Gateway, built by Emperor Augustus around 30 B.C. Other displays feature jewelry, papyrus, tools, and weapons, as well as objects relating to the Egyptian belief in the afterlife.

Schlossstrasse 70. 📞 **030/32-09-11.** www.smpk.de. Admission 6€ ($6.90) adults, 3€ ($3.45) children; free admission 1st Sun of each month. Tues–Fri 10am–6pm; Sat–Sun 11am–6pm. U-Bahn: Sophie-Charlotte-Platz or Richard-Wagner-Platz.

Bröhan Museum   Berlin's finest collection of Jugendstil (German Art Nouveau) is found here. When Professor Bröhan started the collection, Jugendstil was viewed as having little merit. It's a different story today. The objects include glass, furnishings, silver and gold, paintings, and vases. The outstanding porcelain collection ranges from Gallé to Sèvres and Meissen to Royal Copenhagen.

Schlossstrasse 1A. 📞 **030/32-69-06-00.** Admission 6€ ($6.90); 3€ ($3.45) students and children. Tues–Sun 10am–6pm. U-Bahn: Sophie-Charlotte-Platz or Richard-Wagner-Platz.

Schloss Charlottenburg 👁👁   Schloss Charlottenburg, one of the finest examples of baroque architecture in Germany, was built by Sophie Charlotte. This beautiful and intelligent woman, a patron of philosophy and the arts, was the wife of Friedrich I, crowned as the first king in Prussia (as opposed to "of") in 1701. He nearly bankrupted the state with his extravagant ways.

The residence was begun as a summer palace but got out of hand, eventually growing into the massive structure you see today. When you pass through the heavy iron gates and enter the courtyard, you'll immediately encounter a baroque equestrian statue of Friedrich I himself, by Andreas Schlüter. The main entrance to the palace is directly behind this, marked by the 48m-high (157-ft.) cupola and capped by a gilded statue of Fortune. Inside, you'll find a columned rotunda with stucco reliefs depicting the virtues of Prussian princes in mythological terms. From this vestibule, you can take guided tours of the Historical Apartments. English translations of the guide's lecture are sold at the ticket counter.

The main wing of the palace contains the apartments of Friedrich and his "philosopher queen." Of special interest in this section is the **Reception Chamber.** This large room is decorated with frieze panels, vaulted ceilings, and mirror-paneled niches. The tapestries on the walls (1730) are based on Plutarch's *Lives;* included are such classical scenes as Pericles in battle and the sacrifice of Theseus on Delos. At the far end of the west wing is the **Porcelain Chamber,** containing a fine collection of Chinese porcelain.

The **new wing,** known as the Knobelsdorff-Flügel and built from 1740 to 1746, contains the apartments of Friedrich the Great. Today these rooms serve as a museum of paintings, many of which were collected or commissioned by the king. The king's finest paintings are on the upper floor. Works by Watteau include *The Trade Sign of the Art Dealer Gersaint,* purchased by Friedrich in 1745 for the palace's music hall. Also note the decoration on the walls and ceilings.

At the far eastern end of the Schloss is the **Schinkel Pavillon,** an Italian style summer house. Karl Friedrich Schinkel, the leading architect of the day, constructed this villa in 1825. Today it holds a small but noteworthy museum, containing paintings, drawings, and sketches from the early 1800s. Some of the sketches are by Schinkel himself, who was both an architect and an artist.

At the far end of Schlossgarten Charlottenburg is the **Belvedere,** close to the Spree River. This former royal teahouse contains exquisite Berlin porcelain, much of it from the 1700s.

Luisenplatz. (✆ **030/32-09-1275.** Combination ticket for all buildings and historical rooms 7€ ($8.05) adults, 5€ ($5.75) children under 14. Ticket counter sells English translation of guide's lecture. Palace Tues–Fri 9am–5pm; Sat–Sun 10am–5pm; Museum Tues–Fri 10am–6pm. Gardens (free admission) daily 6:30 am-8pm U-Bahn: Sophie-Charlotte-Platz or Richard-Wagner-Platz.

MUSEUMINSEL MUSEUMS

Alte Nationalgalerie ⚘   Known for its collection of 19th-century German as well as French Impressionist art, this museum also has the world's largest collection of the works of one of Berlin's best known artists, Adolph von Menzel (1815–1905). We especially like his piece titled *Das Balkonzimmer.* Although the Nazis sold or destroyed many of the museum's early 20th century works they considered "degenerate," the collection still includes a gallery of art from the romantic and classical movements as well as the Biedermeier era, the latter especially well represented by Caspar David Friedrich and Schinkel. Allow at least an hour and a half to take in canvasses by everyone from Pissarro to Cézanne, from Delacroix to Degas, and from van Gogh to Monet. We are especially fond of the works of Max Liebermann and Max Beckmann.

Museumsinsel. ℂ **030/20905555.** www.smpk.de. Admission 6€ ($6.90) adults, 3€ ($3.45) children. Tues–Sun 10am–6pm. S-Bahn: Hackescher Markt. Tram: 1, 2, 3, 4, 5, 6, or 53.

Altes Museum   Karl Friedrich Schinkel, the city's greatest architect, designed this structure, which resembles a Greek Corinthian temple, in 1822. On its main floor is the **Antikensammlung (Museum of Greek and Roman Antiquities).** This is a great collection of world-famous antique decorative art. Some of the finest Greek vases of the black-and-red-figures style, from the 6th to the 4th century B.C., are here. The best-known vase is a large Athenian amphora (wine jar) found in Vulci, Etruria. It dates from 490 B.C. and shows a satyr with a lyre and the god Hermes. One of several excellent bronze statuettes, the Zeus of Dodone (470 B.C.) shows the god about to cast a bolt of lightning. You can also see a rare portrait of Cleopatra (from Alexandria). In the Brandenburg-Prussian art collection is an exceptional bronze statue of the goddess Luna descending from the firmament. The Prussians called it "the pearl of the collection."

Bodestrasse 1–3, Museumsinsel. ℂ **030/20-90-50.** www.smpk.de. Admission 6€ ($6.90) adults, 3€ ($3.45) children. Tues–Sun 10am–6pm. U-Bahn/S-Bahn: Friedrichstrasse. Bus: 100 to Lustgarten, 147, 157, 257.

Pergamon Museum ℛℛℛ   Pergamon Museum houses several departments, but if you have time for only one exhibit, go to the **Department of Greek and Roman Antiquities,** housed in the north and east wings of the museum, and enter the central hall to see the **Pergamon Altar** ℛℛℛ (180–160 B.C.), which is so large that it has a huge room all to itself. Some 27 steps lead from the museum floor up to the colonnade. Most fascinating is the frieze around the base. It shows the struggle of the Olympian gods against the Titans and is strikingly alive, with figures that project as much as a foot from the background. If you explore further, you'll find a Roman market gate discovered in Miletus as well as sculptures from many Greek and Roman cities, including a statue of a goddess holding a pomegranate (575 B.C.), found in southern Attica, where it had been buried for 2,000 years. It was so well preserved that flecks of the original paint are still visible on her garments.

The **Near East Museum** ℛ, in the south wing, contains one of the largest collections anywhere of antiquities from ancient Babylonia, Persia, and Assyria. Among the exhibits is the Processional Way of Babylon with the Ishtar Gate, dating from 580 B.C., and the throne room of Nebuchadnezzar. Cuneiform clay tablets document

A New Berlin Wall

Berliners aren't likely to forget the **Berlin Wall** any time soon, but just in case, their government has reconstructed a partial stretch of the wall at Bernauer Strasse and Ackerstrasse (U-Bahn: Bernauer Strasse), at a cost of $1.3 million. The 70m-long (230-ft.) memorial consists of two walls that include some of the fragments of the original wall (those fragments not bulldozed away or carried off by souvenir hunters). The memorial is mostly made of mirrorlike stainless steel. Slits allow visitors to peer through. A steel plaque reads "In memory of the division of the city from 13 August 1961 to 9 November 1989." Critics have called the construction "a sanitized memorial," claiming it does little to depict the 255 people shot trying to escape its predecessor.

a civilization that created ceramics, glass, and metal objects while Europe was still overrun with primitive tribes. The museum's upper level is devoted to the **Museum of Islamic Art.** Of special interest are the miniatures, carpets, and woodcarvings.

Kupfergraben, Museumsinsel. ℭ **030/20-90-50.** www.smpk.de. Admission 6€ ($6.90) adults, 3€ ($3.45) children; free admission 1st Sun of each month. Tues, Wed, Fri, Sat & Sun 10am–6pm; Thurs 10am–10pm. U-Bahn/S-Bahn: Friedrichstrasse. Tram: 1, 2, 3, 4, 5, 13, 15, or 53.

TIERGARTEN MUSEUMS

Bauhaus-Archiv Museum für Gestaltung (Bauhaus Design Museum)
The Bauhaus Museum houses a permanent exhibition of photos and architectural designs relating to the Bauhaus school. Even if you're not a student of architecture, this museum is fascinating; it will bring you closer to the ideas and concepts that inspired modern design.

Klingelhoferstrasse 14. ℭ **030/2-54-00-20.** Admission 4€ ($4.60) adults, 2€ ($2.30) children under 12. Wed–Mon 10am–5pm. U-Bahn: Nollendorfplatz.

Gemäldegalerie (Picture Gallery) 🎨🎨🎨
This is one of Germany's greatest art museums. Several rooms are devoted to early German masters, with panels from altarpieces dating from the 13th to 15th centuries. Note the panel *The Virgin Enthroned with Child* (1350), surrounded by angels that resemble the demons in the works of Hieronymus Bosch. Eight paintings make up the Dürer collection, including several portraits.

Most of the great European masters are represented. The Italian collection contains five Raphael Madonnas, along with works by Titian *(The Girl with a Bowl of Fruit)*, Fra Filippo Lippi, Botticelli, and Correggio *(Leda with the Swan)*. There are early Netherlandish paintings from the 15th and 16th centuries (van Eyck, van der Weyden, Bosch, and Brueghel) as well. Several galleries are devoted to 17th-century Flemish and Dutch masters, with no fewer than 15 works by Rembrandt, such as his famous *Head of Christ. The Man with the Golden Helmet,* long famous as a priceless Rembrandt, was proven in 1986 to be by another hand. This remarkable painting is now accepted as a fine independent original.

Mattäiskirchplatz 4. (C) **030/20-90-55-55**. www.smpk.de. Admission 6€ ($6.90) adults, 3€ ($3.45) children. Tues–Sun 10am–6pm (Thurs to 10pm). U-Bahn: Potsdamer Platz, then bus 148. Bus: 129 from Ku'damm (plus a 4-min. walk).

Kunstgewerbemuseum This museum displays applied arts and crafts from the Middle Ages through the 20th century. Its outstanding exhibition is the Guelph Treasure, a collection of medieval church articles in gold and silver. The basement rooms show contemporary design from the Bauhaus school to Charles Eames and Memphis. Venetian glass, Italian majolica, German Renaissance goldsmiths' work, and 18th-century porcelain figurines are also displayed. Notable are such Art Nouveau works as a translucent opal-and-enamel box by Eugène Feuillâtre. There's a cafeteria inside, open from 10am to 4:30pm.

Matthäikirchplatz (opposite the Philharmonie), Tiergartenstrasse 6. (C) **030/2662-902**. Admission 3.05€ ($3.50) adults, 1.55€ ($1.80) children. Tues–Fri 10am–6pm; Sat–Sun 11am–6pm. U-Bahn: Potsdamer Platz. Bus: 129 from Ku'damm to Potsdamer Brücke.

Neue Nationalgalerie (Staatliche Museum zu Berlin) ⊛ In its modern glass-and-steel home designed by Ludwig Mies van der Rohe (1886–1969), the Neue Nationalgalerie is a sequel of sorts to the art at Dahlem. It contains a continually growing collection of modern European and American art. Here you'll find works of 19th-century artists, with a concentration on French Impressionists. German art starts with Adolph von Menzel's paintings from about 1850. The 20th-century collection includes works by Max Beckmann and Edvard Munch, and E. L. Kirchner's *Brandenburger Tor* (1929), as well as paintings by Bacon, Picasso, Ernst, Klee, and American artists such as Barnett Newman. There's food service in the cafe on the ground floor, open 10:30am to 5:45pm.

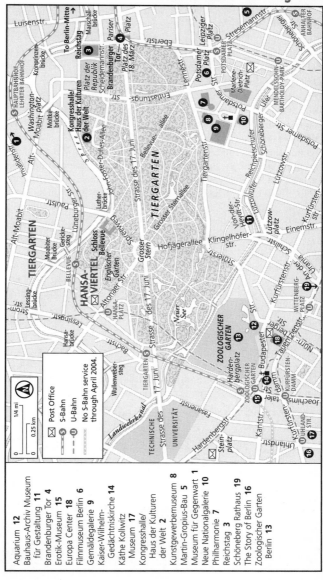

Aquarium **12**
Bauhaus-Archiv Museum
für Gestaltung **11**
Brandenburger Tor **4**
Erotik-Museum **15**
Europa Center **18**
Filmmuseum Berlin **6**
Gemäldegalerie **9**
Kaiser-Wilhelm-
Gedächtniskirche **14**
Käthe Kollwitz
Museum **17**
Kongresshalle/
Haus der Kulturen
der Welt **2**
Kunstgewerbemuseum **8**
Martin-Gropius-Bau **5**
Museum für Gegenwart **1**
Neue Nationalgalerie **10**
Philharmonie **7**
Reichstag **3**
Schöneberg Rathaus **19**
The Story of Berlin **16**
Zoologischer Garten
Berlin **13**

Potsdamerstrasse 50 (just south of the Tiergarten). (© **030/2-66-26-62**. www.smpk. de. Permanent collection 6€ ($6.90) adults, 3€ ($3.45) children and students; temporary exhibitions 3€ ($3.45). Tues–Fri 10am–6pm; Sat–Sun 11am–6pm. S-Bahn: Potsdamer Platz.

OTHER MUSEUMS & SIGHTS

Dahlemer Museen 🏛🏛 After extensive reorganizing, this complex of museums now occupies one mammoth structure in the heart of Dahlem's Freie Universität. If you only have time for one, visit the greatest ethnological collection on earth at the **Ethnologisches Museum** 🏛🏛🏛. The 500,000-plus artifacts represent all five continents, even prehistoric America. The Incan, Mayan, and Aztec stone sculpture alone equal the collections of some of the finest museums of Mexico. Displays also include an intriguing assemblage of pre-Columbian relics, including gold objects and antiquities from Peru, and you can hear folk music. We highly recommend its collection of authentic boats from the South Pacific.

The **Museum für Ostasiatische Kunst** (Museum of Far Eastern Art) 🏛🏛 is a gem of a museum devoted primarily to Japan, Korea, and China, with artifacts dating back to as far as 3000 B.C. Launched in 1906 as the first Far Eastern museum of art in Germany, this is one of Europe's finest in presenting an overview of some of the most exquisite ecclesiastical and decorative art to come out of the Far East. It rivals collections in Paris. In essence, the museum represents the loot acquired during a massive "shopping expedition" the Germans took to the Orient where they even managed to garner the 17th-century imperial throne of China, all lacquered and inlaid with mother-of-pearl. The Japanese woodblock prints, each seemingly more exquisite than the next, are reason enough to visit.

Germany's greatest collection of Indian art is on exhibit at the **Museum für Indische Kunst,** covering a span of 40 centuries. It's an international parade of some of the finest art and artifacts from the world of Buddhism, representing collections from such lands as Burma, Thailand, Indonesia, Nepal, and Tibet.

Outside the Dahlem museum complex, but only a 5-minute walk away, the **Museum Europäischer Kulturen** (© **030/83901-279**) is devoted to the German people themselves—not the aristocrats but the middle class and the peasant stock who built the country. It is a true "museum of the people," tracing artisans and homemakers through four centuries. Household items are displayed along with primitive industrial equipment such as a utensil for turning flax into linen. Furnishings, clothing, pottery, and even items used in religious observances are shown, along with some fun and whimsical depictions of pop culture from the 1950s through the 1980s.

Lansstrasse 8. © 030/83011. www.smpk.de. Admission 3€ ($3.45) adults, 1.50€ ($1.75) students and children. Tues–Fri 9am–6pm; Sat–Sun 11am–6pm. U-Bahn to Dahlem-Dorf.

Deutsche Guggenheim Berlin

This state-of-the-art museum is devoted to modern and contemporary art. The exhibition space is on the ground floor of the newly restored Berlin branch of Deutsche Bank. The Guggenheim Foundation presents several exhibitions at this site annually, and also displays newly commissioned works created specifically for this space by world-renowned artists. The bank supports young artists from the German-speaking world by purchasing their work and displaying it throughout the company's offices and public spaces. Exhibitions have ranged from the most avant-garde of modern artists to Picasso, Cézanne, and Andy Warhol.

Unter den Linden 13–15 (at the intersection with Charlottenstrasse). © 030/2020-930. Admission 3€ ($3.45) adults, 2€ ($2.30) children. Free on Mon. Daily 11am–8pm; Thurs till 10pm. S-Bahn: Unter den Linden.

Die Sammlung Berggruen: Picasso und Seine Zeit (The Berggruen Collection: Picasso and His Era)

This unusual private museum displays the awesome collection of respected art and antiques dealer Heinz Berggruen. A native of Berlin who fled the Nazis in 1936, Berggruen later established a mini-empire of antique dealerships in Paris and California before returning, with his collection, to his native home in 1996. Sometime during your visit, there's a good chance that 80-year-old Mr. Berggruen, who has an apartment nearby, will be conducting a lecture on his favorite painter, or spontaneously strolling among his paintings. The setting is a renovated army barracks designed by noted architect August Stütler in 1859. Although most of the collection is devoted to Picasso, there are also works by Cézanne, Braque, Klee, and van Gogh. The Picasso collection alone, which covers all his major periods, is worth the trip.

Schlosstrasse 1 (entrance across from the Egyptian Museum, in Charlottenburg). © 030/326-95815. www.smpk.de. Admission 8€ ($9.20) adults, 4€ ($4.60) students and children. Tues–Fri 10am–6pm; Sat–Sun 11am–6pm. Closed Mon. U-Bahn: Richard-Wagner Platz, followed by a 10-min. walk.

Erotik-Museum

This "museum" lies on the corner of the seediest-looking block in Berlin. You start out on the third floor and work your way down (no sexual pun intended). Believe it or not, this is

Berlin's fifth most visited museum. The collection shelters some 5,000 sexual artifacts from around the world, including many Indian and Asian miniatures of erotic positions, large carved phalli from Bali, and African fertility masks. Life-size dioramas explore such topics as S&M and fetishism. There are some Chinese wedding tiles from the 18th and 19th century that were supposed to provide sexual education to a newly married couple. The museum also honors the "queen of the Rubber Willy" herself, Beate Uhse, a household name in Germany. Her life is documented from her Luftwaffe days to pictures of her at the helm of a large speedboat. This septuagenarian opened the world's first shop devoted to "marital hygiene," ultimately championing the right to sell contraceptives. Today she still heads the world's largest sex-related merchandising business. Downstairs are video cabins filled with middle-aged men in raincoats and a "sex superstore."

Joachimstaler Strasse 4. ⓒ **030/886-06-66.** Admission 5€ ($5.75), 4€ ($4.60) students and seniors. Daily 9am–11pm. U-Bahn/S-Bahn: Zoologischer Garten.

Filmmuseum Berlin ⓡ   A thematic and chronological tour through the saga of the much-troubled German cinema is on show here. The link between Berlin and Hollywood is one of the main focuses of the collection, which is supplemented with special exhibitions. Currently the museum also owns some 9,000 German and foreign films, both silents and talkies. The collection here owns a million stills of scenes, portraits, and productions along with 30,000 screenplays, 20,000 posters, and 60,000 film programs. Germany's only world-class star, Marlene Dietrich, comes alive again in one wing. Berlin acquired part of her extensive estate of memorabilia in 1993. Photos, costumes, props, letters, and documents recall the remarkable life of this diva, who startled the world with her performance in Josef von Sternberg's *Der Blaue Engel* in 1930. Highlights of other films include props from *The Cabinet of Dr. Caligari*, the most famous German film of the Weimar Republic. One room is devoted to the controversial Leni Riefenstahl, the star director of the fascist era whose key films *Triumph des Willens* and *Olympia* established her as one of the world's major filmmakers and the leading exponent of Nazi propaganda.

Potsdamer Strasse 2. ⓒ **030/300-903-0.** www.filmmuseum-berlin.de. Admission 6€ ($6.90) adults, 4€ ($4.60) students, children, and senior citizens. Tues–Wed, Fri–Sun 10am–6pm; Thurs 10am–8pm. U-Bahn/S-Bahn: Potsdamer Platz.

Friedrichswerdersche Kirche-Schinkelmuseum   This annex of the Nationalgalerie is located in the deconsecrated Friedrichswerdersche Kirche, which was designed in 1828 by Karl Friedrich Schinkel

(1781–1841). It lies close to Unter den Linden, not far from the State Opera House. The twin Gothic portals of the old church shelter a bronze of St. Michael slaying a dragon. Inside, the museum is devoted to the memory of Schinkel, who designed many of Berlin's great palaces, churches, and monuments. Memorabilia and documents record his great accomplishments. There are also exhibitions of neo-classical sculptures, portraits, and tombs by Johann Gottfried Schadow, Christian Daniel Rauch, Friedrich Tieck, and Berthel Thor-valdsen, the Danish sculptor.

Werderstrasse (at the corner of Niederlagstrasse). ℂ 030/2-08-13-23. Admission 3€ ($3.45) adults, 1.50€ ($1.75) children. Tues–Sun 10am–6pm. U-Bahn: Hausvogteiplatz.

Kaiser-Wilhelm Gedächtniskirche (Kaiser Wilhelm Memorial Church)

There is no more evocative site in the western sector of Berlin to remind us of the horrors of war. The massive red sandstone church that originally stood here was dedicated in 1895 as a memo-rial to Kaiser Wilhelm II. In 1945, during the closing months of World War II, a bomb dropped by an Allied plane blasted it to pieces, leaving only a few gutted walls and the shell of the neo-Romanesque bell tower. After the war, West Berliners decided to leave the artfully evocative ruins as a reminder of the era's suffering and devastation. In 1961, directly at the base of the ruined building, they erected a small-scale modern church designed by Egon Eierman.

Tips **The Best Sightseeing Deal**

You can purchase a *Tageskarte* for 6€ ($6.90), which allows you entry to all of the state-owned museums on the same day. A 3-day card for 10€ ($12) allows entry to all state-owned museums for 3 consecutive days. Admission will be higher for special exhibitions. The card can be purchased at any state-owned museum.

Take advantage of free admission to all the state muse-ums on the first Sunday of every month, including the Per-gamon, Alte Nationalgalerie, Altes Museum, Ägyptisches Museum, Gemäldegalerie, Neue Nationalgalerie, Sammlung Berggruen, and the Museum for Gegenwart at Hamburger Bahnhof, Dahlemer Museen. Just remember: You won't be the only one doing so.

Always irreverent, Berliners, noting the avant-garde architecture and geometric design of the new church, nicknamed it "the lipstick and powder box." Its octagonal hall is lit solely by thousands of colored glass windows set into a honeycomb framework. On its premises, you can visit a small museum with exhibitions and photographs documenting the history of the original church, and the destructive ravages of war. The new church can hold up to 1,200 worshippers, and 10-minute religious services—conceived for office workers heading home—are held there every day at 5:30 and at 6pm. Between June and August, English-language services are conducted daily at 9am, and free organ concerts are presented here every Saturday, year-round, at 6pm.

Breit-Scheidplatz. (C) 030/218-50-23. Free admission. Ruined church Mon–Sat 10am–4pm; new church daily 9am–7pm. U-bahn: Zoologischer Garten or Kurfürstendamm.

Käthe-Kollwitz-Museum ⚘ This museum has been called a personalized revolt against the agonies of war. Many works express the sorrow of wartime separation of mother and child, inspired in part by the artist's loss of a son in World War I and a grandson during World War II. Berlin-born Käthe Kollwitz (1867–1945) was an ardent pacifist and socialist whose works were banned by the Nazis. The first woman ever elected to the Prussian Academy of the Arts, she resigned her position in 1933 to protest Hitler's rise to power. Her husband, Karl Kollwitz, was a physician who chose to practice among the poor on a working-class street (now called Kollwitzstrasse). In 1943, Allied bombing drove Käthe to the countryside near Dresden, where she died in 1945, a guest of the former royal family of Saxony in their castle at Moritzburg.

The lower floors of the museum are devoted to woodcuts and lithographs, the upper floors to particularly poignant sculptures. *Note:* The collection is closed twice a year for special exhibits.

Fasanenstrasse 24. (C) 030/882-52-10. Admission 5€ ($5.75) adults, 2.50€ ($2.90) children and students. Wed–Mon 11am–6pm. U-Bahn: Kurfürstendamm or Uhlandstrasse. Bus 109, 119, 129, 219 or 249.

Märkisches Museum The full cultural history of Berlin is displayed in one of the most prominent buildings on the banks of the Spree; 42 rooms contain collections of artifacts from excavations, plus such art treasures as Slav silver and Bronze Age finds. You can learn about Berlin's theaters and literature, the arts in Berlin and Brandenburg, and the life and work of Berlin artisans. Most visitors like the array of mechanical musical instruments that can be played

Wednesday 3 to 4pm and Sunday 11am to noon, for an extra 1€ ($1.15).

Am Källnischen Park 5. (✆ **030/30-86-60**. www.smpk.de. Admission 4.10€ ($4.70) adults, 2.05€ ($2.35) children. Tues–Sun 10am–6pm. U-Bahn: Märkisches Museum. Bus: 147, 240, or 265.

Martin-Gropius-Bau   When this gallery opened in 1981, the *New York Times* called it one of the "most dramatic museums in the world." It contains the **Museum Berlinische Galerie,** with works of art, architecture, and photography from the 19th and 20th centuries; the **Jewish Museum;** and the **Werkbund Archiv.** On the ground floor are changing exhibitions. The building lies near the site of the former Berlin Wall, and its eastern section opens onto the leveled former Gestapo headquarters. It's fascinating to look at the adjoining building with its unrestored exterior terra-cotta friezes—some damaged, some destroyed, and some left intact.

Stresemannstrasse 110. (✆ **030/25-48-60**. Admission 6€ ($6.90) adults, 3€ ($3.45) children. Tues–Sun 10am–8pm. U-Bahn: Potsdamer Platz. S-Bahn: Anhalter Bahnhof.

Museum für Gegenwart   This Museum of Contemporary Art opened in 1996 north of the Spree River in the old Hamburger Bahnhof, the oldest train station in Berlin. The structure was the terminus of the 290km (180-mile) train run from Hamburg. Today, the 19th-century station no longer receives trains but is a premier storehouse of postwar art, a sort of Musée d'Orsay of Berlin. Traces of its former function still are evident, including the high roof designed for steam engines. The modern art on display is some of the finest in Germany; the nucleus of the collection was donated by the Berlin collector Erich Marx (no relation to Karl Marx). You can view everything from Andy Warhol's now legendary Mao to an audiovisual Joseph Beuys archive. The museum houses one of the best collections of the work of Cy Twombly in the world because the curator, Heiner Bastian, was once his assistant. Other works are by Rauschenberg, Lichtenstein, and the recently deceased Dan Flavin. Beuys is also represented by 450 drawings.

Invalidenstrasse 50–51. (✆ **030/20-90-55-55**. www.smpk.de. Admission 6€ ($6.90) adults, 3€ ($3.45) children. Tues–Fri 10am–6pm; Sat–Sun 11am–6pm. U-Bahn: Zinnowitzer Strasse. Bus: 157, 245, 248, or 340.

Museum Haus am Checkpoint Charlie   Exhibits in this small building evoke the tragic events connected with the former Berlin Wall. You can see some of the instruments of escape used by East Germans, including chairlifts, false passports, hot-air balloons, and even a minisub. Photos document the construction of the wall, the establishment of escape tunnels, and the postwar history of both parts of Berlin from 1945 until today, including the airlift of 1948 to 1949. One of the most moving exhibits is the display on the staircase of drawings by schoolchildren, who, in 1961 to 1962, were asked to depict both halves of Germany in one picture.

Friedrichstrasse 44. ℂ **030/253-72-50.** Admission 7€ ($8.05) adults, 4€ ($4.60) children and students. Daily 9am–10pm. U-Bahn: Kochstrasse. Bus: 129.

Olympia-Stadion   Built in 1936 by Werner March for the XI Summer Olympic Games, the Olympia-Stadion, which seats 100,000 people, was the first in Europe to supply all the facilities necessary for modern sports. Hitler expected to see his "master race" run off with all the medals in the 1936 Olympics, but his hopes were dashed when an African American, Jesse Owens, took four golds for the U.S. team.

The stadium area covers a total of 136ha (330 acres), but the main attraction is the arena. The playing field in its center lies 14m (47 ft.) below ground level. For a panoramic view of Berlin, take the elevator to the top of the 80m (260-ft.) platform, where the Olympic bell hangs. Sporting or cultural events are still presented here about once a week during spring, summer, and autumn. For ticket sales and information for sporting events within the stadium, call **Herta-BSC (Herta-Berlin Soccer Club)** at ℂ **030/3-00-92-80.** For information about the occasional live concerts, call **Conzert Concept** at ℂ **030/ 81-07-50.**

Olympischer Platz 3. ℂ **030/30-06-33.** Free admission. June–Sept daily 9am–5pm; off-season daily 9am–4pm. U-Bahn: Olympia-Stadion.

Sachsenhausen Memorial & Museum   Just north of Berlin, Saschsenhausen was one of the most notorious death camps of the Nazi empire and was liberated by Allied troops in 1945. The freedom was short lived. The Soviet secret police turned it into a prison camp, and the misery and death continued until it was shut down 5 years later. The largest prison camp in East Germany, Sachsenhausen was home to some 12,000 inmates from 1945 to 1950. Mass graves of the former prisoners were only discovered in 1990. A museum has opened exhibiting the enslavement by the Nazis and Soviets. In World War II, Sachsenhausen was the administrative headquarters for all the concentration camps, winning the praise of dreaded SS chief Heinrich Himmler. The SS learned its methods of mass killing at this camp. Most of the 30,000 or so Nazi victims were prisoners of war, including Stalin's oldest son. The Soviet prisoners included

Moments **Night of Shame**

Best visited at night, when it is more evocative, **Bebelplatz** is a square along Unter den Linden, approached just before you reach Staatsoper. Here is an eloquent memorial to the notorious Nazi book-burning that took place here on the night of May 10, 1933. Through a window set in the pavement, you can look below to a small library lined with empty bookshelves.

6,000 Nazi officers and other functionaries, as well as Russian soldiers who contracted sexually transmitted diseases from German women.

Strasse der Nationen 22. Oranienburg. ✆ 03301/2000. Free admission. Apr–Sept daily 8:30am–6pm; Oct–Mar daily 8:30am–4pm. 22 miles (35km) north of Berlin. S-Bahn: Oranienburg. 25 min. walk from station (it's signposted).

Schöneberg Rathaus   This former political and administrative center of West Berlin is of special interest to Americans. It was the scene of John F. Kennedy's memorable (if grammatically shaky) "Ich bin ein Berliner" speech on June 26, 1963. Berliners have renamed the square around the building the John-F.-Kennedy-Platz. From the 72m-high (237-ft.) tower, a Liberty Bell replica is rung every day at noon. This Freedom Bell, a gift from the American people in 1950, symbolized U.S. support for the West Berliners during the Cold War. The document chamber contains a testimonial bearing the signatures of 17 million Americans who gave their moral support to the struggle.

John-F-Kennedy-Platz. ✆ 030/75-600. Free admission. Daily 9am–6pm. Tower closed Nov–Mar. U-Bahn: Rathaus Schöneberg.

Spandauer Zitadelle (Spandau Citadel)   The Hohenzollern electors of Brandenburg used this citadel as a summer residence, and over time it became the chief military center of Prussia. The citadel—located at the confluence of the Spree and Havel rivers in northwestern Berlin—was besieged by everybody from the French to the Prussians. The Juliusturm (Julius Tower) and the Palas, constructed in the 13th to 15th centuries, are the oldest buildings in Berlin. The main structure, accessible by footbridge, houses a local-history museum.

Am Juliusturm. ✆ 030/354-944-200. Admission 2.50€ ($2.90) adults, 1.50€ ($1.75) students. Tues–Fri 9am–5pm; Sat–Sun 10am–5pm. U-Bahn: Zitadelle.

The Story of Berlin   This multimedia extravaganza portrays 8 centuries of the city's history through photos, films, sounds, and colorful displays. Beginning with the founding of Berlin in 1237, it chronicles the plague, the Thirty Years' War, Frederick the Great's reign, military life, the Industrial Revolution and the working poor, the Golden 1920s, World War II, divided Berlin during the Cold War, and the fall of the Wall. Lights flash in a media blitz as you enter the display on the fall of the Wall, making you feel like one of the first East Berliners to cross to the West, wondering what they will find. Conclude your tour on the 14th floor with a panoramic view over today's Berlin. Allow at least 2 hours to see the museum. Though the displays are a bit jarring and the historical information is too jumbled to be truly educational, the museum does leaves a lasting impression.

Ku'damm-Karree, Kurfürstendamm 207–208 (at the corner of Uhlandstrasse). ✆ 01805/99-20-10. www.story-of-berlin-.de. Admission 9.30€ ($11) adults, 7.50€ ($8.65) students/children, 21€ ($24) families. Daily 10am–8pm (you must enter by 6pm). S-Bahn: Ulandstrasse.

2 Exploring Berlin-Mitte

The best street for strolling in eastern Berlin is the famous **Unter den Linden,** beginning at Brandenburg Gate.

Alexanderplatz, named for Russian Czar Alexander I, was the center of activity in the old East Berlin. This square has brightened considerably since reunification, though aesthetically speaking it's got a long way to go. Neon lights and bright murals now coexist alongside the dull and fading GDR-era structures, and street musicians and small markets give the area new life.

The massive 335m (1,100-ft.) **Fernsehturm (TV tower)** on Alexanderplatz is the second-highest structure in Europe. It's worthwhile to take the 60-second elevator ride to the observation platform, 186m (610 ft.) above the city. From this isolated vantage you can clearly distinguish most landmarks, and on the floor above, you can enjoy cake and coffee in the revolving Tele-Café. The elevator to the top costs 4.50€ ($5.20) for adults and 2€ ($2.30) for children. The tower is open daily March to October 9am to 1am, and November to February daily 10am to midnight.

At the foot of the Fernsehturm stands Berlin's second-oldest church, the brick Gothic **Marienkirche (St. Mary's Church),** Karl-Liebknecht-Strasse 8 (✆ 030/2-42-44-67), dating from the 15th century. Inside you can see the painting *Der Totentanz (The Dance*

Attractions in Berlin-Mitte

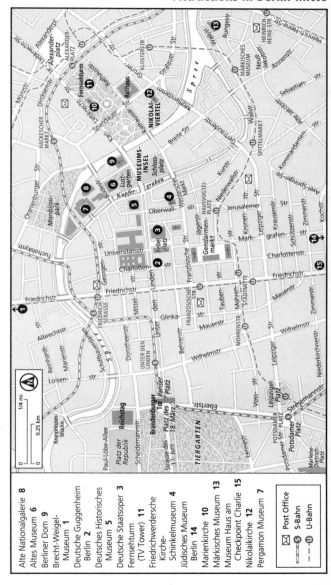

Alte Nationalgalerie **8**
Altes Museum **6**
Berliner Dom **9**
Brecht-Weigel-
Museum **1**
Deutsche Guggenheim
Berlin **2**
Deutsches Historisches
Museum **5**
Deutsche Staatsoper **3**
Fernsehturm
(TV Tower) **11**
Friedrichwerdersche
Kirche-
Schinkelmuseum **4**
Jüdisches Museum
Berlin **14**
Marienkirche **10**
Märkisches Museum **13**
Museum Haus am
Checkpoint Charlie **15**
Nikolaikirche **12**
Pergamon Museum **7**

⊠ Post Office
Ⓢ S-Bahn
Ⓤ U-Bahn

of Death), painted in 1475 then discovered in 1860 beneath a layer of whitewash in the church's entrance hall. Also worth seeing is the marble baroque pulpit carved by Andreas Schlüter (1703). The cross on the top of the church annoyed the Communist rulers of the former East Germany—its golden form was always reflected in the windows of the Fernsehturm. The church is open Monday to Thursday 10am to noon and 1 to 4pm, Friday to Sunday noon to 4pm. Free tours are offered Monday to Thursday at 1pm and Sunday at 11:45am.

Berliner Dom   The cathedral of Berlin took some devastating hits in the British serial bombardments of Berlin in 1940, but it was restored to some of its former glory in the post-war decades, reopening in 1993. Unlike many European capitals where the cathedral is among the top two or three attractions, you can safely miss Berlin's Dom without feeling cultural deprivation. That said, the best way for an overview of this 19th-century cathedral is from the **Dome Gallery** *&,* reached after climbing 270 steps. From here, you get a good glimpse of the Dom's ceiling and the rest of its much-restored interior. The reconstruction of this cathedral into its classic form was completed in 1822. Its most notable features include a gilded wall altar with the 12 apostles by Karl Friedrich Schinkel, and the magnificent Sauer organ containing 7,000 pipes.

The stained-glass windows are especially stunning, depicting such scenes as the Resurrection, as symbolized by an Angel holding a palm branch. The tombstones of Prussian royals are displayed in the crypt; the most impressive tombs being those of Frederick I and his queen, Sophie Charlotte. *Tip:* The best time to visit is for one of the organ concerts, conducted year-round, usually on Saturday at 6pm. An announcement is printed within the church listing hours of all ecclesiastical and musical events.

In the Lustgarten, Museum Island. ℭ **030/202-69-136.** Admission 5.10€ ($5.85) adults, 3.05€ ($3.50) students/seniors. Free for ages 13 and under. Mon–Sat 9am–7pm, Sun noon–7pm (until 6pm in winter). S-Ban: Alexanderplatz or Hackescher Markt.

Brandenburg Gate (Brandenburger Tor) *&&*   This triumphal arch—now restored—stands in the very heart of Berlin, and once was the symbol of the divided city. In the heyday of East Germany, the structure was integrated into the Berlin Wall, which followed a north-south axis as it made its wicked way to the Potsdamer Platz. Six Doric columns hold up an entablature that was inspired by the Propylaea of the Parthenon at Athens. Surrounded by the famous and much photographed Quadriga of Gottfried Schadow from 1793, the gate was designed by Carl Gotthard Langhans in 1789. Napoléon liked the original Quadriga so much he ordered them taken down and shipped to Paris, but they were returned to Berlin in 1814. In Berlin's heyday before World War II, the gate marked the grand western extremity of the "main street," Unter den Linden. In the Room of Silence, built into one of the guardhouses, visitors still gather to meditate and reflect on Germany's past.

Unter den Linden. Free admission. Room of Silence daily 11am–6pm. S-Bahn: Unter den Linden. Bus: 100.

Brecht-Weigel-Museum   This building was occupied by poet and playwright Bertolt Brecht (1898–1956) and his wife, noted actress Helene Weigel (1900–72), from 1953 until their deaths. Brecht, who lived in the United States during World War II, returned to East Berlin after the war. Here he created his own "epic theater" company, the acclaimed Berliner Ensemble. The museum is in an old apartment house. It displays the artists' living and working rooms and the Brecht and Weigel archives, containing 350,000 manuscripts, typescripts, collections of his printed works, press cuttings, and playbills. All visitors are guided around the museum by an attendant. There's a restaurant downstairs (see chapter 5, "Where to Dine").

Chausseestrasse 125. (℡ 030/282-99-16. Admission 4.50€ ($5.20) adults, 2.25€ ($2.60) children and students. Tues– Fri 10–noon; and Thurs 5–6:30pm; Sat 9:30am–1:30pm; Sun 11am–6pm. Visits by guided tour only. U-Bahn: Zinnowitzer Strasse.

The Heartbeat of Berlin

The Potsdamer Platz Arcades contain 140 specialist shops, restaurants, and cafes, inviting you to shop and relax in a civilized urban atmosphere. One of the most visited attractions at the center includes the **Sony Center am Potsdamer Platz** (℡ 030/20-94-54-00), with two cinemas—the CineStar Multiplex and the Cinestar IMAX 3D. The 10-story office building offers a panoramic view that embraces the Philharmonie, the Kulturforum, and the Tiergarten. Around Marlene-Dietrich-Platz, prominent companies offer a whole range of leisure and entertainment facilities. They include the Berlin IMAX-Theater, the Stella Musical-Theater, the Grand Hyatt Hotel, the Madison City Suites, the Berlin Casino, and the Cine-Max cinema center.

Deutsches Historisches Museum   The big museum news coming out of Berlin will be the reopening of this museum sometime in the life of this edition (perhaps late 2002). From the Neanderthals to the Nazis, the whole saga of German history is presented. The collection includes extensive posters and documents of the history of the workers' movement as well as a few remains from the former Zeughaus (arsenal) collection, which before World War II had been the largest collection of militaria from the history of Brandenburg and Prussia. The museum also owns tons of the old GDR communist art (naturally all the workers are depicted with smiling faces). There will be a permanent exhibition on German history in the main building, with temporary exhibitions in an annex.

Under den Linden 2. ℭ 030/20-30-40. Free admission. 9am-6pm Thurs-Tues. U-Bahn: Friedrichstrasse.

Reichstag (Parliament) ℛ   The night of February 17, 1933, was a date that lives in infamy in Germany's history. On that night, a fire broke out in the seat of the German house of parliament, the Reichstag. It was obviously set by the Nazis on orders of Hitler, but the German Communist Party was blamed. That was all the excuse Hitler's troops needed to begin mass arrests of "dissidents and enemies of the lawful government." Because of this mysterious fire, democracy came to an end in Germany. The Reichstag was in for even greater punishment as it faced massive allied bombardment in World War II.

Today it's come back and is once again the home of the country's parliament in the wake of the collapse of the Berlin Wall and subsequent reunification in 1990. The building still evokes the neo-Renaissance style it had when it opened in 1894. Today it's crowned by a new glass dome designed by Sir Norman Foster, the famous English architect. You can go through the west gate for an elevator ride up to the dome, where a sweeping vista of Berlin opens before you. There's both an observation platform and a rooftop restaurant (the view is better than the food).

Platz der Republik 1. ℭ 030/2273-2152. Free admission. Daily 8am–midnight (last entrance at 10pm). S-Bahn: Unter den Linden. Bus: 100.

THE HISTORIC NIKOLAI QUARTER

The historic **Nikolaiviertel** (U-Bahn: Klosterstrasse) was restored in time for the city's 750th anniversary in 1987. Here, on the banks of the Spree River, is where Berlin was born. Many of the medieval and baroque buildings in the neighborhood were completely and

---

Moments **In Memory of . . .**

At the corner of Lewetzov and Jagow streets is a **Jewish War Memorial** to the many Berliners who were deported—mostly to their deaths—from 1941 until the end of the war in 1945. The memorial is a life-size sculpture of a freight car with victims being dragged into it. Behind it is a 15m (50-ft.) structure listing the dates of the various death trains and the number of prisoners shipped out. The memorial stands on the site of a former synagogue destroyed by the Nazis.

---

authentically reconstructed after World War II. Subsequently, some of the city's old flavor has been recaptured here.

The area is named for the **Nikolaikirche (Church of St. Nicholas),** Nikolaikirchplatz, off Spandauerstrasse (© **030/24-00-20**). The church, the oldest in Berlin, was originally constructed in the 14th century on the remains of a 13th-century Romanesque church. The restored building now displays the finds of postwar archaeological digs; during the reconstruction, 800-year-old skeletons were found. It's open Sunday 2 to 4pm and Saturday noon to 3pm; a visit can be arranged on weekdays if you call in advance. Admission to the church and tower is free.

3 Other Architectural Sights

Just north of the Tiergarten is the **Hansaviertel,** or Hansa Quarter (U-Bahn: Hansaplatz). The architecture of this area was an outgrowth of the great INTERBAU 1957 (International Builder's Exhibition), when architects from 22 nations designed buildings for the totally destroyed quarter. The diversity here is exciting: 50 architects took part, including Gropius, Niemeyer, and Duttman.

Le Corbusier also submitted a design for an apartment house for INTERBAU 1957, but the structure was so gigantic that it had to be built near the **Olympic Stadium** (U-Bahn: Olympia-Stadion). The **Corbusier House,** called *Strahlende Stadt* (radiant city), is one of Europe's largest housing complexes—its 530 apartments can house up to 1,400 people. Typical of the architect's style, this tremendous building rests on stilts.

The architects of rebuilt Berlin were also encouraged to design centers for the performing arts. One of the most controversial projects was the **Congress Hall (Kongresshalle),** on John-Foster-Dulles-Allee, in the Tiergarten, just west of Brandenburg Gate (S-Bahn: Unter den Linden). This building was conceived as the American contribution to INTERBAU 1957. The reinforced concrete structure has an 18m-high (60-ft.) vaulted ceiling that reminds some viewers of an oversize flying saucer. Berliners immediately christened it "The Pregnant Oyster." The building today, now called The House of World Cultures (Haus der Kulturen der Welt) is used mainly for conventions. More successful was the **Philharmonie,** new home of the Berlin Philharmonic, and its adjacent chamber-music hall, next to the Tiergarten. The tent-like roof arches up in a bold curve, and the gold-colored facade glitters.

Berlin's tallest building sits in the midst of the city's busiest area. The 22-story **Europa Center,** just across the plaza from the Kaiser Wilhelm Memorial Church (U-Bahn: Kurfürstendamm), is the largest self-contained shopping center and entertainment complex in Europe. This town-within-a-town opened in 1965 on the site of the legendary Romanisches Café, once a gathering place for actors, writers, and artists in the flamboyant 1920s. Berliners dubbed it "Pepper's Manhattan," after its owner, K. H. Pepper. In addition to three levels of shops, restaurants, nightclubs, bars, and cinemas, it contains dozens of offices, a parking garage, and an observation roof. At the Tauentzienstrasse entrance, you can find two pieces of the former Berlin Wall. The building is open daily 9am to midnight (to 10pm in winter). Admission to the observation roof is 2€ ($2.30).

BERLIN'S JEWISH HERITAGE

Haus der Wannsee-Konferenz   This was the site of one of the most notorious conferences in history: a meeting of Nazi bureaucrats and SS officials to plan the annihilation of European Jewry. The minutes of the conference were kept by Adolf Eichmann, the sallow-faced SS functionary who later mapped out transport logistics for sending millions of Jews to their deaths.

The villa is now a memorial to the Holocaust. It includes a selection of photographs of men, women, and children who were sent to concentration camps. This exhibit is not for the squeamish. Nearly all the pictures on display are official Nazi photographs, including some of Nazi medical experiments. As noted at the trials at Nürnberg, "No government in history ever did a better job of photographing and documenting its crimes against humanity."

Am Grossen Wannsee 56. ℂ 030/80-50-01-0. www.ghwk.de/engl/kopfengl.htm. Free admission. Daily 10am–6pm. S-Bahn: Wannsee, then bus 114.

Jüdischer Friedhof (Jewish Cemetery)   This famous Jewish cemetery was opened in 1880. It contains 110,000 graves of Jewish residents of Berlin. Many distinguished artists, musicians, and scientists, as well as religious leaders, are buried here. Some tombs are of Jewish soldiers who fought for Germany in World War I. A memorial honors Jewish victims murdered during the Nazi era. You may have a hard time finding the cemetery on your own, so we recommend a taxi.

Herbert-Baum-Strasse, Weissensee (a suburb east of Berlin). ℂ 030/9-25-33-30. Mar–Nov daily 8am–5pm; Dec–Feb Mon–Thurs 8am–4pm, Fri 8am–3pm. Tram: 23 or 24, or taxi.

Jüdisches Museum Berlin (Jewish Museum Berlin) 𝄐𝄐   The most talked about museum in Berlin, the Jewish Museum is housed in a building that is one of the most spectacular in the entire city. Called "the silver lightning bolt," it was designed by architect Daniel Liebeskind. To some viewers, the building suggests a shattered Star of David by its building plan and the scarring in the zinc-plated facade. Odd-shaped windows are haphazardly embedded in the building's exterior.

Inside, the spaces are designed to make the visitor uneasy and disoriented, simulating the feeling of those who were exiled. A vast hollow cuts through the museum to mark what is gone. When the exhibits reach the rise of the Third Reich, the hall's walls, ceiling, and floor close in as the visitor proceeds. A chillingly hollow Holocaust Void, a dark, windowless chamber, evokes much that was lost.

The exhibits concentrate on three themes: Judaism and Jewish life, the devastating effects of the Holocaust, and the post–World War II rebuilding of Jewish life in Germany.

Europe's largest Jewish Museum presents the panorama of German-Jewish history, its cultural achievements and its horror. The history of German Jewry is portrayed through objects, works of art, and documentation.

The roots of this museum were in an older museum opened in 1933 shortly before Hitler's rise to power. That collection of art and Judaica was shut down by the Gestapo in 1938, and all of its holdings were confiscated.

The on-site **Liebermanns Restaurant** features a world cuisine, with an emphasis on Jewish recipes—all strictly kosher.

Lindenstrasse 9–14. ℂ 030/25-99-33. Admission 5.10€ ($5.85); kids 5 and under free. Family ticket 10.20€ ($12) for 2 adults and up to 4 children. Mon 10am–10pm; Tues–Sun 10am–8pm. U-Bahn: Hallesches Tor or Kochstrasse.

The New Synagogue (Neue Synagoge Berlin-Centrum Judaicum) Originally consecrated on Rosh Hashanah in 1866, and capped with what's remembered as one of the most spectacular domes in Berlin, this synagogue was vandalized in 1938 during Kristallnacht, torched by Berliners in 1944, blasted by Allied bombs in 1945, and finally, after about a decade of further deterioration, demolished by the Communist East Germans in the 1950s. During its heyday, with 3,200 seats and a design inspired by the Moorish architecture of the Alhambra in Granada, Spain, it was the largest synagogue in Germany. In recent times, it was partially rebuilt, and capped with a gilded dome that's visible for many surrounding blocks. Inside, there's a replica, using some of the original carvings, of some of the original synagogue's entrance vestibules and ante-rooms, within which are exhibitions detailing the events that transpired in this building since its original construction. The bulk of the synagogue was never rebuilt. In its place is a gravel-covered plot of land where markers indicate the original layout of the building. If you visit you'll gain a disturbing and unnerving insight into the destruction of a way of life that used to be, and a sense of the passion with which Berlin's Jewish and German communities commemorate the memory of their murdered kinfolk.

Oranienburgerstrasse 31. ℭ **030/880-28-316.** Admission 2.55€ ($2.95) adults, 1.55€ ($1.80) for children under 14. Sun–Thurs 10am–6pm; Fri 10am–2pm. Last entrance 30 min. before closing. S-Bahn: Oranienburger Tor or Hackescher Markt.

4 The Parks & Zoo

The huge **Botanischer Garten (Botanical Garden),** Königin-Luise-Strasse 6–8 (ℭ **030/83-85-01-11;** www.bgbm.org/BGBM/; S-Bahn: Botanischer Garten or Rathaus Steglitz), near the Dahlem Museums, contains vast collections of European and exotic plants. The big palm house is one of the largest in the world. There's a large arboretum here as well as several special collections, such as a garden for blind visitors and another with water plants. Admission is 4€ ($4.60) for adults, 2€ ($2.30) for children, and free for children under 6. The gardens are open daily 9am to 8pm April and August; 9am to 9pm May, June, and July; 9am to 7pm September; 9am to 6pm March and October; 9am to 5pm February; and 9am to 4pm November, December, and January; the museum is open daily, year-round from 10am to 6pm.

Tiergarten ⟨ℛ⟩ is the largest green space in central Berlin, covering 2.5 sq. km. (just under 1 sq. mile), with more than 23km (14 miles) of meandering walkways. It was originally laid out as a private park for the electors of Prussia by a leading landscape architect of the day, Peter Josef Lenné. The park was devastated during World War II, then the trees that remained were chopped down for fuel as Berliners shivered through the winter of 1945–46. Beginning in 1955, trees were replanted, and walkways, canals, ponds, and flowerbeds were restored to their original patterns. The park is popular with joggers and (sometimes nude) sunbathers. Inside the park is the Berlin Zoo-Aquarium (see below).

Among the park's monuments is the **Siegessäule (Victory Column),** a golden goddess of victory perched atop a soaring red-granite pedestal. The monument stands in the center of the wide boulevard (Strasse des 17 Juni) that neatly bisects the park. A 48m- (157-ft.-) high observation platform can be reached by a climb up a 290-step spiral staircase. It's open on Monday 3 to 6pm and Tuesday to Sunday 9:30am to 6:30pm. Admission is 1€ ($1.15) for adults and .50€ (60¢) for children. For information, call © **030/391-29-61.**

Zoologischer Garten Berlin (Berlin Zoo-Aquarium) *, Hardenbergplatz 8 (© **030/25-40-10;** U-Bahn/S-Bahn: Zoologischer Garten), founded in 1844, is Germany's oldest zoo. It occupies almost the entire southwest corner of the Tiergarten. Until World War II, the zoo boasted thousands of animals—many were familiar to Berliners by nickname. By the end of 1945, however, only 91 had survived. Today, more than 13,000 animals live here, many of them in large, open natural habitats. The most valuable residents are the

---

Kids Fun for Kids

Children love the **Berlin Zoo-Aquarium** (see below). Its most famous residents, the giant pandas, are perennial favorites. The zoo also has playgrounds and a children's section, where the animals welcome a cuddle. Another place to take the kids is **Grips-Theater,** Altonaerstrasse 22 (© **030/39-74-74-77;** U-Bahn: Hansaplatz), known for its bright, breezy productions. Children are sure to enjoy the music and dancing (if not the simple German-language dialogue). Tickets cost 9.50€ ($11) for students and persons under 16, and 17€ ($20) for adults. Call to ask about current productions. Most performances begin at 7:30pm, although there are some matinees as well, depending on the production. The theater is closed from late June to mid-August.

giant pandas. The zoo also has Europe's most modern birdhouse, with more than 550 species.

The **aquarium** is as impressive as the adjacent zoo, with more than 9,000 fish, reptiles, amphibians, insects, and other creatures. Crocodiles, Komodo dragons, and tuataras inhabit the terrarium within. You can walk on a bridge over the reptile pit. There's also a large collection of snakes, lizards, and turtles. The "hippoquarium" is a new attraction.

Admission to the zoo is 8€ ($9.20) for adults and 4€ ($4.60) for children. A combined ticket costs 13€ ($15) for adults and 6.50€ ($7.50) for children. The zoo is open April to October daily 9am to 5pm; November to March daily 9am to 5:30pm. The aquarium is open year-round daily 9am to 6pm. S-Bahn/U-Bahn: Zoologischer Garten.

5 Organized Tours

WALKING TOURS

For an excellent introduction to Berlin and its history, try one of the walking tours offered by **Berlin Walks** (© **030/301-9194** or e-mail: BerlinWalks@compuserve.com for information). "Discover Berlin" is a 3-hour introductory tour that takes you past the New Synagogue, the Reichstag, and the Brandenburg Gate, among other major sites. This walk starts daily at 10am and 2:30pm (in winter at 10am only). "Infamous Third Reich Sites" focuses on the sites of major Nazi buildings in central Berlin, such as Goebbels' Propaganda Ministry and Hitler's New Reichschancellery; it starts at 10am on Saturdays, Sundays, Tuesdays, and Thursdays in summer, less frequently in the off-season. "Jewish Life in Berlin" takes you through the pre-war Jewish community; sights include the Old Cemetery and the former Boys' School. The tour starts at 10am Monday and Thursday, April to mid-October. For all tours, reservations are unnecessary—simply meet the guide, who will be wearing a Berlin Walks badge, outside the main entrance to Bahnhof Zoologischer Garten (Zoo Station), at the top of the taxi stand. Tours last from 2½ to 3 hours and cost 9€ ($10) for those under 26 and 10.90€ ($13) for everyone else. This summer, Berlin Walks will be inaugurating a new 5-hour tour to Potsdam, starting every Wednesday and Saturday at 9am; meet at the same place.

BUS TOURS

Berlin is a far-flung metropolis whose interesting neighborhoods are often separated by extended areas of parks, monumental boulevards, and Cold War wastelands. Because of these factors, organized bus tours can be the best way to navigate the city.

Some of the best are operated by **Severin+Kühn,** Kurfürstendamm 216 (© **030/880-41-90;** U-Bahn: Kurfürstendamm), located on the second floor of a building across from the Kempinski Hotel. This agency offers a half-dozen tours of Berlin and its environs. Their 2-hour "14-Stops-City Tour" departs daily every half hour November to April 10am to 3pm and May to October 10am to 4pm. Tickets cost 18€ ($21) per person. The tour passes 12 important stops in Berlin, including the Europa Center, the Brandenburg Gate, and Potsdammer Platz, provides taped audio commentary in eight languages, and offers the option of getting on and off the bus at any point during the hour. Retain your ticket stub to reboard the bus.

Severin+Kühn also offers the 3-hour "Big Berlin Tour," which departs at 10am and 2pm daily and costs 22€ ($25) per person. This tour incorporates more sites than the 14-Stops-City Tour. All tours include a live guide who delivers commentaries in both German and English.

One of the most interesting tours visits Potsdam, site of the famed World War II conference and of Sans Souci Palace, former residence of Frederick the Great. The price is 35€ ($40) per person. Departures are Tuesday, Thursday, Saturday, and Sunday at 10am, May to October; there are additional departures Friday, Saturday and Sunday at 2:15pm.

BOAT TOURS

It may not be the obvious choice for transportation in Berlin, but a boat ride can offer visitors a good change of pace. The networks of canals that bisect the plains of what used to be known as Prussia were an engineering marvel when they were completed in the 19th century. Today, transport through the lakes, locks, and canals around Berlin retains its nostalgic allure, and affords unusual vistas that aren't available from the windows of more conventional modes of transport. Berliners boast that their city has more bridges than Venice. Local waterways include the Spree and Havel rivers—ranging in size from narrow channels to large lakes—as well as many canals. You can take short tours that offer close-up views of the city or daylong adventures along the Spree and Havel; the latter often turn into beer-drinking fests.

The city's best-known boat operator is **Stern- und Kreisschiffahrt,** Pushkinallee 60–70 (© **030/5-36-36-00**). Since Germany's reunification, the company has absorbed the piers and ferryboats of its former East German counterparts. "Historische Stadtfahrt" is a ride along the banks of the Spree, the river that helped build Berlin. 2-, 3-, and 4-hour tours (in German only) depart at 10am and 2pm from a quay near Berlin's cathedral, Am Palast Ufer. These trips offer good views of the Reichstag, the Pergamon Museum, the Königliche Bibliothek (Royal Library), and the monumental heart of the former East Berlin. The tours lasting 1 hour cost 9.50€ ($11) per person; tours lasting 2 hours cost 12€ ($14); tours lasting 4 hours are 16€ ($18).

Stern- und Kreisschiffahrt also has a cruising yacht, *Moby Dick,* a whale-shaped boat that usually sails along the waters of the Eglersee and looks like something that might have been developed by the staff at Disneyland. It departs from a point near the Alt-Tegel U-Bahn station, on the city's northwestern edge. Walk for about 10 minutes through the suburb of Tegel to the Greenwich Promenade, and then to the Stern- und Kreisschiffahrt pier. Boats head southward from Tegel, passing along the Havel River and many of its lakes. Reservations are usually necessary for all boat rides described here. Rides operate only April to either late October or early December, depending on the tour. Prices and actual itineraries change seasonally; call for more details.

6 Sports & Outdoor Pursuits

BIKING

The best place to rent bikes in Berlin is at **Fahradstation,** GmbH, Bergmannstrasse 9 (© **030/215-1566;** U-Bahn: Platz de Luftbrüke), in Kreuzberg. Rentals cost 15€ ($17) per day or 35€ ($40) per week, plus a one-time insurance fee of 3€ ($3.45). The city maintains a labyrinth of bike paths, marked by red bricks on the walkways, through the central core of Berlin and in its parks, especially the Tiergarten. The best places for biking are the Tiergarten in central Berlin, and farther afield in the Grunewald Forest (S-Bahn: Grunewald).

JOGGING

Head for the vast and verdant leafiness of the **Grunewald,** on the city's western edge, which is crisscrossed with pedestrian and bike paths. This area is appropriate for very long endurance tests. Closer to the center is the **Tiergarten,** which allows you to soak up a little history on your morning jog thanks to its many monuments and memorials. The grounds of **Schloss Charlottenburg** are also good for jogging.

SPECTATOR SPORTS

Among Berliners, **soccer** is the most popular sport. For information about which teams are playing, ask your hotel receptionist, or refer to a daily newspaper or the weekly magazine *Berlin Programm.*

SWIMMING & SAUNAS

Berlin has dozens of pools. One of the best equipped is the **S.E.Z. Landsberger,** Landsberger Allee 77 (© **030/421-820;** U-Bahn: Alexanderplatz). Here you'll find a swimming pool, a diving pool, a wave pool, an assortment of waterfalls, a jet pool, sauna and solarium facilities, a weight room, about half a dozen restaurants and snack bars, and a bowling alley. The cost is 6€ ($6.90) for adults and 3€ ($3.45) for children for 2 hours of swimming.

A worthy competitor (just east of Tempelhof Airport) is the **Club Paradise,** Buschkrugallee 64 (© **030/6-06-60-60;** U-Bahn: Grenzallee), which has indoor and outdoor pools, saunas, a steam room, solariums, and a 120m (393½-ft.) water slide. Its latest attraction, called "Crazy River," sends you down a river in water tubes. A 4-hour pass costs 12€ ($14) for adults and 9€ ($10) for children ages 2 to 12. It's open daily 10am to 11pm.

Perched on the top floor of the Europa Center's parking garage *(Parkhaus Europa Center),* you'll find a health and exercise club called **Thermen,** Nürnberger Strasse 9 (© **030/2-61-60-32;** U-Bahn: Wittenbergplatz), offering an array of heated pools, saunas, massage facilities, and solariums. A full-day pass costs 18€ ($21), but if you want to limit your exposure to just 3 hours, you'll pay 9.20€ ($11) for arrivals between 10am and 9pm, and 16€ ($18) if you arrive between 9pm and closing. Both men and women share the same saunas. If you just want to use the pool, and bypass the saunas and exercise facilities, you'll pay 9€ ($10) for a 2-hour immersion, regardless of the time of day. Massages cost 22€ ($25) for 30 minutes. Hours are Monday to Saturday 10am to midnight and Sunday 10am to 9pm.

For outdoor swimming during the hot months, head to one of Europe's largest lake beaches at **Wannsee.** Take the S-Bahn to Nikolaisee and follow the hordes of bathers heading toward the water's edge.

TENNIS & SQUASH

At **Sports Treffe,** Buschkrugallee 84 (© **030/6-06-60-11;** U-Bahn: Grenzall), indoor courts rent for 30€ ($35) for a 1-hour session, depending on when you play. There are also five squash courts that each rent for around 16€ ($18) for a 1-hour session. Somewhat

closer to Berlin's center is the **Squash & Tennis Center,** Treuenbri-
etzenerstrasse 36 (② **030/4-15-30-11;** U-Bahn: Wittenau, then bus
124 or X-21), which has similar rates. There are also courts in the
Preussen Park, Kamenzerstrasse 34, Lankwitz (② **030/7-75-10-
51;** U-Bahn: Mariendorfer), open 7am to 11pm year-round with
rates beginning at 24€ ($27) per hour.

7

A Walking Tour of Berlin

In August 1961, the Berlin Wall was hastily erected between East and West Berlin. For more than 28 years, the Wall dramatized a nation's division. As you take this tour, bear in mind that there were actually two walls, separated by a desolate and very dangerous "no-man's land." In some places, the two barriers were only a few yards apart; in other places, spaces the size of a football field separated them.

In 1989, after the East German regime lifted travel restrictions between East and West Berlin, the wall began to be dismantled. By 1990, its demolition was in full swing, much to the delight of souvenir hunters around the world. Collectors purchased pieces of the wall for as much as $100,000 and hauled them off as relics of a dying era.

Today, this former no-man's land between the eastern and western zones is prized real estate. Consortiums of German and foreign companies have begun constructing office buildings here, so you'll sometimes walk beneath scaffolding because of construction projects.

WALKING TOUR	FROM THE SITE OF THE BERLIN WALL TO UNTER DEN LINDEN

Finish:	Nikolaikirche.
Time:	4 hours.
Best Time:	Daylight hours during clement weather.
Worst Time:	After dark, when bad lighting and the possibility of ongoing construction make access hazardous.

Your tour begins in the district of Kreuzberg, in the formerly western zone, at:

① Moritzplatz

Before World War II, Moritzplatz was known as the publishing center of the German-speaking world. Its importance, however, waned almost overnight after the Communist regime suppressed newspapers. During the Cold War, Moritzplatz served as the only authorized gateway to and from East Berlin for West Germans not residing in Berlin. The neighborhood was viewed as a wasteland of border controls.

From here, walk a few paces west along Oranienstrasse; then veer right (north) onto:

❷ Stallschreiber Strasse

Within less than a block, this street will traverse what was known for almost 30 years as the "Death Zone," claiming the lives of all but a lucky handful of people trying to escape from the eastern zone. Turn left at Alter-Jakob-Strasse, a residential street once divided midway along its length by the Berlin Wall. Vestiges of the street's past are quickly being swept away.

Turn right onto Kommandanten, then left onto Lindenstrasse. At the corner of Lindenstrasse (a small length of which was renamed "Axel Springer Strasse" in honor of its most famous corporate resident) and Oranienstrasse, you'll see the headquarters of:

❸ Axel Springer Verlag (Axel Springer Publishers)

The company's pugnacious director deliberately constructed this building adjacent to the Berlin Wall as a symbol of defiance against the East German regime. Today, the expanded structure houses the executive offices for three of Germany's most powerful newspapers and magazines: *Berliner Morgenpost, Bild,* and *Die Welt.*

Now retrace your steps north for a block along Lindenstrasse, turning left (west) onto Zimmerstrasse. Here both walls ran along the entire length of the street, separated by only a few feet of tightly patrolled space. Within 3 blocks, you'll come to the:

❹ Corner of Zimmerstrasse and Charlottenstrasse

Here you'll see the site where one of the most widely publicized dramas of the Cold War occurred. A cross, a plaque, and, usually, bouquets of faded flowers mark the spot where in 1962, 18-year-old Peter Fechter was shot as he attempted to climb over the Berlin Wall, within sight of a horrified crowd of West Berliners, photojournalists, and U.S. soldiers.

From here, walk another block west to the corner of Zimmerstrasse and Friedrichstrasse, where you'll see the:

❺ Site of Checkpoint Charlie

For decades, this spot was the tensest border crossing in the world. Checkpoint Charlie (named for Brig. Gen. Charles Frost Craig, commander of U.S. forces in Berlin) was created in 1961, when U.S. tanks moved up Friedrichstrasse and a crane lowered a prefabricated metal-sided hut into the middle of the street. The action

From the Site of the Former Wall to Unter den Linden

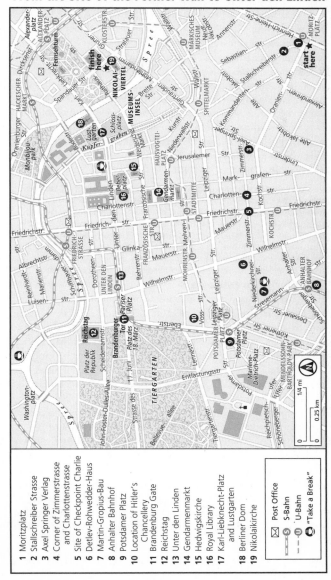

1 Moritzplatz
2 Stallschreiber Strasse
3 Axel Springer Verlag
4 Corner of Zimmerstrasse and Charlottenstrasse
5 Site of Checkpoint Charlie
6 Detlev-Rohwedder-Haus
7 Martin-Gropius-Bau
8 Anhalter Bahnhof
9 Potsdamer Platz
10 Location of Hitler's Chancellery
11 Brandenburg Gate
12 Reichstag
13 Unter den Linden
14 Gendarmenmarkt
15 Hedwigskirche
16 Royal Library
17 Karl-Liebknecht-Platz and Lustgarten
18 Berliner Dom
19 Nikolaikirche

⊠ Post Office
Ⓢ S-Bahn
Ⓤ U-Bahn
--- "Take a Break"

provoked three of the tensest weeks of the Cold War, as U.S. and Soviet troops stared at each other over the armor of their tanks. For years, this border crossing funneled merchants, spies, and members of the non-German public through its forbidding series of double-locked doors, past television monitors, luggage inspectors, and humorless, heavily armed guards. Ironically, Charlie was the only border crossing between the two Germanys forbidden to all Germans. In 1992, the much-photographed metal hut was sold to a group of American investors for its souvenir value. While here, you might visit the **Checkpoint Charlie Museum** (Museum Haus am Checkpoint Charlie), Friedrichstrasse 43-45 (© **030/253-7250**), described in chapter 6, "Exploring Berlin."

Now continue to walk west along Zimmerstrasse, looking for occasional remnants of the ruined, once-mighty wall. The street will eventually change its name to Nieder-Kirchner-Strasse after it crosses the Wilhelmstrasse. (Some street signs and maps may refer to this section of the Wilhelmstrasse as either the Toleranz-Strasse or the older Otto-Grotewohl-Strasse.) Continue walking west along Nieder-Kirchner-Strasse. On its right-hand (northern) edge, you'll see the gray-colored (unmarked) back side of one of the largest, most architecturally boring, and most transmogrified buildings in German history, the:

6 Detlev-Rohwedder-Haus

Filling an entire city block, its bureaucratic-looking bulk was originally designed as the headquarters for the Third Reich's air ministry, directed by Hermann Göring. Between 1945 and the collapse of the East German regime, it served as the regime's Haus der Ministerien (cabinet offices). After that, its offices supervised the transition of East German industry to the free-market economy. During the rebellion of June 16, 1953, it was the site of some of the fiercest fighting, and consequently, some of the most brutal repression by the communist government. At this writing, it was being reconfigured as the home of the new German Ministry of Finance.

Continue walking west along Nieder-Kirchner-Strasse. During the lifetime of this edition, the city of Berlin will probably transform a small temporary exhibition "Topography of Terror" into a full-fledged, albeit very small, museum. The exhibition is located within the basement of what was once used as a torture chamber by the Gestapo. There was no phone number at press time. During your tour, look for its location near the junction of the Nieder-Kirchner Strasse and the Wilhelmstrasse.

From here, turn left onto Stresemannstrasse. At no. 110, you'll find one of the most interesting museums in Berlin, the:

❼ Martin-Gropius-Bau

The Martin-Gropius-Bau (© **030/25-48-60**) was deliberately constructed near the site of the Wall, adjacent to the former headquarters of the Nazi Gestapo. Its unusual art collection is described in chapter 6, "Exploring Berlin."

TAKE A BREAK
The Martin-Gropius-Bau Café, Stresemannstrasse 110 (© **030/ 25-48-60**), a cafe inside this museum (see above), serves sandwiches, coffee, drinks, and platters of food in a setting enriched with a sense of the ironies of 20th-century art.

After your visit, exit the museum onto Stresemannstrasse, turn left (south), and walk for about 2 blocks. You'll soon see the markings for the S-Bahn station of Anhalter Bahnhof. A short distance to the east of the S-Bahn station lies the site of what during the 1920s was the third-largest railway station in Europe, the:

❽ Anhalter Bahnhof

During the rule of the German Kaisers, this railway station received many of the crowned heads of Europe on official visits. Later, it was used as the setting for many of Hitler's propaganda films. When the Berlin Wall blocked most of the station's feeder lines and access routes, West Berlin officials demolished those parts of the station that weren't already devastated by the wartime bombings. Today, the premises contain an S-Bahn Station, lots of rather ugly concrete, and little more than memories of the grand ceremonies that used to be broadcast from here throughout Germany, Europe, and the world.

Now retrace your steps and walk north along Stresemannstrasse. Bypass the Martin-Gropius-Bau, site of your earlier visit, and continue on past a landscape that alternates roaring traffic with Cold War wastelands and what seems like an unending cycle of urban renewal. Soon you'll reach what before the war was one of the most glamorous addresses in Europe:

❾ Potsdamer Platz

Its hotels, cafes, and town houses were once legendary bastions of privilege and chic. Its street lamps represented Europe's first electric illumination. During its heyday, more than 550 trams passed through the Platz every hour. In 1920, with the advent of the motorcar, Germany's first traffic light was installed here, and during the height of the Third Reich, the Platz bordered the most important power centers of the Nazi empire, including the now-demolished chancellery. In Allied air raids, most of its monuments and all its grandeur were bombed into dust. During the Cold War, any hope of rebuilding the area was squashed by its division into three occupied zones—American, British, and Soviet. For decades it languished, little more than a depressing expanse of shattered concrete and busy traffic.

Since the collapse of the Wall, Potsdamer Platz was the site of one of the most raging controversies in Berlin. Despite the hope of civic planners to return the plaza to its prewar glory, at least half the surrounding landscape was snapped up in 1990 at deflated prices by Daimler Benz, and the remainder by such companies as Sony and ABB, GmbH. The square quickly became Europe's largest construction site.

Architects Wilmer and Sattler redeveloped the square and several nearby blocks. The major projects here include landmark towers, a shopping arcade, and even apartment buildings. Eye catchers include the Debis Tower, the Sony Center, an IMAX theater, and an office tower, plus a large new underground station, shopping arcade, and entertainment complex.

Exit from the Potsdamer Platz and walk north along the eastern edge of Ebertstrasse. During World War II, the neighborhood you're traversing was filled with the densest concentration of Nazi administrative buildings in Germany, known collectively as the Regierungsviertel (Government Quarter). Throughout the Cold War, one of the most politically sensitive areas in Berlin was an understated bump in the hard-packed earth located east of Ebertstrasse and beside the northern edge of Vossstrasse. Although recent increases in the land's value and massive urban development have obliterated the once-famous mound almost completely, the site is remembered as the:

⑩ Location of Hitler's Ruined Chancellery

During World War II, Hitler directed the German military machine from here. In 1945, reluctant to have the site of Hitler's suicide canonized by defeated Germans, the Soviets demolished the once-massive building brick by brick and in its place established what became, during the Cold War, the broadest point of the impassable no-man's land. According to Soviet legend, none of the guard dogs patrolling the site during the Cold War would ever go near where the chancellery had stood unless forced to do so, and no vegetation ever grew in the poisoned soil around it. The city of Berlin is planning to build a Holocaust Museum somewhere near this site.

At this point, facing north along Ebertstrasse, you'll be within sight of the world-famous:

⑪ Brandenburg Gate (Brandenburger Tor)

The Propylea of the Acropolis in Athens was the inspiration behind this monument. Originally constructed in 1789 as a focal point for the grand avenues that radiate from it, its neoclassical grandeur later marked the boundary between East and West Berlin. Ironically, the monument represents an early act of cooperation between the sectors of the once-divided city. When the Quadriga (a chariot drawn by four horses) atop the gate was destroyed during the war and the gate badly damaged, the West Berlin senate arranged for a new Quadriga to be hammered in copper as a gift to the administration of East Berlin.

From the base of the Brandenburg Gate, walk north a short distance, toward the Spree River, to the large square called Platz der Republik. At the eastern edge of the square rises the:

⑫ Reichstag (Parliament)

This building is now the official seat of the German government. It was designed in the late 19th century in a neo-Renaissance style and rebuilt in a more streamlined style after World War II. The Reichstag, despite a rich history that predates the rise of Hitler, continues to evoke memories of the Nazi period. In 1933, a fire mysteriously broke out in its chambers and nearly destroyed the building. Declaring Communist enemies of Germany responsible, Hitler used the fire as an excuse to assume dictatorial powers. Many historians believe that the Nazis themselves were the arsonists; at any rate, the Reichstag was not repaired during the Nazi period.

Now retrace your steps south to the base of the Brandenburg Gate, and notice the broad, eastward-stretching panorama of one of the most famous thoroughfares in Europe:

⑬ Unter den Linden

The palaces and cafes that once lined this boulevard were legendary throughout Europe for a clientele that included virtually every famous artist and politician in the German-speaking world. The street is lined with symmetrical rows of trees, so admired by the Great Elector, Friedrich Wilhelm, that he decreed that anyone cutting down one of his lindens should have his hand amputated. (Hitler, in defiance of the monarchical tradition, cut all of them down to widen the boulevard for his military parades.) The East Germans replanted the trees after World War II and restored many of the neoclassical palaces and Humboldt University buildings that line it today. Despite these efforts, the prewar gaiety and glamour of Unter den Linden has never returned. Despite its formal beauty, much of the east-to-west expanse remains monumental, monotonous, and lifeless. One of its most famous landmarks is the equestrian statue of Frederick the Great. In 1945, this statue was shipped to Potsdam, but it was returned in 1980.

At Unter den Linden 8 (House #1) is the **Deutsche Staatsbibliothek** (National Library) (© **030/266-1217**). It was constructed in a neobaroque style between 1903 and 1914, and contains more than 8.7 million volumes. It's open Monday to Friday from 9am to 9pm and on Saturday from 9am to 5pm.

TAKE A BREAK
The most famous coffeehouse of prewar Berlin, the Operncafé, Unter den Linden 5 (© **030/20-26-83**), occupied a section of a palace destroyed during Allied bombing raids. Now restored, the cafe has plenty of old-world charm and dispenses all sorts of drinks, light meals, snacks, and ice cream. It also offers a big breakfast buffet for 9.90€ ($11), every day from 9am to noon. It's open daily from 8am to midnight. Check out the beautiful terrace during extended summertime hours. Upstairs, you can order complete lunches and dinners.

Turn right at the third street on your right, Charlottenstrasse, which within 3 blocks runs into one of the most monumental squares in the former eastern section:

⑭ Gendarmenmarkt

Frederick the Great designed this graceful baroque square in the 1780s. Despite its antique appearance, the Gendarmenmarkt was reduced to a pile of rubble during World War II, but was later restored by the East Germans. The square's centerpiece remains the neoclassical theater (Schauspielhaus) designed by Karl Friedrich Schinkel in 1821. Restoration of the French Cathedral here was completed in 1983, and the property was returned to the French Reformed Church. The Schauspielhaus reopened in 1984 as a concert hall.

Exit from the square's northeast corner and walk east for a short block along Französische Strasse. Turn left at Hedwigskirchgasse. When it funnels into Bebelplatz, admire the enormous dome of the baroque:

⑮ Hedwigskirche

The Hedwigskirche (© **030/2-03-48-70**) now functions as the Roman Catholic cathedral of the Berlin diocese. Begun in 1747 by Frederick the Great, probably as a gesture to appease his troublesome subjects in Catholic Silesia, it was the only Catholic church in Berlin until the mid-1880s. Architect Georg Wenzeslaus von Knobelsdorf modeled it on the Pantheon in Rome, adding a coppersheathed dome. Plagued with structural problems early in its construction, it's a much simpler building than the one originally hoped for by Frederick. The restoration done between 1952 and 1963 preserved the original structure of the dome, although the interior is modern. The church is open Monday to Saturday from 10am to 5pm and on Sunday from 1 to 5pm.

Also on Bebelplatz, across from the cathedral, is the:

⓰ Königliche Bibliothek (Royal Library)

This library is part of Humboldt University, which was completed in 1780. The library is modeled on the Royal Palace (Hofburg) in Vienna. Its curved wings prompted Berliners to christen it the Kommode (chest of drawers). Despite its illustrious contribution to German scholarship over the years, the library is remembered as the site of Hitler's infamous book burnings. On the eastern edge of Bebelplatz rises the Berlin State Opera (Staatsoper), and on the northern edge of the square you'll once again see Unter den Linden.

Continue your walk east along Unter den Linden, which becomes narrower as it crosses over a branch of the Spree River and then ends at:

⓱ Karl-Liebknecht-Platz and the Lustgarten

Before reunification, their boundaries were collectively known as Marx-Engels-Platz. Once the much-heralded site of the Kaiser's Palace, which was completely demolished by the Communists as a symbol of bourgeois decadence, the square is now a monument to the bad architectural taste of the defunct East German regime. Many of the graceless and angular buildings here were declared unfit for use after reunification because of the massive amounts of asbestos used in their construction during the 1960s and 1970s.

Another landmark here is the:

⓲ Berliner Dom

The Berliner Dom (✆**030/202-69-136**) was constructed from 1894 to 1905, in the style of the High Renaissance. It's the largest Protestant cathedral in Germany. Visitors are asked for a 2.55€ ($2.95) donation for ongoing restoration. The main church is open Monday through Saturday from 9am to 7:30pm and Sunday from 11:30am to 7:30pm. The imperial staircase is open Monday through Saturday from 9am to 6pm and on Sunday from 11:30am to 6pm. Visits to the dome gallery depend on weather conditions.

Exit from Karl-Liebknecht-Platz and the Lustgarten by walking northeast along Karl-Liebknecht-Strasse. (This boulevard is the eastward continuation of Unter den Linden.) Within several blocks, turn right onto Spandauerstrasse. Within 2 blocks you'll reach one of Germany's proud achievements in historic restorations—a neighborhood that is quickly blossoming into a haven of coffeehouses, art galleries, and nightspots, the Nikolaiviertel. The neighborhood's most prominent building and centerpiece is the:

⑲ Nikolaikirche

Berlin's oldest parish church was built in the 14th century. It has two spires, which have become the symbol of the reunited city. The church boasts a refreshingly simple interior. On this site, in 1307, Berlin and its neighbor, Cölln, decided to unite their borders and form a single city.

8

Shopping

Although hardly a rival of London or Paris, Berlin is great for shopping. It's filled with department stores, antiques shops, art galleries, specialty shops, and outdoor markets. Prices here are often regrettably high, but there are bargains for those willing to look.

Most stores in Berlin are open Monday to Friday from 9 or 10am to 6 or 6:30pm. Many stay open late on Thursday evenings, often to 8:30pm. Saturday hours are usually 9 or 10am to 2pm.

1 The Top Shopping Streets

The **Ku'damm** (or Kurfürstendamm) is the Fifth Avenue of Berlin. It's filled with quality stores but also has outlets hustling cheap souvenirs and T-shirts. Although Berliners themselves shop on the Ku'damm, many prefer the specialty stores on the side streets, especially between **Breitscheidplatz** and **Olivaer Platz.** You might also want to check out **Am Zoo** and **Kantstrasse.**

Another major shopping street is the **Tauentzienstrasse** and the streets that intersect it: **Marburger, Ranke,** and **Nürnberger.** This area offers a wide array of stores, many specializing in German fashions for women. Stores here are often cheaper than on the Ku'damm. Also on Tauentzienstrasse (near the Ku'damm) is Berlin's major indoor shopping center, the **Europa Center** (© **030/3-48-00-88**), with around 75 shops, as well as restaurants and cafes. At the end of this street lies the **KaDeWe,** the classiest department store in Berlin and the biggest in continental Europe. A new, upmarket version of the Europa Center is the **Uhland-Passage,** at Uhlandstrasse 170, which has some of the best boutiques and big-name stores in Berlin. Shoppers interested in quality at any price should head to **Kempinski Plaza,** Uhlandstrasse 181–183, a pocket of posh with some of the most exclusive boutiques in the city, featuring haute-couture women's clothing. Trendy and avant-garde boutiques are found along **Bleibtreustrasse.** Head to **Wilmersdorferstrasse** for a vast number of discount stores, although some of the merchandise is second-rate. Try to avoid impossibly overcrowded Saturday mornings.

In eastern Berlin, not that long ago, you couldn't find much to buy except a few souvenirs. All that is changed now. The main street, **Friedrichstrasse,** offers some of Berlin's most elegant shopping. Upmarket boutiques—selling everything from quality women's fashions to Meissen porcelain—are found along **Unter den Linden.** The cheaper stores in eastern Berlin are around the rather bleak-looking **Alexanderplatz.** Many specialty and clothing shops are found in the **Nikolai quarter.** The largest shopping mall in eastern Berlin, with outlets offering a little bit of everything, is at the **Berliner Markthalle,** at the corner of Rosa-Luxemburg-Strasse and Karl-Liebknecht-Strasse.

2 Shopping A to Z
ANTIQUES

Astoria   Astoria, whose buyers frequently scour the antiques markets of France, England, and Germany, pays homage to the decorative objects of the 1920s and '30s. You'll find antique mirrors, lamps, tables, and jewelry here, as well as a handful of reproductions. Bleibtreustrasse 42. ✆ 030/8-83-81-81. S-Bahn: Savignyplatz.

Harmel's   Most of Harmel's inventory was gathered in England and France, a commentary on the relative scarcity of genuine German antiques because of wartime bombing. The carefully chosen collection stresses furniture, jewelry, and accessories from the Victorian and Edwardian eras. Damaschkestrasse 24. ✆ 030/3-24-22-92. U-Bahn: Adenauerplatz.

Kunstsalon   Don't expect everything in this shop to be tasteful. Instead, you'll find the kind of rococo art objects that Liberace might have used in a stage set, or that a hip Berliner nightclub or brothel might buy as a means of creating instant kitsch. Everything is a castoff from previous productions of the Komische Oper (Comic Opera), including both the stage props and the costumes. Come here for the wigs, gowns, and waistcoats that clothed the partiers during *The Merry Widow,* the candelabra that lit up Violetta when she died in *Traviata,* and the associated trash and treasures that evoke smiles from virtually anyone who understands their origin. The store also sells CDs, posters, and reproductions of rare portraits of Garbo, Dietrich, and Charlie Chaplin with Pola Negri during a holiday they enjoyed at the nearby Adlon Hotel in 1929. Unter den Linden 41. ✆ 030/20-45-02-03. S-Bahn: Under den Linden.

L. & M. Lee   This is one of several sophisticated antiques stores on the Ku'damm's eastern end. The inventory includes mostly German-made porcelain, silver, and glass from the early 20th century, and an assortment of 19th-century pieces from other European countries. Kurfürstendamm 32. ℂ 030/8-81-73-33. U-Bahn: Kurfürstendamm.

Stilbruch Antiquitäten & Schmuck   It's far from being the largest antiques store in Berlin, but something about its dense inventories of Biedermeier-era furniture, tableware, and jewelry might appeal to your sense of schmaltz and nostalgia. Owner Margareta Wojcieszak makes sure that objects are waxed and polished to a high sheen. Everything seems to evoke a story about other places, other priorities, and other eras. Bleibtreustrasse 50. ℂ **030/312-83-04.** S-Bahn: Savignyplatz.

ART GALLERIES

Galerie Brusberg   One of Germany's most visible and influential art galleries, Galerie Brusberg was established in 1958 by Dieter Brusberg. The gallery has handled the work of Max Ernst, Salvador Dalí, Paul Delvaux, Henri Laurens, Pablo Picasso, and René Magritte, plus German artists Altenbourg, Antes, and Klapheck. Long before unification, it promoted painters of the old Eastern bloc, notably Bernhard Heisig, Harald Metzkes, and Werner Töbke. No one will mind if you drop in just for a look. Kurfürstendamm 213. ℂ 030/8-82-76-82. U-Bahn: Kurfürstendamm.

Galerie Pels-Leusden and Villa Grisebach Auktionen   This building, constructed in the 1880s by architect Hans Grisebach as his private home, is a historic monument in its own right. Two floors are devoted to 19th- and 20th-century art, mainly German. Prices begin at around 100€ ($115) for the least expensive lithograph, and go much higher. The building also functions as headquarters and display area for an auction house. Sales are held every spring and fall. Fasanenstrasse 25. ℂ 030/8-85-91-50. U-Bahn: Uhlandstrasse.

Prüss & Ochs Gallery   This gallery's setting resembles a fortress from the Industrial Revolution. Built of red brick, it's accessible via a labyrinth of alleyways that lead in from one of the oldest and most historic streets in the neighborhood. Exhibits change regularly, but the temporary venue is likely to be as offbeat and iconoclastic as the arts scene in Berlin itself. The company's main branch is in arts-conscious Cologne; this one gives the sense of exploring the artistic

Finds   Treasures in the Barn District

At the very heart and soul of Berlin's fashion and art revival is the Scheunenviertel, or "barn district" (S-Bahn: Hackescher Market). The name comes from a period in the 17th century when hay barns were built far from the city center for fear of fires. In time the city's growth overtook the area, and it became Berlin's Jewish quarter. For some reason, many of its oldest buildings survived World War II bombing assaults.

The remains of a grand 1909 shopping arcade—which occupies most of the block formed by Oranienburger, Rosenthaler, Grosse Hamburger Strasse, and Sophien-strasse—have been turned into a series of galleries, studios, and theaters. Worth a visit is **Tacheles** ("talking turkey" in Yiddish), Oranienburger Strasse 53–56 (© **030/282-61-85;** S-Bahn: Hackescher Markt). It's an alternative arts center. One of the several cutting-edge shops in the immediate Hackesche Hofe neighborhood includes **Lisa D.,** Hackescher Hof–Hof 4, Rosenthalerstrasse 40–41 (© **030/282-9061;** S-Bahn: Hackescher Markt), a sought-after designer whose women's clothing comes in shades other than the black that has been favored in Berlin and New York for so long. Clothing includes a sophisticated mixture of sportswear, office wear, and eveningwear.

frontiers of Berlin, with special emphasis on counterculture art that's being produced in Asia and the Balkans. Sophienstrasse 18. © **030/ 28391-387.** U-Bahn: Weinmeisterstrasse.

BOOKSHOPS

This literate and culture-conscious city boasts lots of bookshops catering to a multilingual clientele. For English and American literature and recent periodicals, go to the **British Bookshop,** Mauer-strasse 83–84 (© **030/2-38-46-80;** U-Bahn: Stadtmitte). An outfit richly stocked with works from German publishing houses is **Literaturhaus Berlin,** Fasanenstrasse 23 (© **030/8-82-50-42;** U-Bahn: Uhlandstrasse). The leading gay bookstore of Berlin, containing both erotica and upscale literature in several different languages, is **Prince Eisenherz,** Bleibtreustrasse 52 (© **030/3-13-99-36;** S-Bahn: Savignyplatz).

The more prestigious galleries are found along August-strasse. **Galerie Wohnmaschine,** Tucholskystrasse 34–36 (✆ 030/3087-20-15), became the area's first gallery when it opened in 1988. Some of the best artists in the city are on exhibit here, most of them of a conceptual or minimalist bent. One of the most prestigious and respected of these galleries is viewed today as a pioneer that made its way eastward within a few weeks of reunification: **Eigen & Art Gerd Harry Lybke,** Auguststrasse 26. (✆ 030/28-31-002; U-Bahn: Rosenthaler Platz; S-Bahn: Oranienburger Strasse). They represent a roster of artists that include, among others, Leo Rauch and Carsten Nicolai.

Other shopping highlights include **Tools & Gallery,** Rosen-thaler Strasse 34–35 (✆ 030/2859-9343; U-Bahn: Weinmeis-terstrasse), which sells both formal and elegantly casual clothes for both sexes, including exclusive labels such as Givenchy, Balenciaga, and Kenzo. **Johanna Petzoldt,** Sophienstrasse 9 (✆ 030/282-6754; U-Bahn: Weinmeister-strasse), sells handcrafts from the old Erzgebirge region, including wooden toys and assorted curiosities, such as scenes fitted into a matchbox.

CHINA & PORCELAIN

KPM This prestigious emporium was founded in 1763, when Frederick the Great invested his personal funds in a lackluster porce-lain factory, elevated it to royal status, and gave it a new name: **Königliche Porzellan-Manufaktur (Royal Porcelain Factory).** It was Prussia's answer to Meissen in Saxony. Since then, the factory has become world-famous for its artistry and delicacy. Each hand-painted, hand-decorated item is carefully packed for shipment to virtually anywhere in the world. Patterns are based for the most part on traditional 18th- and 19th-century designs. All objects carry a distinctive official signature, an imperial orb, and the letters KPM. There's also an array of high-quality trinkets for visitors.

You can also visit the **factory** itself at Wegelystrasse 1 (✆ 030/39-00-90; U-Bahn: Tiergarten). Guided tours let you look at the craftsmanship of the employees, and you can also buy pieces here.

Tours are provided once a day from Monday to Thursday at 10am. The charge is 2.55€ ($2.95), which is applied to any purchase. Children under 16 are prohibited, as are video cameras and photography. Kurfürstendamm 27, in the Kempinski Hotel Bristol. © **030/88-67-21-10**. U-Bahn: Kurfürstendamm.

Meissener Porzellan This is one of the most famous porcelain outlets in Europe. It offers the finest array of exquisite Meissen dinner plates in Berlin, and also displays and sells sculptures and chandeliers. Kurfürstendamm 26A. © **030/88-68-35-30**. U-Bahn: Kurfürstendamm.

Rosenthal Head here for contemporary Rosenthal designs from Bavaria. In addition to Rosenthal porcelain, you'll find Boda glassware and elegantly modern tableware. Kurfürstendamm 226. © **030/8-85-63-40**. U-Bahn: Kurfürstendamm.

DEPARTMENT STORES
Kaufhaus des Westens (KaDeWe)
This huge luxury department store, known popularly as KaDeWe (pronounced kah-day-vay), was established some 90 years ago. It's best known for its sixth-floor food department, where more than 1,000 varieties of German sausages are displayed along with delicacies from all over the world. Sit-down counters are available. After fortifying yourself here, you can explore the six floors of merchandise. KaDeWe is more than a department store—one shopper called it a "collection of first-class specialty shops." Tauentzienstrasse 21. © **030/2-12-10**. U-Bahn: Kurfürstendamm or Wittenbergplatz.

Wertheim This centrally located store is good for travel aids and general basics. It sells perfumes, clothing for the entire family, jewelry, electrical devices, household goods, photography supplies, and souvenirs. It also has a shoe-repair section. Shoppers can fuel up at a large restaurant with a grand view over half the city. Kurfürstendamm 231. © **030/88-00-30**. U-Bahn: Kurfürstendamm.

FASHION
Anette Peterman
This shop is noteworthy because of its limited number of carefully chosen dresses, each of which is displayed, and priced, like an art object in its own right. Sheer, shimmering, and undeniably sexy, they're the kind of design that might be worn to dinner at a posh schlosshotel in the country. Bleibtreustrasse 40. © **030/323-2556**. S-Bahn: Savignyplatz.

Bleibgrün It's small, it's fashionable, and it's sought after by well-dressed and well-heeled women from Berlin and its suburbs. And best of all, the staff is charming and helpful. Come here for access to things that are terribly chic and contemporary, including dresses by Jean-Paul Gaultier, Paul Smith, Marithé François Girbaud, and a handful of other currently fashionable trendsetters. Bleibtreustrasse 30. ✆ 030/885-0080. S-Bahn: Savignyplatz.

Bogner Zenker-Berlin   This three-story shop has sold garments to three generations of clients. Its selection of women's clothing includes everything from formal evening gowns to sportswear. Many of the items are made in Germany, Austria, or Italy. Kurfürstendamm 45. ✆ 030/8-81-10-00. S-Bahn: Savignyplatz.

Chapeaux Hutmode Berlin   There are only about 10 hatmakers left in Berlin today, and of those 10, only two or three have earned the respect and patronage of the city's couture crowd. This is the most appealing of the lot and also the most whimsical. Andrea Curti, owner and designer, draws her inspirations from vintage fashion magazines, old movies, and anything that looked good on Greta Garbo. The result is an artfully arranged inventory of veiled, feathered, or minimalist hats. Come here with a sense of glamour, a sense of humor, a sense of theatricality, and some open-ended ideas about what makes you look good. Bleibtreustrasse 51. ✆ 030/312-09-13. S-Bahn: Savignyplatz.

Modenhaus Horn   Berlin is one of the world's most fashion-conscious cities, and here you'll see examples of what's au courant for chic women. Kurfürstendamm 213. ✆ 030/8-81-40-55. U-Bahn: Kurfürstendamm.

Sonia Rykiel   This stylish showcase is the only shop in Germany devoted exclusively to Ms. Rykiel, the successful French fashion mogul. She designed the store's interior herself. *Beware:* Even a Sonia Rykiel T-shirt is expensive. There's both a children's shop and a women's shop. Kurfürstendamm 186. ✆ 030/8-82-17-74 for women, or 030/882-28-85 for children. U-Bahn: Adenauerplatz.

To Die For   Clothing here follows trends so obsessively that you're likely to find inventories configured exclusively in tones of gray, black, and apple green (though these examples are guaranteed to change before your visit). Don't expect to find anything suitable unless you're in relatively good shape. Svelte men or women can find what they need here to assimilate themselves into many of Mitte's emerging bars and clubs. Neue Schönhauser Strasse 10. ✆ 030/28-38-68-34. U-Bahn: Rosenthaler Platz.

Triebel   This elegant store offers everything you might need for a weekend retreat at a private hunting lodge, such as clothing, shoes, boots, or sporting equipment. If you dream of looking like the lord of a Bavarian manor in a loden coat and feather-trimmed hat, or if you've been invited on a spontaneous fox hunt, come here first. The inventory includes a selection of hunting rifles and shooting equipment. Schönwalder Strasse 12, Spandau. ✆ 030/3-35-50-01. U-Bahn: Rathaus Spandau. S-Bahn: Spandau.

Werner Scherer   The arrival of this upscale menswear emporium symbolized to some extent the rebirth of the Unter den Linden as a glamorous shopping destination. Set on the street level of the Adlon Hotel, it's the showplace of Munich-based designer Werner Scherer, who makes the kind of clothes that millionaires love to buy. Expect well-made shirts, silk neckties, and curiosities that include bomber jackets crafted from a mixture of silk and linen, and buttery soft black leather coats. Despite its high prices, the shop does a roaring business with the glam crowd, many of whom wouldn't consider buying their shirts anywhere else. Unter den Linden 77. ✆ 030/22-67-98-93. S-Bahn: Unter den Linden.

JEWELRY

Galerie Lalique   One of the more unusual jewelry stores in Berlin, this emporium stocks the original designs of about 50 German-based designers. Most pieces are modern interpretations, using diamonds and other precious stones. Even though the store's name is similar to that of the French glass designer, no crystal or glassware is sold here. Bleibtreustrasse 47. ✆ 030/8-81-97-62. S-Bahn: Savignyplatz.

Treykorn   This outlet displays the most avant-garde jewelry in Berlin. Owners Andreas and Sabine Treykorn provide a showcase for more than three dozen of the boldest and often most controversial jewelry artisans in the city. Prices for some pieces are in the thousands, there are many more reasonable selections as well. Savignyplatz 13-Passage. ✆ 030/312-4275. S-Bahn: Savignyplatz.

Wurzbacher   Everything this small store sells is crafted on-site from either gold or platinum, often with accents of precious or semiprecious stones. Most designs are modern and streamlined. Some pieces are noteworthy for their heft. Most of the jewelry here is for women, although a scattering of rings, tie clips, and cuff links are for men. Kurfürstendamm 36. ✆ 030/8-83-38-92. U-Bahn: Uhlandstrasse. S-Bahn: Savignyplatz.

KITCHENWARE

VMF   The inventory here is a restaurant owner's fantasy, with appealing kitchen gadgets that cooks will love. Be warned that most appliances here are incompatible with North American electric current. But if you're interested in glassware (from Nachtmann and Eich), stoneware, kitchen cutlery, or Hummel and Goebel porcelain figurines, you'll find this place fascinating. Kurfürstendamm 229. ℂ 030/8-82-39-41. U-Bahn: Kurfürstendamm.

MARKETS

Antik & Flohmarkt   You might want to check out the finds at this flea market in the S-Bahn station. Some 60 vendors try to tempt buyers with assorted bric-a-brac, including brassware and World War II mementos. Friedrichstrasse S-Bahn station, Berlin-Mitte. ℂ 030/2-08-26-45. U-Bahn/S-Bahn: Friedrichstrasse.

Berliner Trödelmarkt   This flea market lies near the corner of the Bachstrasse and the Strasse des 17. Juni, at the western edge of the Tiergarten, adjacent to the Tiergarten S-Bahn station. It's the favorite weekend shopping spot of countless Berliners, who come here to find an appropriate piece of nostalgia, a battered semiantique, or used clothing. The market is held every Saturday and Sunday (also Easter Mon) 10am to 5pm. Strasse des 17. Juni. ℂ 030/26-55-00-96. S-Bahn: Tiergarten.

MILITARY FIGURES

Berliner Zinnfiguren   A mecca for collectors since 1934, this shop carries an impressive inventory of German-language books on military history and more than 10,000 different pewter figurines of soldiers from many different imperial armies, up to the Franco-Prussian War of 1870. Also included are hand-painted models of Roman and ancient Greek foot soldiers. Flat, hand-painted pewter figures are sold only in sets of 12 or more and cost from 90€ ($104) to 180€ ($207); fully detailed depictions of Prussian soldiers from the 1870s can range as high as 150€ ($173) to 180€ ($207) each, or even 2,000€ ($2300) for special pieces. Knesebeckstrasse 88. ℂ 030/315-700-0. S-Bahn: Savignyplatz.

MUSIC

Musik Riedel   Most of the professional musicians of Berlin have a working familiarity with the layout of this well-established store, as it's been selling musical instruments and sheet music since 1910. Regardless of how esoteric, you're likely to find the score to whatever it is that interests you—sometimes in used folios that have some historic interest in their own right. There's a second branch of this outfit in the Schauspielhaus, on the Gendarmenmarkt (ℂ 030/204-1136; U-Bahn: Französische Strasse), but most of the old-time clients of this place continue to patronize the branch on Uhlandstrasse. Uhlandstrasse 38. ✆ 030/882-7395. U-Bahn: Uhlandstrasse.

PERFUME

Harry Lehmann   This is the kind of shop where German mothers and grandmothers might have bought their perfume between the two world wars. Don't expect big names you'd find at a duty-free airport shop. Most scents here are family recipes, distilled from flowers, grasses, and leaves. The reasonable prices might surprise you—10g (.35 oz.) for as little as 5€ ($5.75). Coming here is a cheap and amusing way to experience the scents of a Prussian spring. Kantstrasse 106. ✆ 030/3-24-35-82. U-Bahn: Wildersdorferstrasse.

PUNK MEMORABILIA

Kaufhaus Schrill   Few other stores mingle a sense of junkiness and kitsch with such artful abandon. Its stocks would gladden any punk-rocker's heart, especially if he or she were on the lookout for Elvis-era memorabilia, hair barrettes that glow in the dark, and jewelry that might appeal to Courtney Love for her date with a group of bikers. Don't come here expecting anything tasteful—that isn't its style. Partly because of that, and partly because the place evokes a vivid sense of the long-ago rebelliousness of the '60s, the place is something of an icon for disaffected, or counterculture, youth. Bleibtreustrasse 46. ✆ 030/882-40-48. S-Bahn: Savignyplatz.

SCULPTURE

Gipsformerei der Staatlichen Museen Preussischer Kulturbesitz (Plaster Works of the State Museums of Prussia)   This company has duplicated the world's great sculptures as plaster casts since 1819. Today, there's an inventory of more than 6,500 of them, everything from busts of Queen Nefertiti to a faithful reproduction of the Farnese Bull. Prices begin at 14€ ($16). Objects can be crated and shipped around the world. Sophie-Charlotte-Strasse 17. ✆ 030/3267690. S-Bahn: Westend.

SHOPPING ARCADES

One of the many surprising aspects of the rebuilt and redesigned Potsdamer Platz is the **Potsdamer Platz Arkaden** (U-Bahn/S-Bahn: Potsdamer Platz), one of the most comprehensive shopping malls in Berlin. In a deliberate rejoinder to more outdated Ku'damm malls, such as the Europa Center, it contains at least 100 shops scattered over three levels, many offering cost-cutting clothing and house-wares. Foreign visitors visit **The Museum Company** (✆ 030/25-29-69-21) for high-quality reproductions of the ancient Greek, Roman, and Egyptian sculptures and jewelry sold in Berlin's muse-ums, and **La Bottega de Mamma Ro** (✆ 030/25-29-63-68), which specializes in Tuscan pottery, linens, table settings, and kitchenware, much of it in bright Mediterranean colors.

9

Berlin After Dark

In Berlin, nightlife runs around the clock, and there's plenty to do at any time. There are at least three magazines that list happenings in the city. The English-language monthly, *Checkpoint Berlin,* is available for free at hotel reception desks and tourist offices and sold at news kiosks. The German-language *Berlin Programm* is available at newsstands. The most detailed listings are found in *zitty,* a biweekly publication in German.

Berlin is famous not only for its opera, classical music, and theater, but also for its cabaret and nightclub entertainment. If you'd like to arrange tickets from America for shows and entertainment in Berlin, contact **Global Tickets** (② **800/223-6108** or 212/398-0154; fax 212/302-4251; www.keithprowse.com). This company can mail actual tickets to your home in most cases or leave tickets at the box office for you. There's a 25% markup (more for opera and ballet) over the box office price, plus a U.S. handling charge of up to $9. Tickets are available for musicals, cabaret, opera, and dance.

1 The Performing Arts

OPERA & CLASSICAL MUSIC

Berliner Philharmonisches Orchester (Berlin Philharmonic Orchestra)   The Berlin Philharmonic, directed by Claudio Abbado, is one of the world's premier orchestras. Its home, **the Philharmonie,** in the Kulturforum, Herbert-von-Karajan Strasse 1 (② **030/254-88-0;** www.berlin-philharmonic.com; U-Bahn: Potsdamer Platz), is a significant piece of modern architecture; you may want to visit even if you do not attend a performance. None of the 2,218 seats are more than 30m (100 ft.) from the rostrum. The box office is open Monday to Friday 3:30 to 6pm and Saturday and Sunday 11am to 2pm. You can place orders by phone at ② **030/25-48-89-99.** If you're staying in a first-class or deluxe hotel, the concierge can usually obtain seats for you. Herbert-von-Karajan-Strasse 1. ② **030/254-88-132.** Tickets 15€–51€ ($18–$59) ; special concerts 26€-128€ ($29–$147). S-Bahn: Potsdamer Platz.

Deutsche Oper Berlin   This opera company performs in Charlottenburg in one of the world's great opera houses, a notable example of modern theater architecture that seats 1,885. The company tackles Puccini favorites, Janácek rarities, or modern works, and has a complete Wagner repertoire. A ballet company performs once a week. Concerts, including Lieder evenings, are also presented on the opera stage. Bismarckstrasse 35. ℂ **030/3-43-84-01**. Tickets 15€–102€ ($18–$118). U-Bahn: Deutsche Oper and Bismarckstrasse.

Deutsche Staatsoper (German State Opera)   The German State Opera performs in the Staatsoper Unter den Linden. This was for years the showcase of the opera scene of East Germany. Originally constructed in 1743 and destroyed in World War II, the house was rebuilt in the 1950s, reproducing as closely as possible the original designs of Georg Knobelsdorff. Some of the world's finest opera as well as concerts and ballet are presented here. The box office is open Monday to Friday 10am to 6pm, Saturday and Sunday noon to 6pm. The opera closes from late-June to the end of August. Unter den Linden 7. ℂ **030/20-35-45-55**. Tickets, opera 11€–82€ ($13–$94); concerts 7.65€–61€ ($8.80–$71). U-Bahn: Französische Strasse. S-Bahn: Friedrichstrasse.

Komische Oper Berlin   The Komische Oper has become one of the most highly regarded theater ensembles in Europe, presenting many avant-garde opera productions as well as ballet and musical theater. The box office is open Monday to Saturday 11am to 7pm and Sunday 1pm until 1½ hours before the performance. Behrensstrasse 55–57. ℂ **030/20-26-00**. Tickets 7.65€–54€ ($8.80–$62). U-Bahn: Französische Strasse. S-Bahn: Friedrichstrasse or Unter den Linden.

Konzerthaus Berlin   This 1821 building was created by Friedrich Schinkel. It offers two venues for classical concerts, the Grosser Konzertsaal for orchestra and the Kammermusiksaal for chamber music. Its organ recitals are considered the finest in Germany. Performances are often daring and innovative. The Deutsches Sinfonie-Orchester is also based here. In the Schauspielhaus, Gendarmenmarkt. ℂ **030/203-09-21-01**. Tickets 10€–70€ ($12–$81). U-Bahn: Französische Strasse.

2 Theater

Berlin has long been known for its theater. Even if you don't understand German, you may enjoy seeing a production of a familiar play or attending a musical.

Perhaps the most famous theater is the **Berliner Ensemble,** Am Bertolt-Brecht-Platz 1 (ℂ **030/284-08-155;** U-Bahn/S-Bahn:

Friedrichstrasse), founded by the late playwright Bertolt Brecht. His wife, Helene Weigel, played an important role in the theater's founding and was the ensemble's longtime director. Works by Brecht and other playwrights are presented here. Seats are reasonably priced.

Moments   The Love Parade

The **Love Parade** is the techno-rave street party to end all parties. On the second weekend of July, around 1 million (mostly) young people converge in the center of Berlin for 48 decidedly hedonistic hours. What began in 1988 as a DJ's birthday party with about 150 friends has grown into an immense corporate event that wreaks havoc on the rest of the city's usually impeccable organization (particularly the public transportation system).

The center of Berlin becomes awash with litter and good-natured debauchery. Because of the frenzied jiggling, gyrating, and very noisy good times, anyone wanting an even remotely peaceful weekend should follow the little old ladies and rock fans on the fast train out of town. The event starts off on Saturday afternoon, when a booming caravan of floats carries the best DJs in Europe from Ernst-Reuter-Platz to the Brandenburg Gate. If you want to see the procession, come early and grab as high a view as possible.

Everything imaginable is imbibed in high quantities, and every year serious worries are voiced over the deluge of urine in the Tiergarten, site of the evening celebrations. The entire city, in fact, transforms itself into a huge party. The BVG (public transport system) offers a 5.10€ ($5.85) "no limit" ticket to speed you from one rave to another. Traveling revelers should note that club prices skyrocket during the weekend.

Lots of fuss and bother or a really good time? It all depends on your point of view. This is a must for anybody with a love of synthesizers and a lot of steam to let off: The Love Parade has become an international fixture to rival Mardi Gras.

The most important German-language theater in the country is **Schaubühne am Lehniner Platz,** Kurfürstendamm 153 (© **030/ 89-00-23;** U-Bahn: Adenauerplatz), at the east end of the Ku'-damm, near Lehniner Platz. There are three different stages here.

Finally, **Theater des Westens,** between the Berlin Zoo and the Ku'damm at Kantstrasse 12 (© **030/31-90-30;** U-Bahn/S-Bahn: Zoologischer Garten), specializes in plays, musical comedies, and the German equivalent of Broadway extravaganzas. The theater was built in 1896. Performances are held Tuesday to Saturday at 8pm and Sunday at 6pm. Ticket prices range from 20€–90€ ($23–104).

3 The Club & Music Scene
CABARET

Very popular among visitors to Berlin is the kind of nightspot depicted in the musical *Cabaret,* with floor-show patter and acts that make fun of the political and social scene.

Die Stachelschweine Since the beginning of the Cold War, the "Porcupine" has poked prickly fun at the German and American political scenes. The performance is delivered in rapid-fire German and evokes the legendary Berliner sense of satire, which can often be scathing in its humor. Although you need to understand German to really appreciate what goes on here, you'll still recognize some of the names (George W., Al Gore, and Hillary), and there's likely to be a deliberately corny selection of popular ditties ("Life is a cabaret, old chum") thrown in. Shows take place Tuesday to Friday at 7:30pm and Saturday at 6 and 9pm. The box office is open Tuesday to Friday 11am to 2pm and 3 to 7:30pm and Saturday 10am to 2pm and 3 to 8:45pm. It's closed in July. Tauentzienstrasse and Budapesterstrasse (in the basement of Europa Center). © **030/2-61-47-95.** Cover 11€–24€ ($12–$27). U-Bahn: Kurfürstendamm.

Wintergarten The largest and most nostalgic Berlin cabaret, the Wintergarten offers a variety show every night, with magicians, clowns, jugglers, acrobats, and live music. The most expensive seats are on stage level, where tiny tables are available for simple suppers costing from 12.80€ ($15) to 24€ ($27). Balconies have conventional theater seats, but staff members pass frequently along the aisles selling drinks. Shows last around 2¼ hours each and begin Monday to Friday at 8pm, Sunday at 6pm, and Saturday at 6 and 10pm. Potsdamer Strasse 96. © **030/23-08-82-30.** Cover Fri–Sat 47€–53€ ($54–$61), Sun–Thurs 37€–43€ ($43–$50) per person, depending on the seat. U-Bahn: Kurfürstenstrasse.

DANCE CLUBS

Big Eden   Everyone from Paul McCartney to Sylvester Stallone has danced here. This club accommodates some 1,000 dancers nightly on its huge dance floor, where top DJs play the latest international hits. The light effects and superstereo are impressive. There's a nightly happy hour. Kurfürstendamm 202. ✆ **030/8-82-61-20.** Cover 5€– 10€ ($5.75–$12) Fri–Sat (includes 1 drink). Sun–Thurs 9pm–5am; Fri–Sat 9pm–6am. U-Bahn: Uhlandstrasse.

Café Keese   This dance club caters to a more traditional clientele, most aged 35 to 40. Here women can ask the men to dance, and the management even reserves the right to kick out any male patron

Life Is a Cabaret in Berlin

Cabaret life in between-the-wars Berlin was a legend that inspired writers that included Christopher Isherwood, among many others. These emporiums of *schmaltz* have been reborn in the former East Berlin—though the satire might be a bit less biting than it was during the Weimar Republic. Today's cabaret shows might remind you of Broadway blockbusters, without much of the intimacy of the smoky and trenchant cellar revues of the 1930s. But for access to talent that includes multilingual comedians and singers, jugglers, acrobats, musicians, plenty of coyly expressed sexuality, and lots of costume changes, consider an evening at the **Friedrichstadt-Palast,** Friedrichstrasse 107 (✆ **030/23-26-23-26;** U-Bahn/S-Bahn: Friedrichstrasse). Although showtimes might vary with whatever revue is featured at the time of your visit, they tend to begin Tuesday to Saturday at 8pm, with additional performances every Saturday and Sunday at 4pm. The most visible and well-publicized competitor is **Wintergarten,** Potsdamer Strasse 96 (✆ **030/230-88-230;** U-Bahn/S-Bahn: Kurfursten-strasse). Shows, which are less high-tech than at the richly computerized Friedrichstadt-Palast, are usually presented Monday to Friday at 8pm, Saturday at 6 and 10pm, and Sunday at 6pm and 10pm. Cover Friday and Saturday is 47€ ($54) to 53€ ($61), Sunday to Thursday 37€ ($43) to 43€ ($49), depending on the performance and the seat. Price includes first drink.

who turns down a request. The orchestra plays a lot of slow music, and the place is often jammed, especially on Saturday nights. The Keese sees itself as something of a matrimonial bureau and is always announcing statistics about the number of people who met on its premises and got married. Formal attire is requested. Open Tuesday to Thursday 8pm to 3am, Friday to Saturday 8pm to 4am, Sunday to Monday 4pm to 1am. Bismarckstrasse 108. ℂ 030/3-12-91-11. No cover, but a drink minimum of 6€ ($7) Fri and Sun, 8€ ($9) Sat. U-Bahn: Ernst-Reuther-Platz.

Clärchen's Ballhaus   This place has been around since 1913, and it's schmaltzy enough to remind sentimental newcomers of the nostalgic old days. A renewed interest in ballroom dancing has kept it going. Live music from a dance band is the norm, with recorded music to fill in when the band takes a break. On Wednesday, women are encouraged to ask men to the dance floor. Open Tuesday, Wednesday, Friday, and Saturday 8:30pm to around 3am. Auguststrasse 24–25. ℂ 030/2-82-92-95. Cover 8€ ($9.20). U-Bahn: Rosenthaler Platz. S-Bahn: Oranienburger Strasse.

Far Out   Large and artfully drab, this industrial-looking disco plays danceable rock from the '70s to the '90s for hundreds of high-energy dancers. You'll see lots of students and artists, many dressed up in bizarre clothing. The place only really comes alive after midnight. Open Tuesday to Sunday 10pm to between 4 and 6am, depending on the crowd. Kurfürstendamm 156. ℂ 030/320-00-717. Cover 5.10€–7.65€ ($5.85–$8.80). U-Bahn: Adenauerplatz.

Metropole   On the outside, this club—originally built as a theater around 1906—boasts one of the great proto–Art Deco facades of Berlin. Inside, you'll find a replica of an ancient Egyptian temple, but with accessories that might have been designed for an early Hollywood stage set by Busby Berkeley. Most patrons are in their 20s, dancing the night away every weekend 9pm until dawn. Don't confuse this place with the Kit Kat Club, an independent, more notorious venue that occupies the building's cellar (see "Gay & Lesbian Berlin," below). Nollendorfplatz 5, Schöneberg. ℂ 030/21-73-680. Cover 7.65€ ($8.80). U-Bahn: Nollendorfplatz.

SO36   The lines begin to form here about 30 minutes before the place even opens, but they move quickly as Berliner hipsters get into the spirit of one of the city's more witty and unconventional clubs. Its name derives from the postal code SO36 applied to this district before World War II. Inside, you'll find two very large rooms, a stage, an ongoing rush of dance music, and a scene combining a senior prom in the high school gym with some of the more bizarre aspects of Berlin nightlife. Many women come here, both gay and straight, as well as a higher percentage of heterosexual men than you might have expected along this strip of bars in Kreuzberg. If you're lucky enough to be in town for the once-per-month Turkish drag night, you'll find one of the most amusing drag shows in Berlin, where Fatima the belly dancer is likely to be male, beguiling, and well-versed in the satirical aspects of life in a Turkish harem. The club is open most nights, based on an evolving schedule, 10:30pm to at least 4am. Oranienstrasse 190, Kreuzberg. ℭ **030/61-40-13-06.** Cover 6€–14€ ($6.90–$16). U-Bahn: Prinzenstrasse.

Tresor Globus   One of Berlin's best techno venues, this club really packs them in. The building was once part of Globus Bank; downstairs there's a bunker-like atmosphere, with prison-type metal bars and harsh acoustics. The spacious dance floor upstairs has lighter house sounds. There's a bar in the back. In summer, tables are placed outside, and food is served. The club is open from 10pm Wednesday and from 11pm Friday to Sunday. Leipzigerstrasse 8. ℭ **030/2-29-06-11.** Cover 6€–14€ ($6.90–$16); 3.60€ ($4.14) on Wed only. U-Bahn: Mohrenstrasse.

LIVE MUSIC

A Trane   This small and smoky jazz house is an excellent choice for either beginning or ending an evening of bar-hopping in the neighborhood. It features musicians from all over the world. It's open daily at 9pm; music begins around 10pm. Closing hours vary. Pestalozzistrasse 105. ℭ **030/3-13-25-50.** Cover 7.65€–15€ ($8.80–$18). S-Bahn: Savignyplatz.

Knaack-Klub   This four-story club features a live-music venue, two floors of dancing, and a games floor. There are usually four live rock shows a week, with a fairly even split between German and international touring bands. Show days vary. There's dancing on Wednesday, Friday, and Saturday nights. Hours are nightly from 10pm. Greifswalderstrasse 224. ℭ **030/4-42-70-60.** Cover 2.55€–5.10€ ($2.95–$5.85). S-Bahn: Alexanderplatz.

Oxymoron   This is a good example of Berlin's newest crop of hyper-trendy, high-visibility hangouts where the food is served almost as an afterthought to an exhibitionistic/voyeuristic scene that can be a lot of fun and in some cases, intriguing. The setting is a high-ceilinged room with old-fashioned proportions and enough battered kitsch to remind you of a turn-of-the-century coffeehouse in Franz-Josef's Vienna. Local wits refer to it as a *Gesamtkunstwerk*—a self-obsessed, self-sustaining work of art that might have been appreciated by Wagner. Most nights after around 11pm, a slightly claustrophobic, much-used annex room—all black with ghostly flares of neon—opens for business as a disco, usually for a 75% hetero and 100% iconoclastic clientele. If live bands appear, it will usually be on a Thursday. Open daily 11am to 2am. In the courtyard of the complex at Rosenthaler Strasse 40–41. ✆ 030/283-91-88-6. Cover 5.10€–10.20€ ($5.85–$12). S-Bahn: Hackescher Markt.

Quasimodo   This is the top Berlin jazz club. Although many different styles of music are offered here, including rock and Latin, jazz is the focus. Local acts are featured on Tuesday and Wednesday, when admission is free. Summer visitors should check out the "Jazz in July" festival. The club is open Tuesday to Saturday 9pm to 3am, with shows beginning at 10pm. Kantstrasse 12A. ✆ 030/3-12-80-86. Cover 7€–22€ ($8.05–$25). U-Bahn: Zoologischer Garten.

Wild at Heart   This club, with its kitschy knickknacks, colored lights, and wine-red walls, is dedicated to the rowdier side of rock. Hard-core punk, rock, and rockabilly bands from Germany and elsewhere are featured. Live performances take place Wednesday to Saturday nights. It's open Monday to Friday 8pm to 3am, Saturday and Sunday 8pm to 10am (yes, you may miss breakfast). Wienerstrasse 20. ✆ 030/6-11-70-10. Cover 8€ ($9.20) for concerts only. U-Bahn: Görlitzer Bahnhof.

DRAG SHOWS

Chez Nous   The famous show at Chez Nous is played to an essentially straight crowd in a mock Louis XIV setting. Some of the world's best drag show acts appear here, from a sultry, boa-draped star from Rio de Janeiro to a drag queen who looks like a gun moll from the 1940s. Shows are nightly at 8:30 and 11pm. Marburgerstrasse 14. ✆ 030/2-13-18-10. Cover 35€ ($40), includes 1 drink. U-Bahn: Wittenbergplatz.

La Vie en Rose   This club offers a highly polished, Vegas-style revue to a straight clientele, often businessmen. This is where "Barbra," "Dolly," and "Judy" are likely to appear. The box office is open daily 10am to 11pm. Shows start at 9pm Sunday to Thursday and at 10pm on Friday and Saturday. Europa Center. ✆ 030/3-23-60-06. Cover 37€ ($43). U-Bahn: Zoologischer Garten.

4 Gay & Lesbian Berlin

Traditionally, lesbian and gay life centered around the **Nollendorf-platz** (U-Bahn: Nollendorfplatz), the so-called "Pink Village." There is a history of homosexuality here at the **Schwules Museum,**

Mehringdamm 61 (© **030/693-11-72**), open Wednesday to Monday from 2 to 6pm. Admission is 5.50€ ($6.35) adults, 3€ ($3.45) students. The **State-Supported Spinnboden-Lesbenarchiv,** Anklamerstrasse 38 (© **030/448-58-48**), caters to all sorts of lesbian cultural events. **Man-o-Meter,** Motzstrasse 5 (off Nollendorfplatz) (© **030/216-80-08**), is a gay information center.

Today, Motzstrasse is the location of many gay and lesbian bars. A trio of popular gay bars, **Tom's,** the **Prinzknecht,** and the **Knast Bar,** are sometimes referred to as "the Bermuda Triangle."

In the latter half of June, the **Lesbisch-Schwules Stadtfest** (Lesbian & Gay Men's Street Fair) takes place at Nollendorfplatz. This is topped in size, though not in exuberance, the last week in June by the **Christopher Street Day** parade, when 200,000 people congregate to have fun and drop inhibitions.

Begine Café Bistro Bar Exklusiv für Frauen   This is a center for feminists and one of Berlin's best places for women to meet other women. It has a changing array of art exhibitions, and features poetry readings, German-language discussions, lectures, and other social events. Call in advance for the schedule. The premises are occasionally transformed into a disco. Potsdamerstrasse 139. © **030/215-43-25.** No cover. Mon–Sat 5pm–1am. U-Bahn: Bulowstrasse.

Connection Disco   Other discos occasionally challenge its entrenched grip on gay nightlife in Berlin, but somehow Connections continues to endure as an after-dark staple. It's very large, with two floors and a network of independently operated shops and specialty bars. Come here to dance to techno and trance music, but know in advance that this place is proud of the darkened labyrinth of cellar rooms it maintains for trysts—management cites them as the largest network of back rooms in Berlin. It's open Friday and Saturday from 11pm to 4am. Fuggerstrasse 31–33. © **030/218-1432.** Cover 8€ ($9.20). U-Bahn: Wittenbergplatz.

Kit Kat Klub   In Liza Minnelli's cinema version of *Cabaret,* Sally Bowles was an entertainer at the Kit Kat Club. Today's incarnation of that fictional club presents far more than dominatrix-style singers with hearts of gold. You'll check most of your clothes at the door (retain your shoes), and enter an ultra-permissive lounge, bar, and disco where Mr. or Ms. Right will probably show you all their charms on the first date. Tuesday, Wednesday, Friday, and Saturday, are for heterosexuals; Thursday and Sunday are all-gay and all-male. On those nights, clients must enter between 9 and 11pm, after which the doors are locked to newcomers, and the partying continues until much later. In the basement of the Metropole, Nollendorfplatz 5, Schöneberg. *©* 030/21-73-680. Cover 11€–15€ ($13–$18). U-Bahn: Nollendorfplatz.

Knast Bar   Dark and amiably battered, this is one of the two or three bars in Berlin most frequently cited for a macho-looking crowd that appreciates the allure of leather, rubber, and anything that even begins to resemble a uniform. Open daily 8pm to dawn. Fuggerstrasse 34. *©* 030/2-18-10-26. U-Bahn: Wittenbergplatz.

Kumpelnest 3000   Gay or straight, you're welcome here. All that's asked is that you enjoy a kinky good time in what used to be a brothel. This crowded and chaotic place is really a bar now, but there's also dancing to disco classics. Berliners often show up here for early morning fun after they've exhausted the action at the other hot spots. Open daily 5pm to 5am, even later on weekends. Lützow-strasse 23. *©* 030/2-61-69-18. U-Bahn: Kurfürstenstrasse.

Lenz die Bar   It's convivial, it attracts lots of neighborhood acquaintances, and at its best, it can be a lot of fun. Caipirinhas are one of the enduringly popular drinks. Priced at 8€ ($9.20) each, they bring a bit of Brazilian samba to foggy Berlin on a cold dark night. It's open nightly 8pm to 4am. Eisenacherstrasse 3. *©* 030/217-7820. No cover. U-Bahn: Viktoria-Luise-Platz.

Prinzknecht   It's large, brick-lined, and mobbed with ordinary guys who just happen to be gay, and who just happen to be involved in computers, media, the building trades, and show business. The combination can be unpretentious and a lot of fun, especially when frothy pink Hemingways are bought by friends for friends, and when the stories start getting raunchy. If you want a place that manages to be both high class and earthy, within walking distance of lots of other gay options, this might be appropriate. It's open daily 3pm to 3am. Fuggerstrasse 33. *©* 030/23-62-74-44. No cover. U-Bahn: Viktoria-Luise-Platz.

SchwuZ   If you hadn't been warned in advance, you might not even know that this was a nightclub, hidden as it is behind the con-ventional-looking facade of the Café Sundström. You'll descend into a battered-looking warren of basement rooms, outfitted in a surreal combination of glossy stainless steel that alternates with structural beams and cinderblock. The mostly gay, mostly male, and mostly under 35-year-old crowd comes to dance the night away, every day 11pm until around 4am. There are two separate dance floors, one with cutting edge, the other with more traditional dance music.

Mehringdamm 61, Berlin-Kreuzberg. © 030/693-70-25. Cover 5€–7€ ($5.75–$8.05). U-Bahn: Mehringdamm.

Tom's Bar Tom's becomes crowded after 11pm with young gay men. Most of the clients show up here in rugged-looking T-shirts, flannel, jeans, and/or black leather, evocative of a Tom of Finland drawing. Upstairs, the porno action is merely on the screen; downstairs it's real. Monday nights feature two-for-one drinks. There's a cover charge for special occasions only. Motzstrasse 19. © 030/2-13-45-70. Daily 10pm–6am. U-Bahn: Nollendorfplatz.

5 The Bar & Cafe Scene

BEER GARDENS & WINE CELLARS

Historischer Weinkeller This squat and unpretentious inn might be the site of one of your more interesting evenings in Berlin. The setting is a highly atmospheric vaulted cellar. In winter the staff performs the medieval ceremony of "burning the punch," during which a sugar cone is lighted in your punch. As it burns, you're supposed to make a wish. The ritual takes place three times a week on Wednesday, Friday, and Saturday between 11 and midnight. The punch, a kind of hot spiced wine, costs 5€ ($5.75) per glass. You can also order beer or one of more than 100 German wines, as well as full meals that cost 14€ ($16) to 35€ ($40). (If you plan to dine, make reservations in advance.) An outdoor rustic beer garden is open in the summer. Open daily noon to midnight. Alt-Pichelsdorf 32 (about 1.5km/1mile west of the Olympia-Stadion). © 030/3-61-80-56. Reservations required. U-Bahn: Olympia-Stadion.

Joe's Wirthaus zum Löwen This cozy pub in the city center is attractively decorated with traditional Teutonic accessories. Even in winter, when you're snug and warm inside, you get the feeling you're sitting out under the chestnut trees. The kitchen offers good plain German food, including Bavarian specialties and some Italian dishes. Open daily 11am to 1am; the best time to come here is 7pm to midnight. Hardenbergstrasse 29 (opposite the Kaiser Wilhelm Memorial Church). © 030/2-62-10-20. U-Bahn: Zoologischer Garten.

Loretta im Garten (Pupasch) This surprisingly rustic indoor/outdoor beer garden is large, sometimes rowdy, and very German. It's outfitted with durable wooden banquettes, battered accessories, a large outdoor area, and a children's play area with its own Ferris wheel. Menu items include platters of sausage with sauerkraut and potatoes, spareribs, and stuffed baked potatoes. There's no live music; this a place for talk, gossip, and beer drinking. Many locals also come here for lunch. It's open April to early October only, daily 11am to 3am. Lietzenburgerstrasse 89. ℂ **030/8-82-33-54.** U-Bahn: Uhlandstrasse.

THE BEST BARS

Bar am Lützowplatz   Many hip locals cite this as their favorite bar, partly because it manages to be beautiful, chic, breezy, and artsy, and partly because it provides a concentrated kind of conviviality within a neighborhood that otherwise is prosperous but just a bit staid. Known as one the longest and narrowest bars in Berlin, it presents a flattering and almost reverential portrait of Mao-Tse-Tung as its visual focal point, the humor of which cannot be lost on the devoted capitalists and *bons vivants* who come here to see, be seen, and flirt. It's open daily 3pm until 4am. Lützowplatz 7. ℂ **030/26-26-807.** U-Bahn: Nollendorferplatz.

Green Door   No, the name wasn't taken from one of the 20th-century's most famous porno flicks, *Beyond the Green Door.* There is actually a green door here at this intimate, cozy, and classic cocktail lounge. Like the famous movie itself, there is a '70s retro feel to the place. Exotic cocktails perfectly prepared by the waitstaff are one of the best features of this place, and all of them have such names as "Hot Kiss" or "Burning Bush." We'd rank their martinis as among the best in town. Open daily 6pm to 3am. Winterfeldstrasse 50. ℂ **030/ 215-2515.** U-Bahn: Nollendorf.

Greenwich Bar—a.k.a. Cookie's   Its decor evokes the body of the Michelin Guide's animated tire, because of the foam-padded bands of florescent green Naugahyde that surround the room. That, along with built-in rows of bubbling aquariums and the refusal of management to post a sign identifying the location of this very in spot, create an iconoclastic setting where about 30% of the clients are openly gay and the remainder mysteriously undefined. It's open daily 6pm to 6am, serving stiff, party-colored drinks and martinis priced from 5.10€ ($5.85) each. Recorded music plays, usually focusing on soul, drum and bass, and house music. Gipstrasse 5. No phone. U-Bahn: Weinmeisterstrasse.

Harry's New York Bar   Harry's is an aggressively stylized bar with minimalist decor, pop art, and photographs of all the American presidents. It's modeled after the famous watering hole, Harry's New York Bar, in Paris. Its drink menu is a monument to the oral traditions of the IBF (International Bar Flies) Society, and includes such favorites as "Mizner's Dream" (created in 1962 for the Boca Raton

Hotel Club in Florida) and the 1964 classic, "The Petrifier" (ingredients unlisted), for two. The menu lists almost 200 drinks, as well as a limited selection of food. Open 24 hours a day, 7 days a week. In the Grand Hotel Esplanade, Lützowufer 15. ℭ 030/25-47-88-21. U-Bahn: Nollendorfplatz, Wittenbergplatz, or Kurfürstenstrasse.

Juleps New York Bar The roaring '20s and the turbulent '30s of America are evoked at this Speakeasy type bar, with its bare brick walls. The only thing they don't have is Prohibition, as the liquor flows. We counted more than 120 different cocktails on the drink menu alone. On a tree-lined street in Charlottenburg, this is a warm, intimate, and welcoming place, with a long oaken bar. If you're hungry, check out those big and yummy bacon cheeseburgers, or else dig into a pasta or order chicken satays. The kitchen even turns out fabulous desserts such as Mississippi Mud Cake. The mohitos here are as good as those in Cuba. Open Sunday to Thursday 5pm to 1am, Friday and Saturday 5pm to 2am. Giesebrechtstrasse 3. ℭ 030/881-8823. U-Bahn: Adener Plazt.

Kurvenstar One of the most quirky and famous offbeat bars in Hackescher Höfe celebrates an artfully tacky decor that elevates the worst of the decorative and plasticized excesses of the 1970s into an art form of the highest degree of kitsch. Come here for ideas on how to recycle everything you might have stashed within your attic. Also visit for a drink, priced at around 7.50€ ($8.65), a dialogue, perhaps a snack, but not a full meal. Open daily 7pm until the last patron leaves, usually around 3 or 4am. Grossepräsidentumstrasse 1. ℭ 030/28-59-97-10. U-Bahn: Hackescher Markt.

Lore Berlin This is the bar most often cited by hipsters as a watering hole that combines cutting-edge design, fabulous dance music, and a stimulating mix of clients from all branches of Berlin society. The setting is a long and narrow, eerily backlit bar area where theatrical lighting makes almost everyone look attractive. Most clients remain at the bar, talking, flirting, and gossiping about the new Berlin, except for the high-energy danceaholics. These migrate to a blackened semicellar, where the hulking remains of what was originally built in the 19th century as a coal-fired heating station add visual interest. Even the washrooms and washbasins here are worth a comment, designed like poured-concrete reinterpretations of ancient Roman aqueducts. Neue Schönhauser Strasse 20. ℭ 030/28-04-51-34. U-Bahn: Weinmeisterstrasse.

Newton Bar There have been more reviews about Berlin's Newton Bar than virtually any other watering hole in town. You might be rejected at the door by a bouncer who disapproves of your sense of style. Here's what you'll get if you're admitted: a high-ceilinged, well-proportioned room that evokes 1960s modernism at its best and a deeply ingrained sense of the well-heeled and socially conscious *bourgeoisie* looking for like-minded people. It's condemned for its sense of *chicki-miki* (self-conscious chic) by clients of counterculture bars in less expensive neighborhoods. But regardless of how you feel, you can't help but be intrigued by a huge black-and-white mural that sweeps an entire runway of naked fashion models across your field of vision, and service rituals inspired by Old Prussia. Love it or hate it, it's hard to ignore the Newton Bar. It's open daily 10am till at least 2am. Charlottenstrasse 57. ℂ 030/20-61-29-99. U-Bahn: Stadtmitte.

Reingold   This bar is elegant and chic, stretching along the length of a long and narrow room. The overall effect has been called "Manet meeting Hopper." An aquarium seems *de rigueur* for Berlin bars, but the one here is modest. The beautiful people descend nightly to see and be seen. The truly beautiful ones show up after midnight. Novalisstrasse 11. ℂ 030/2838-7676. U-Bahn: Friedrichstrasse.

Roses   It might have been known 30 years ago as a storefront selling food supplies to the neighborhood's *Hausfrauen,* but it's very different from that today. You'll find a claustrophobic pair of rooms whose level of kitsch has been elevated to an art form; flickering candles, lavish graffiti, a Jamaican Gastarbeiter selling cookies reputed to have been baked with hashish, and gay and straight clients who seem very, very hip to whatever is happening in Berlin's *Nacht-szene.* It's open nightly 10pm until at least 5am. Oranienstrasse 187. Kreuzberg. ℂ 030/615-6570. U-Bahn: Kottosser Tor.

Times Bar   The cozy and intimate Times Bar has a quiet charm reminiscent of a wood-paneled private library in someone's home. The bar is dedicated to the *Times* (of London), whose latest edition is often displayed in the window. Guests sit in leather-upholstered chairs and read English-language newspapers. Menu items range from lobster soup to ice cream. Open daily 11am to 2am. In the Savoy Hotel, Fasanenstrasse 9–10. ℂ 030/31-10-30. U-Bahn: Zoologischer Garten.

FINDING A *KNEIPE*

A *Kneipe* is a cozy rendezvous place, the equivalent of a Londoner's local pub. The typical Berliner has a favorite Kneipe for relaxing after work and visiting with sympathetic friends. There are hundreds in Berlin. Here's a handful to get you started.

Gaststätte Hoeck (Wilhelm Hoeck) The oldest Kneipe in Charlottenburg (1892) still sports original wood panels with inlaid glass on the walls. It also has a brightly illuminated facade jammed with local beer slogans. You (and half of the neighborhood) can have a drink in the very rowdy, sometimes raucous bar area, where (among other oddities) a clown may be playing the harmonica. The separate dining room serves traditional food. More than a dozen kinds of beer are offered (if in doubt, just ask for our favorite, Pilsner Urquell), as well as wine by the glass. Main courses cost 6.50€ ($7.50) to 16€ ($18); hot food is served Monday to Saturday 11am to 10:30pm. Regular hours, however, are 8am to midnight. Wilmersdorferstrasse 149. ℂ **030/3-41-81-74.** U-Bahn: Bismarckstrasse.

Lutter und Wegner 1811 This place was named after a gastronomic and social landmark, Lutter und Wegner, a hangout for actors in the 19th century. You can have a drink in the stand-up bar, or make reservations in advance to dine. Try the local specialty, Königsberger Klopse, with potatoes and a fresh salad. We also recommend the wiener schnitzel or pot roast with horseradish and sekt. The wide selection of drinks ranges from single-malt Scottish whiskies to Italian grappas. Main courses range from 16€ ($18) to 25€ ($29). The restaurant is open daily 6pm to midnight; the bar is open daily 6pm to 1:30am or even later, depending on business. In summer, you can sit on a terrace and observe the passing parade. Schlüstrasse 55. ℂ **030/8-81-34-40.** S-Bahn: Savignyplatz.

CAFE LIFE

At its mid–19th century zenith, Berlin was famous for its cafes. Max Krell, an editor, once wrote: "Cafes were our homeland. They were the stock exchange of ideas, site of intellectual transactions, futures' market of poetic and artistic glory and defeat." They've changed with the times, but cafes are still going strong in Berlin—particularly, these days, in what used to be East Berlin. In the heart of the old East German capital is a complex of about 100 bars, shops, and restaurants, called *Die Hackenschen Höfe* (S-Bahn: Hackescher Markt). This stylish mini-mall attracts hip counterculture denizens who wander between galleries, boutiques, and cafes. It has become one of the most prominent places in the city to go drinking.

Cafe Aedes Tucked away within what were once small 19th-century factories, this is a trendy and convivial cafe with a counterculture clientele that's very, very hip to the changing face of Berlin and its cultural scene. The decor includes lots of shimmering glass and free-form concrete, and the clientele includes a mixed collection of merchants, artists, performers, writers, and business people. Whisky with soda costs 8€ ($9.20), platters of simple food range from 7.50€ to 13€ ($8.65–$15). Beef consommé, salmon steaks with mango sauce, pasta with tuna and fresh tomatoes, and all vegetarian salads are what it's all about—that and ongoing dialogues. Open daily 10am to midnight. Rosenthaler Strasse 40–41. ℭ 030/285-82-75. U-Bahn: Weinmeisterstrasse.

Café/Bistro Leysieffer This cafe opened in the early 1980s in what used to be the Chinese embassy. Some of the embassy's ornate moldings and lighting fixtures are still in place; a pair of gilded lions still guards the entrance. On the street level is a pastry and candy shop, but you can climb the flight of stairs to a marble-and-wood-sheathed cafe with a balcony overlooking the busy Ku'damm. The elegant breakfast menu here features Parma ham, smoked salmon, freshly baked baguettes, French butter, and, to round it off, champagne. Meals range from 11€ to 19€ ($13–$22). Open daily 10am to 7pm. Kurfürstendamm 218. ℭ 030/8-85-74-80. U-Bahn: Kurfürstendamm.

Café Silberstein From the outside, this place looks like an art gallery, but once inside, you'll see that it's an artsy cafe, one of Berlin's trendiest, with sushi, ambient music, and an ultra-hip clientele. This is one of the best places to enjoy "new Berlin" in the formerly grim eastern sector. Open Monday to Friday 10am to 4am and Saturday and Sunday 10am to 5am. Oranienburger Strasse 27. ℭ 030/2-81-20-95. S-Bahn: Oranienburger Tor.

Cafe Wintergarten in Literaturhaus Berlin Set within a Tuscan-style brick villa that was built in 1885 1 block south of the Ku'damm, a few steps from the Käthe-Kollwitz-Museum, this cafe is part of a private foundation that's devoted to the promotion—through lectures and research—of German literature. In addition to a prestigious and respectable bookshop that fills the building's basement, it contains lecture halls, offices that have links to Germany's academic community, and exhibition space for temporary exhibitions that cost from 3€ to 5€ ($3.45–$5.75) to see. The best way to unlock the secrets of this place is by heading for the cafe and restaurant, whose tables fill two old-fashioned Berliner-style rooms and spill into a much sought-after garden during clement weather. If you're hungry, the cheerful, old-Berliner-style staff will serve platters of noodles with cheese, rigatoni with beef strips, Argentinian steaks with herbs, and cucumber and tuna salads. Open daily 9:30am to 1am. Fasanenstrasse 23. ℭ 030/882-54-14. U-Bahn: Kurfurstendam.

Dachgarten This cafe is installed in the dome of Germany's Parliament, the Reichstag. Sad to say, the food is hardly the city's finest, although we find the setting and panorama so overpowering we recommended a visit if only for coffee and pastry. If you are a customer here, you can also avoid the long lines waiting to enter the dome. Stylishly redesigned by Sir Norman Foster, the cafe looks like a modern art museum. Even the Reichstag chef admits most diners come for the view and not the continental menu. A waiter recently confided "Come back in the morning for breakfast. We get the least complaints about the food then." Platz der Republik, Tiergarten. ℭ **030/2262-9933**. Main courses from 14€ to 36€ ($16–$41), fixed-price menus 35€ to 40€ ($40–$46). Open daily 9am to 2:30pm and 6:30pm to 11:30. U-Bahn: Unter den Linden.

6 A Casino

It's brassy, it sparkles with lots of chrome, and the staff is about as jaded as any you'll find in a city that's legendary for its jaded citizens. Berlin's only casino, **Spielbank Berlin,** is a high-ceilinged, scarlet affair that might remind you of an airport. The basement is devoted to slot machines; the upper floors (Casino Royale) to a battery of more sophisticated gambling devices that include roulette and baccarat. Men must wear a necktie for access to the Casino Royale, but not to the basement-level slot machines.

The cover charge of 5€ ($5.75) is refunded in the form of a casino chip. There are no maximum bets—the amount you lose, or can bet on any one play, depends on your credit rating with the casino. Slot machines are accessible daily 11:30am to 3am; the rest of the complex is available for bets daily 2pm to 3am. I.D. in the form of a passport is required to enter the casino. This is really the only casino in Berlin: Its only competition is a simple and rather small facility within the Forum Hotel, on Alexanderplatz. Marlene Dietrich Platz 1 (Potsdamer Platz). ℭ **030/255-990**. U-Bahn: Potsdamer Platz.

10

Side Trips from Berlin

The best day trip from Berlin is to the town of **Potsdam,** sometimes called "Germany's Versailles." It's only about half an hour away by rail, S-Bahn, bus, or car. Another great trip in the summertime is to the forest of the **Spreewald.**

1 Potsdam

The baroque town of Potsdam, located on the Havel River about 24km (15 miles) southwest of the city, has often been called Germany's Versailles. The town has many historic sights, as well as parks and a beautiful chain of lakes formed by the river. It was beautifully planned, with large parks and many green areas. The palaces and gardens of **Sans Souci Park,** which lies to the west of Potsdam's historic core, are the major attractions here. A mile northwest of Sans Souci is the **Neuer Garten** on the Heiliger See, which contains the **Schloss Cecilienhof.**

From the beginning of the 18th century, Potsdam was a residence and garrison town of the Prussian kings. Soviet propagandists called it a "former cradle of Prussian militarism and reactionary forces." World attention focused on Potsdam July 17 to August 2, 1945, when the Potsdam Conference helped shape postwar Europe.

ESSENTIALS

GETTING THERE   By Train   Potsdam Hauptbahnhof is on the major Deutsche Bundesbahn rail lines, with 29 daily connections to the rail stations in Berlin (23 min. to Bahnhof Zoo and 54 min. to Ostbahnhof). There are also 14 trains daily to and from Hannover (3–3½ hr.), and 15 daily trains to and from Nürnberg (6–6½ hr.). For rail information and schedules, call © **018/05-99-66-33.**

Potsdam can also be reached by S-Bahn Lines S3, S4, and S7 from Berlin, connecting at Wannsee station with Lines R1, R3, and R4. Travel time on these lines from Berlin to Potsdam is 30 minutes. For more information, call **BVG Berlin** (© **030/19-449**).

By Bus   **Verkehrsverbund Potsdam** provides regional bus service with frequent connections between Berlin and Potsdam at Wannsee station (bus 133) in Berlin. For travel information and schedules, call **BVG Berlin** (✆ **030/19-449**).

By Car   Access is via the E30 Autobahn east and west or the E53 north and south. Allow about 30 minutes to drive here from Berlin.

VISITOR INFORMATION   Contact **Potsdam–Information,** Friedrich-Ebert-Strasse 5 (✆ **0331/27-55-80**), open April to October, Monday to Friday 9am to 7pm, Saturday and Sunday 9am to 4pm; November to March, Monday to Friday 9am to 6pm and Saturday and Sunday 10am to 2pm.

GETTING AROUND   By Public Transportation   Ask at the tourist office about a **Potsdam Billet,** costing 5€ ($6)and good for 24 hours on the city's public transportation system. In Potsdam, **bus A1,** leaving from the rail station, will deliver you to the Potsdam palaces. Call ✆ **0331/2-80-03-09** for more information.

By Boat   Because the area around Potsdam is surrounded by water, boat tours in fair weather are a popular diversion. Call **Weisse Flotte Potsdam** at ✆ **0331/275-92-10** for more information.

By Bicycle   You can rent a bicycle from **City Rad Potsdam,** at the Potsdam Hauptbahnhof (✆ **0331/619052**), but you can't ride your bike on the grounds of Sans Souci Park. The rental shop is open May to October, Monday to Friday 9am to 7pm, Saturday and Sunday 9am to 8pm. Bicycles rent for 14€ ($16) per day.

EXPLORING THE PARKS & PALACES

A British air raid on April 14, 1945, destroyed much of the old city center, but the major attraction, Sans Souci Park and its palaces, survived.

Neuer Garten   On Heiliger See, or "Holy Lake," in the northern part of Potsdam, lies the Neuer Garten. The nephew and successor to Frederick the Great, Frederick William II, had these gardens laid out.

On Heiliger See, about a mile northwest of Sans Souci. ✆ 0331/2-31-41. Free admission. Same hours as Sans Souci (see below). Bus: 695.

Sans Souci Palace 𝄞𝄞𝄞   Sans Souci Park, with its palaces and gardens, was the work of many architects and sculptors. The park covers an area of about 1.6 km. sq. (1 square mile). Its premier attraction is the palace of Frederick I ("the Great"), **Sans Souci,** meaning "free from care." Frederick was one of the most liberal and

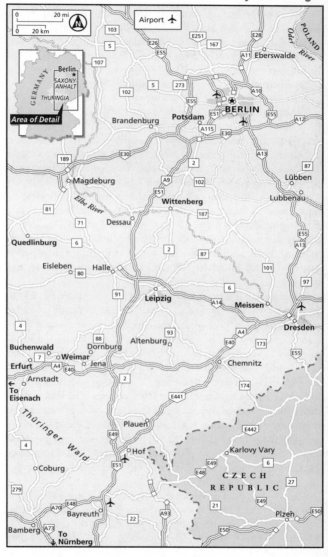

farsighted of the Prussian monarchs. He was a great general, but he liked best to think of himself as an enlightened patron of the arts. Here he could get away from his duties, indulge his intellectual interests, and entertain his friend Voltaire. The style of the buildings he had constructed is called "Potsdam rococo," and is primarily the achievement of Georg Wenzeslaus von Knobelsdorff.

Sans Souci (or Sanssouci) Palace, with its terraces and gardens, was inaugurated in 1747. The long one-story building is crowned by a dome and flanked by two round pavilions. The elliptically shaped Marble Hall is the largest in the palace, but the music salon is the supreme example of the rococo style. A small bust of Voltaire commemorates Voltaire's sojourns here. Sans Souci Palace can only be visited with a guide. *Be warned:* it is best (especially in summer) to show up before noon to buy your tickets for the palace tour. At busy times, all the slots for the rest of the day can be completely filled by noon. The palace is open April to October, Tuesday to Sunday 9am to 5pm; November to March, Tuesday to Sunday 9am to 4pm; closed Mondays. Guided tours (in English) of the palace cost 8€ ($9.20) for adults; 5€ ($5.75) for children under 18 and students; free for children under 8.

Bildergalerie (Picture Gallery), Östlicher Lustgarden (© **0331/ 9694181**), was built between 1755 and 1763. Its facade is similar to that of Sans Souci Palace, and the interior is one of the most flamboyant in Germany. The collection of some 125 paintings features works by Italian Renaissance and baroque artists along with Dutch and Flemish masters. Concerts of the Potsdam Park Festival take place here. The Bildergalerie is open Tuesday through Sundays, only from May 15 to October 15, from 10am to 5pm. The Bildergalerie can be visited with or without a guide, and the crush of visitors here is nowhere near as intense as at Sans Souci Palace. Guided tours cost 3€ ($3.45) for adults; 2.50€ ($2.90) for students and people under 18; free for children under 8. Entrance without a guided tour costs 2€ ($2.30) for adults; 1.50€ ($1.75) for students and people under 18; free for children under 8.

West of the palace is the **Orangerie** (© **0331/969-4280**), built between 1851 and 1864. It was based on Italian Renaissance designs. Its purpose was to shelter southern plants during the cold months. In the central core is the Raphael Hall, which holds 47 copies of that master's paintings. In addition, you can visit five lavishly decorated salons. The Orangerie is open Tuesday through Sundays, only from May 15 to October 15, from 10am to 5pm. The

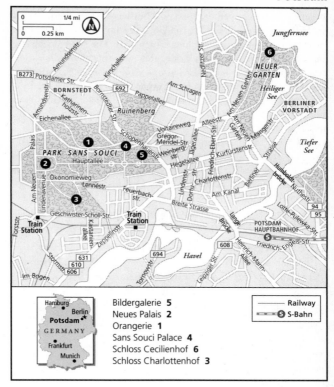

Bildergalerie **5**
Neues Palais **2**
Orangerie **1**
Sans Souci Palace **4**
Schloss Cecilienhof **6**
Schloss Charlottenhof **3**

——— Railway
━━━Ⓢ━━ S-Bahn

Orangerie must be visited with a guide. Though not as severe a situation of overcrowding as you'll find at Sans Souci Palace, you should still try to get your tickets before noon, especially in midsummer. Guided tours cost 3€ ($3.45) for adults; 2€ ($2.30) for students and people under 18; free for children under 8.

The largest building in the park is the extravagant **Neues Palais** (℃ **0331/9694255**), built between 1763 and 1769, at the end of the Seven Years' War. Crowning the center is a dome. The rococo rooms, filled with paintings and antiques, were used by the royal family. The most notable chamber is the Hall of Shells, with its fossils and semiprecious stones. At the palace theater, concerts take place every year April to November. The Neues Palais is open April 1 to October 31, Saturday to Thursday from 9am to 5pm. During other months, it's open Saturday to Thursday from 9am to 4pm. It is always closed on Fridays. It charges 7€ ($8.05) for adults and 6€ ($6.90) for children (guided tour is included). The Neues Palais can be visited with or without a guide, and the crush of visitors isn't as intense as at Sans Souci. Showing up before noon here is not vital. Guided tours cost 7€ ($8.05) for adults; 6€ ($6.90) for students and people under 18; children under 8 enter free. Visits without tours cost 6€ ($6.90) for adults; 3€ ($3.45) for people under 18; children under 8 enter free.

Note: During the summer months, when all four of the attractions are open, you can buy a combination ticket that incorporates guided access to all four of these monuments. It's valid for two days and costs 17€ ($20) for adults; 14€ ($16) for students and people under 18; free for children under 8.

Zur historischen Mühle. ℂ **0331/96-94-202.** Tues–Sun 9am–5pm. Tram: 94 or 96. Bus: 614, 631, or 632 to reach the sights in the park.

Schloss Cecilienhof

This palace was completed in the style of an English country house. Kaiser Wilhelm II had it built between 1913 and 1917 for Crown Prince Wilhelm. The palace was occupied as a royal residence until March 1945, when the crown prince and his family fled to the West. In addition to the regular guided tour, offered in summer, there's a tour of the private rooms of Crown Prince Wilhelm and Princess Cecilie on the upper story. The tour takes place at 11am and 2pm and costs 1.55€ ($1.80) adults and 1€ ($1.15) students and children. Note that you can lunch and spend the night here, if you wish.

Cecilienhof was the headquarters of the 1945 Potsdam Conference, attended by the heads of the allied powers, including Truman, Stalin, and Churchill. You can visit the studies of the various delegations and see the large round table, made in Moscow, where the actual agreement was signed.

In Neuer Garten. ℂ **0331/9-69-42-44.** Admission 9€ ($10) adults, 5.50€ ($6.35) students with guided tour (1.50€ less without); free for children under 6. Tues–Sun 9am–12:30pm and 5–7pm. Bus: 695.

Schloss Charlottenhof

This palace was built between 1826 and 1829 by Karl Friedrich Schinkel, Germany's greatest master of neoclassical architecture. He also designed most of the furniture inside. The nearby **Roman baths** are on the north of the artificial lake known as *Maschinenteich* (Machine Pond). These baths, constructed between 1829 and 1835, were built strictly for the romantic love of antiquity and have no practical purpose. The schloss now closes in winter.

South of Okonomieweg. (②) 0331/969-42-00. Admission 5.10€ ($5.85) adults, 4€ ($4.60) children. Open daily May-Oct 10am-5pm, Nov-Apr Tues-Sun 9am-4pm. Tram: 96.

WHERE TO STAY

Astron Hotel Voltaire 🏨🏨 This hotel, the best in Potsdam, is a radical renovation of the Brühlsche Palace, formerly a dour and crumbling relic built in 1732. Only the palace's baroque facade has been retained. The site belongs to the small Arkona chain. Rooms are scattered over three floors and, in almost every case, overlook the quiet, pleasant garden in back. Each unit comes with a small tiled bathroom with tub or shower. The rooms here are far better furnished and more elegantly appointed than those within its closest rival, Schloss Cecilienhof (see above), although the latter has richer history. The décor is, in fact, so sophisticated here that the Astron accurately labels itself as "a designer hotel." Some of the accommodations are large enough to be used as a triple, with each guest having enough room to move about. Many families book into a suite here, although some of the regular rooms are large enough to accommodate an extra bed. The health club facilities are the best in Potsdam, and include a whirlpool, sauna, and solarium. An added feature is the roof terrace where you're treated to a panoramic view over Potsdam. The garden terrace is the venue for summer barbecues staged by the hotel.

Friedrich-Ebert-Strasse 88, 14467 Potsdam. (②) 0331/2-31-70. Fax 0331/2-31-71-00. www.nh-hotels.com. 143 units. 103-112€ ($118–$129) double; from 150€ ($173) suite. Rates include breakfast. AE, DC, MC, V. Parking 11€ ($13). Tram: 92. **Amenities:** Restaurant; lounge; bike rental; room service; babysitting; laundry/dry cleaning. *In room:* A/C, TV, minibar, hair dryer, safe.

WHERE TO DINE

Juliette 🍴 FRENCH (TRADITIONAL) At last, Potsdam has a world-class restaurant. The cozy and intimate Juliette lies in the center of the restored Holländisches Viertel (Dutch Quarter), 3 blocks north of the Altar Markt. You'll feel at home the moment you enter this restored old house, with its blazing fireplace, low ceilings, and tiny little windows. There is no more romantic choice in the city. Most of the excellent waiters are from France. Menu items include saddle of boar in cranberry sauce, fresh grilled fish, and some wonderful chicken dishes. All the desserts are freshly made on-site.

Jägerstrasse 39. (②) 0331/2701-791. Reservations required. Main courses 21€– 26€ ($24–$29). AE, MC, V. Daily noon–11pm. Tram 94 or 96.

Specker's Gaststätte ☆☆ CONTINENTAL One of Potsdam's most prestigious and popular restaurants happens to be one of its oldest, set within a thick-walled country-baroque building midway between Potsdam's railway station and its historic core. The clients who file in here to enjoy the inventive cuisine of chef Gottfried Specker tend to be deeply involved in German political affairs: Expect to see business-suited representatives from municipal and national bureaucracies lunching or dining with representatives from the European Union—many of whom appreciate the restaurant's somewhat reverentially hushed, conservative ambience. The decor consists of thick walls, rich paneling, and mementos evoking the glory days of Prussia. The cuisine changes with the seasons, the availability of local ingredients, and the inspirations of the chef—as such, it's likely to change every 10 to 14 days. Expect a celebration of whatever is fresh (asparagus, strawberries, game, and seasonal fish are good examples) and specialties that may include a terrine of wild mushrooms and goose liver; a clear oxtail soup loaded with flavor and garnished with spinach leaves; cream of wild mushroom soup; poached crayfish on a bed of black (squid-ink-flavored) risotto; and breast of guinea fowl with a mango-flavored cream sauce.

Am Neuen Markt 10. ☎ 0331/280431. Reservations recommended. Main courses 13€–17€ ($15–$20); set-price lunches 10€–40€ ($12–$46); set-price dinners 30€–55€ ($35–$63). AE, MC, V. Tues–Sat 11am–3pm and 6–11pm. Closed: Jan–Feb. S-Bahn: Potsdamer Hauptbahnhof.

Villa Kellerman ITALIAN One of the most talked-about restaurants in Potsdam is in an 1878 villa, once occupied by author Bernhardt Kellerman. The Italian cuisine here attracts a diverse clientele from finance and the arts. Your meal might include marinated carpaccio of sea wolf; ravioli stuffed with cheese, spinach, and herbs; John Dory in butter-and-caper sauce; or an array of veal and beef dishes. The wine list is mostly Italian.

Mangerstrasse 34–36. ☎ 0331/29-15-72. Reservations recommended. Main courses 14€–24€ ($16–$27); fixed-price menu 45€ ($52). AE, DC, MC, V. Fri–Sun noon–midnight, Tues–Thurs 4–11pm. S-Bahn: Potsdam Stadt. Bus: 92 or 93.

2 The Spreewald

A fascinating side trip, about an hour south of Berlin, is to the history-rich Sorb country of the Spreewald (Forest of the Spree), nearly 100 square miles of woodland, pastures, and canals. The flat, water-soaked landscape has an eerie beauty. Legends abound about spirits that inhabit the thick forests. Over a period of at least 1,000 years, the people of the region channeled the marshlands into a network of canals, streams, lakes, and irrigation channels, building their houses, barns, and chapels on the high points of otherwise swampy ground. Ethnologists consider this area a distinctive human adaptation to an unlikely landscape, and botanists appreciate the wide diversity of bird and animal life that flourishes in the lush and fertile terrain.

The area is inhabited by the Sorbs, descendants of Slavic tribes who settled here in the 6th century. They speak a language similar to Czech and Polish. Over the years, they have often faced tremendous persecution, but have never succumbed. The Sorbs were targeted by the Nazis, who outlawed their language and killed many of them. It's estimated that there are still 100,000 Sorbs living in Germany, 30,000 of whom inhabit the Spreewald. They grow vegetables and fruit in a protected landscape, using labor-intensive methods even today.

ESSENTIALS

GETTING THERE   The main population centers of the area are the towns of Lübben and Lübbenau. From Berlin, take Autobahn 13 until you come to either the first turnoff, to Lübben, or another turnoff, 6 miles further, to Lübbenau. There are also trains from Berlin's Lichtenberg Station to Lübbenau. The trip takes about an hour.

VISITOR INFORMATION   The tourist office in Lübben, the main point of departure for most Spreewald cruises, is on Ernst von Houwald Damm 16 (© **03456/3090**). The tourist office in Lübbenau, a secondary point of departure, is at Am Weg 15 (© **03542/3668**).

EXPLORING THE SPREEWALD

The Spreewald is at its most appealing in early spring and autumn, when the crowds of sightseers depart, and a spooky chill descends with the fog over these primeval forests and shallow medieval canals. Once in either Lübben or Lübbenau, drive toward the port *(Hafen)*. From there, tour companies will take you through the canals via a shallow-draft boat propelled by a long pole, like a Venetian gondola. The guide is often a woman in traditional dress. Several waterside cafes along the canals serve food and drink.

Boat tours cost about 8€ ($9.20) for 2½ hours. Your best bet is simply to wander down to the piers and hop aboard the next departure. Few people speak English. The boat tour companies operate only between May and early October, with departures scheduled every day between 9am and 4pm. The companies include **Kahn-fahrhafen Flottes Rudel,** Eisenbahnstrasse 3 (© **03546/8269**), in Lübben; and in Lübbenau, **Kahn Fahr GmbH,** Dammstrasse (© **03542/2225**).

If you're interested in paddling around the Spreewald on your own, head for **Bootsverleih Gebauer,** Lindenstrasse, Lübben (© **03546/7194**), where canoes can be rented for around 7.50€ ($8.65) for a 2-hour rental.

Index

See also Accommodations and Restaurant indexes below.

FROMMER'S® COMPLETE TRAVEL GUIDES

Alaska
Alaska Cruises & Ports of Call
Amsterdam
Argentina & Chile
Arizona
Atlanta
Australia
Austria
Bahamas
Barcelona, Madrid & Seville
Beijing
Belgium, Holland & Luxembourg
Bermuda
Boston
Brazil
British Columbia & the Canadian
  Rockies
Brussels & Bruges
Budapest & the Best of Hungary
California
Canada
Cancún, Cozumel & the Yucatán
Cape Cod, Nantucket & Martha's
  Vineyard
Caribbean
Caribbean Cruises & Ports of Call
Caribbean Ports of Call
Carolinas & Georgia
Chicago
China
Colorado
Costa Rica
Cuba
Denmark
Denver, Boulder & Colorado Springs
England
Europe
European Cruises & Ports of Call

Florida
France
Germany
Great Britain
Greece
Greek Islands
Hawaii
Hong Kong
Honolulu, Waikiki & Oahu
Ireland
Israel
Italy
Jamaica
Japan
Las Vegas
London
Los Angeles
Maryland & Delaware
Maui
Mexico
Montana & Wyoming
Montréal & Québec City
Munich & the Bavarian Alps
Nashville & Memphis
New England
New Mexico
New Orleans
New York City
New Zealand
Northern Italy
Norway
Nova Scotia, New Brunswick &
  Prince Edward Island
Oregon
Paris
Peru
Philadelphia & the Amish Country
Portugal

Prague & the Best of the Czech
  Republic
Provence & the Riviera
Puerto Rico
Rome
San Antonio & Austin
San Diego
San Francisco
Santa Fe, Taos & Albuquerque
Scandinavia
Scotland
Seattle & Portland
Shanghai
Sicily
Singapore & Malaysia
South Africa
South America
South Florida
South Pacific
Southeast Asia
Spain
Sweden
Switzerland
Texas
Thailand
Tokyo
Toronto
Tuscany & Umbria
USA
Utah
Vancouver & Victoria
Vermont, New Hampshire & Maine
Vienna & the Danube Valley
Virgin Islands
Virginia
Walt Disney World® & Orlando
Washington, D.C.
Washington State

FROMMER'S® DOLLAR-A-DAY GUIDES

Australia from $50 a Day
California from $70 a Day
England from $75 a Day
Europe from $70 a Day
Florida from $70 a Day
Hawaii from $80 a Day

Ireland from $60 a Day
Italy from $70 a Day
London from $85 a Day
New York from $90 a Day
Paris from $80 a Day

San Francisco from $70 a Day
Washington, D.C. from $80 a Day
Portable London from $85 a Day
Portable New York City from $90
  a Day

FROMMER'S® PORTABLE GUIDES

Acapulco, Ixtapa & Zihuatanejo
Amsterdam
Aruba
Australia's Great Barrier Reef
Bahamas
Berlin
Big Island of Hawaii
Boston
California Wine Country
Cancún
Cayman Islands
Charleston
Chicago
Disneyland®
Dublin
Florence

Frankfurt
Hong Kong
Houston
Las Vegas
Las Vegas for Non-Gamblers
London
Los Angeles
Los Cabos & Baja
Maine Coast
Maui
Miami
Nantucket & Martha's Vineyard
New Orleans
New York City
Paris
Phoenix & Scottsdale

Portland
Puerto Rico
Puerto Vallarta, Manzanillo &
  Guadalajara
Rio de Janeiro
San Diego
San Francisco
Savannah
Seattle
Sydney
Tampa & St. Petersburg
Vancouver
Venice
Virgin Islands
Washington, D.C.

FROMMER'S® NATIONAL PARK GUIDES

Banff & Jasper
Family Vacations in the National
  Parks

Grand Canyon
National Parks of the American West
Rocky Mountain

Yellowstone & Grand Teton
Yosemite & Sequoia/Kings Canyon
Zion & Bryce Canyon

FROMMER'S® MEMORABLE WALKS

Chicago
London

New York
Paris

San Francisco

FROMMER'S® WITH KIDS GUIDES

Chicago
Las Vegas
New York City

Ottawa
San Francisco
Toronto

Vancouver
Washington, D.C.

SUZY GERSHMAN'S BORN TO SHOP GUIDES

Born to Shop: France
Born to Shop: Hong Kong,
 Shanghai & Beijing

Born to Shop: Italy
Born to Shop: London

Born to Shop: New York
Born to Shop: Paris

FROMMER'S® IRREVERENT GUIDES

Amsterdam
Boston
Chicago
Las Vegas
London

Los Angeles
Manhattan
New Orleans
Paris
Rome

San Francisco
Seattle & Portland
Vancouver
Walt Disney World®
Washington, D.C.

FROMMER'S® BEST-LOVED DRIVING TOURS

Britain
California
Florida
France

Germany
Ireland
Italy
New England

Northern Italy
Scotland
Spain
Tuscany & Umbria

HANGING OUT™ GUIDES

Hanging Out in England
Hanging Out in Europe

Hanging Out in France
Hanging Out in Ireland

Hanging Out in Italy
Hanging Out in Spain

THE UNOFFICIAL GUIDES®

Bed & Breakfasts and Country
 Inns in:
 California
 Great Lakes States
 Mid-Atlantic
 New England
 Northwest
 Rockies
 Southeast
 Southwest
Best RV & Tent Campgrounds in:
 California & the West
 Florida & the Southeast
 Great Lakes States
 Mid-Atlantic
 Northeast
 Northwest & Central Plains

Southwest & South Central
 Plains
 U.S.A.
Beyond Disney
Branson, Missouri
California with Kids
Central Italy
Chicago
Cruises
Disneyland®
Florida with Kids
Golf Vacations in the Eastern U.S.
Great Smoky & Blue Ridge Region
Inside Disney
Hawaii
Las Vegas
London
Maui

Mexio's Best Beach Resorts
Mid-Atlantic with Kids
Mini Las Vegas
Mini-Mickey
New England & New York with
 Kids
New Orleans
New York City
Paris
San Francisco
Skiing & Snowboarding in the West
Southeast with Kids
Walt Disney World®
Walt Disney World® for
 Grown-ups
Walt Disney World® with Kids
Washington, D.C.
World's Best Diving Vacations

SPECIAL-INTEREST TITLES

Frommer's Adventure Guide to Australia &
 New Zealand
Frommer's Adventure Guide to Central America
Frommer's Adventure Guide to India & Pakistan
Frommer's Adventure Guide to South America
Frommer's Adventure Guide to Southeast Asia
Frommer's Adventure Guide to Southern Africa
Frommer's Britain's Best Bed & Breakfasts and
 Country Inns
Frommer's Caribbean Hideaways
Frommer's Exploring America by RV
Frommer's Fly Safe, Fly Smart

Frommer's France's Best Bed & Breakfasts and
 Country Inns
Frommer's Gay & Lesbian Europe
Frommer's Italy's Best Bed & Breakfasts and
 Country Inns
Frommer's Road Atlas Britain
Frommer's Road Atlas Europe
Frommer's Road Atlas France
The New York Times' Guide to Unforgettable
 Weekends
Places Rated Almanac
Retirement Places Rated
Rome Past & Present